NEW STUDIES IN ARCHAEOLOGY

Editor: David L. Clarke
Fellow of Peterhouse, University of Cambridge

Spatial analysis in archaeology

This is the first book in the series:
other titles are in preparation

Spatial analysis in archaeology

IAN HODDER AND
CLIVE ORTON

CAMBRIDGE UNIVERSITY PRESS

CAMBRIDGE

LONDON · NEW YORK · MELBOURNE

Published by the Syndics of the Cambridge University Press
The Pitt Building, Trumpington Street, Cambridge CB2 IRP
Bentley House, 200 Euston Road, London NWI 2DB
32 East 57th Street, New York, NY 10022, USA
296 Beaconsfield Parade, Middle Park, Melbourne 3206,
Australia

First published 1976

Text set in 10/12 pt Monotype Baskerville, printed by
letterpress, and bound in Great Britain at
The Pitman Press, Bath

Library of Congress Cataloguing in Publication Data

Hodder, Ian.

Spatial analysis in archaeology.

(New studies in archaeology; 1)

Includes bibliographical references and index.

1. Archaeology–Methodology. 2. Archaeology–
Statistical methods. I. Orton, Clive, 1948–
II. Title. III. Series.
CC75.H57   930'.1'0285   75-44582
ISBN 0 521 21080 1

CONTENTS

PREFACE

This book consists largely of the results obtained from research in Cambridge by Ian Hodder from 1971–4. Here much encouragement was received from David Clarke at Peterhouse and from a number of friends doing research at Cambridge in the same period. Great stimulus was obtained through contact with Dr A. Cliff, Department of Geography, Cambridge, without whose time and attention the work would have been impossible. He also wrote some of the computer programmes used in the study. Ian Robertson helped in the solving of some statistical and computational problems, and Ron Martin advised on the model described on page 183. Anything of merit learned as an undergraduate must derive from the staff of the Institute of Archaeology in London in the period from 1968 to 1971, in particular Professor J. Evans and Professor F. R. Hodson.

Clive Orton, until recently in the statistical department of the Ministry for Agriculture, Fisheries and Food, and the Southwark Archaeological Excavation Committee, was encouraged to apply his statistical attention to the problems of archaeology by Professor F. R. Hodson and Professor D. G. Kendall, and this book forms part of the result.

We should like to thank Dr M. Rowlands (middle Bronze Age palstave data) and Dr M. Fulford (Romano-British fine pottery data) for allowing us to use unpublished data, and Dr R. Reece for help with his Roman coin data. Dr J. Alexander drew the work of R. H. Atkin to our attention, Dr R. Coleman provided some useful comments on edge-effects in nearest-neighbour analysis, and A. E. Brown very kindly allowed us to try out our ideas on his extra-mural students. Mrs P. M. E. Altham read and commented on parts of the manuscript. Mrs Jackson helped with some of the typing. Sincerest thanks go to Françoise Hivernel for her time and patience both in typing and in many other ways.

January 1975
I.H.
C.R.O.

I
Introduction

1.1 *General introduction*

The main aim of this work is to suggest to archaeologists that there is a potential for more detailed and systematic study of spatial patterning in archaeological data. The distribution map lies behind some of the most central themes in archaeology such as trade, diffusion and culture. The map of archaeological data also has a value for chronology. For example, Clark (1957) has suggested that the degree of overlap between distributions of different cultural assemblages can give an indication of their contemporaneity (cf. Willey and Phillips 1958, 32). 'The distribution map is one of the main instruments of archaeological research and exposition, but because it is a commonplace of books and papers, do not let us forget what it is trying to do – to accomplish and to demonstrate the totality of information about some archaeological fact, to study the total evidence in space regarding one aspect of the material remains of the past' (Daniel 1962, 80). 'For the past thirty or forty years archaeological distribution maps have been one of the main weapons in the armoury of the prehistorian' (Clark 1957, 153). However, the development of spatial studies in archaeology has been slow. Early prehistorians were mainly concerned with establishing chronological sequences and they did not always concern themselves with the geographical extent of the cultures they examined. 'It was because of this that archaeological mapping made little headway until well into the twentieth century. . . . It was not until 1912 that Crawford first used distribution maps to argue questions of cultural history' (Clark *ibid.*). But it is only in the last few years that systematic methods for the examination of archaeological maps have begun to be used. Because of this past neglect, most of the methods which have been used recently in archaeology and which are employed in the study presented here have been introduced and adapted from other disciplines, in particular geography and plant ecology. 'The distribution of artifacts in space is only now, through the application of locational analysis, undergoing systematic study. All the notions of random and regular spacing, of central place theory and settlement hierarchy, and of correlations among distributions, have yet to be assimilated to prehistoric archaeology' (Renfrew 1973*b*, 250). This work is an attempt to develop such systematic study, although the field is very wide and one cannot hope to cover all aspects nor to solve all the associated problems.

An appraisal of the role of spatial studies in archaeology is felt necessary for three reasons. The first is that previous work in this field has been limited in its aims and methods which were often uncritical and did not aid detailed interpretation. Second, subjective assessments of distributions can be dangerous, and third, some methods are needed to handle the large amounts of distributional information that are now becoming available.

As an illustration of the first point and as an example of the early approach to distribution maps in archaeology, Fox's study of *The personality of Britain* (first edition 1932, revised 1943) may be considered. Fox's aim in this study was as follows. 'I shall endeavour to express the character of Britain in prehistoric and early historic ages, and to indicate the effect of the environment she afforded on the distribution and fates of her inhabitants and her invaders' (Fox 1943, 10). 'The most convenient line of approach is to find out, by the study of distribution maps, where in this island early Man actually lived and laboured' (*ibid.*, 11). 'The essay is concerned to establish principles and not to present the prehistory of Britain' (*ibid.*, 14).

The method employed to achieve this aim was the visual interpretation of a large collection of distribution maps of different periods. General similarities between the distributions were sought. A major difference, for example, was noted between distributions with a western (for example megalithic monuments) and an eastern (for example Beakers) bias. Such differences then had to be explained and interpreted. 'The first question that arises is how these different distributions are to be explained. Must they be considered in isolation, or are there underlying and constant factors to be taken into account in framing any rational explanation of them? In these pages the existence of such dominating factors will be made manifest' (*ibid.*, 14). It was found that 'geographical position and form suffice to explain, in large measure, the two chief variations in distribution' (*ibid.*, 15). Thus, southeast England is well situated for contact with and influences from neighbouring parts of Europe, while the western British Isles absorbed influences moving along the Atlantic routes. The physiography of Britain also played a part, with the western and northern highland zone being markedly different from the lowland zone. 'It is easy to understand why the major physical factors should exert so powerful an influence on distributions. Lowland country, with its insignificant hills and easy contours, is more easily overrun by invaders than highland. The difficulties which mountainous country presents to an invader are well known; moreover, the highlander lives a harder life and is less easily conquered, still less easily displaced, than the lowlander' (*ibid.*, 33). Differences in climate and the impact of these on man's economy were also seen to affect distributions. For example, 'the distribution of the "damp" oak woodland and Man's dislike for it explains many curious features in the prehistoric maps' (*ibid.*, 58).

In modern times, the aims of Fox's study seem limited. In pursuit of his desire to establish general principles, 'a given distributional situation may be, as here, expressed in the simplest terms available, stripped of those complexities which make the pattern of human life and activity so interesting, and which it is the business of the prehistorian and historian to elucidate' (*ibid.*, 14). 'It is true that some of the massed maps show, by a variety of symbols, the diversity of material which goes to build a culture pattern; but usually it is the resultant pattern only which is relevant to my purpose' (*ibid.*, 14). In addition, the visual methods employed often seem uncritical. There is no detailed examination of the degree of correlation between maps nor of whether a distribution indicates patterns of site destruction or fieldwork intensity, an invasion, trade or social contact. An invasion hypothesis is usually preferred although there is little discussion as to why this should be so.

The inadequacy of early studies of distributions of artifacts can also be seen in the common aim to establish prehistoric trade routes. An example is the work of Sprockhoff (1930) discussed by Stjernquist (1966, 8–9). Sprockhoff's network of trade routes for the Bronze Age is shown in fig.1.1. Two methods were combined to produce this map. One was to map out finds of imported goods and finds from hoards. These hoards were not discussed in detail but were assumed to be trade hoards. This method was combined with one in which the author used verifiable stretches of mediaeval trade routes. An assumption was made that the network of trade routes had not changed much during the period from the Bronze Age to the Middle Ages. De Navarro (1925) also constructed 'trans-continental trade routes'. In his case these were derived from the distribution of amber finds. In these and other studies

> none of the scholars engaged on the problems concerning trade routes has tried to analyse the distribution maps in greater detail. The trade routes have been drawn with the intention of indicating the principal direction of the flow of goods. There is no detailed analysis of the economic and topographical conditions, although the topographical aspects have been taken into account in studies of limited areas. The conclusions drawn, however, presuppose the opinion that places where finds of imported objects have been made mark a trade route. There is an underlying hazy conception of what this means and from the literature one can see that there is a confusion in thought between the views on the goods as evidence of a trade route and the goods as evidence of a market [Stjernquist 1966, 14].

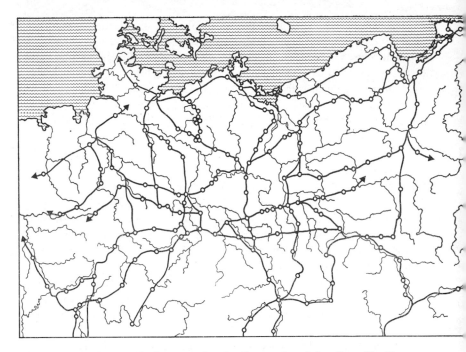

Fig.1.1. Trade routes for the Bronze Age (after Sprockhoff).
Source: Stjernquist 1966.

A second reason for developing spatial studies in archaeology results from the subjectivity involved in map interpretation. 'It has been shown that the ability of the map-user to discriminate and evaluate the information contained in the map is not free from subjective elements and that the more information contained in a map the more ambiguity and uncertainty there is likely to be as regards the interpretation to be put upon it' (Harvey 1969, 377). It is possible, however, to measure some aspects of map information and to develop more rigorous methods of map interpretation. 'Until the recent introduction of a statistical definition of spatial uniformity based on nearest neighbour analysis, . . . it was difficult rigorously to measure dot-patterns. The more traditional "eye-ball" methods are not really satisfactory' (Garner 1967, 310).

The subjectivity of map interpretation may not be immediately apparent and it is perhaps worth providing some examples (see also p. 31). In fig.1.2 to 1.5 points have been allocated at random to a bounded area (point co-ordinates obtained from a random numbers table). By allowing a certain flexibility in the approach to these distributions we can identify structure even though the pattern is random. For example, if the points are considered as sites, in fig.1.2 circles can be drawn around certain of the site points (cf. the approach followed by Stanford 1972). Some pairing and clustering might be

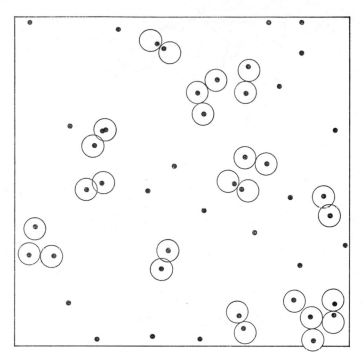

Fig.1.2. Points placed at random in a bounded area. Circles
suggest spheres of influence around 'sites'.

suggested, with an otherwise fairly even scatter of single sites. Depending on the context, a number of hypotheses could be put forward to
explain this 'structured' pattern. For example, the pairings and
clusters might be seen to indicate those sites which have moved location,
the circles reflecting the area of land used up by these shifting agricul-
turalists (cf. Clarke 1972, 25). Alternatively, the regularly spaced
single sites might be seen as major service centres with peripheral
clustering of minor sites in areas of least competition from the main
centres.

In fig.1.3 we can test a hypothesis that the points in part of the study
area are regularly spaced by placing over them a network of hexagons
whose orientation and size we are allowed to alter at will (cf. Clarke
1968, 508–9). We notice that one site occurs in most hexagons and
therefore conclude that the hypothesis of regular spacing is correct.
Since it is the hexagon shape which has been used we might even
invoke aspects of central place theory to explain the distribution. An
'advantage' of archaeological data is its incomplete nature. In cases
where the model does not fit we introduce this factor. For example,
empty cells might be said to predict where further sites will be found or
to suggest where they have been destroyed. Hexagon cells containing

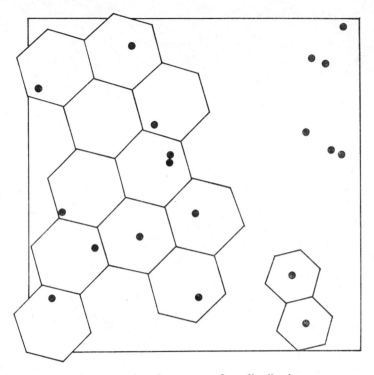

Fig.1.3. Hexagons placed over a random distribution to suggest regular spacing.

two rather than one site could be explained by suggesting that the sites are not precisely contemporaneous.

If a hypothesis of clustering of sites is preferred, contours can be drawn around the same pattern of sites as in fig.1.4. This time (fig.1.5) agglomeration is suggested, not regularity.

These examples serve to underline the dangers of a non-rigorous approach to map analysis and interpretation when, as with archaeological data, little is known of the spatial process which produced the pattern.

Developments in the spatial analysis of archaeological data are needed for a third reason. Recently, large bodies of distributional information have been collected which are difficult to examine without some advance in the available techniques. For example, for one phase of the northwest German early Bronze Age, Bergmann (1970) collected over 112 distribution maps of different artifact types. On each of these, different symbols were used to indicate the context of discovery. Handling the similiarities and variations between all this information is not easy, and a reappraisal (p. 211) identified additional patterning to that noticed in the visual sorting. In a study of 542 middle Bronze Age palstaves in southern England (Rowlands and Hodder, unpublished),

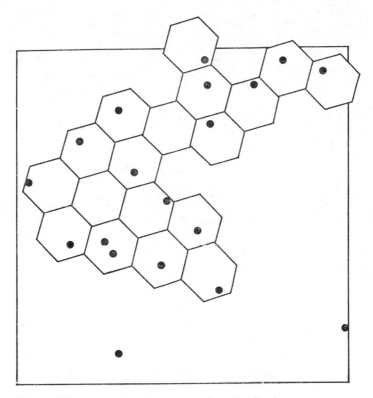

Fig.1.4. Hexagons placed over a random distribution to suggest regular spacing.

the spatial structure of the many palstave types in each of four typological groupings of the material was to be examined for two divisions of the palstaves. To produce the large number of necessary maps would have been time consuming, difficult to present in a published form, and extremely difficult to interpret. By using some of the techniques to be discussed in this work, the problem became manageable.

In response to the need for a development in spatial studies, recent archaeological work has been advancing in two main ways. The first development is an attempt to describe and analyse distributions in a more rigorous way in order to obtain greater precision and reliability. Examples of this approach are the work of Whallon (1973; 1974) and Dacey (1973). These and other examples will be discussed in the following chapters. With more characteristics of the distributions defined there is a better basis for interpretation. In general a quantitative and/or statistical approach is involved. Because of the difficulties in using statistical tests on archaeological data (which will be discussed below), the rigour which is achieved in this way may be more apparent than real. However, some rigour is sometimes found in attempts to use

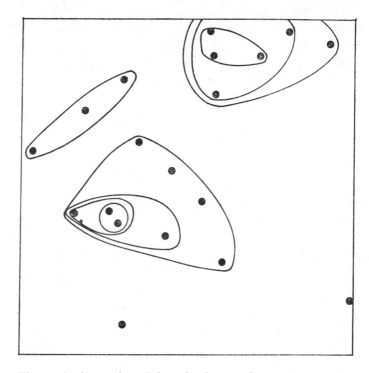

Fig.1.5. An impression of clustering in a random pattern.

clearly defined and repeatable analytical procedures. A second recent change is a greater emphasis on the process leading to the form of an archaeological pattern. This was an area of interest for Fox, but there was no real attempt to distinguish invasion from other mechanisms. With better techniques we can hope to differentiate different processes such as, for example, different types of diffusion. Anomalies in spatial trends might be related to varying social conditions etc. Indeed, along these lines Renfrew (1969; 1972b) has made some generalisations about trade from regression curves, and Hogg (1971) has modelled the process of dispersal of Iron Age coins.

One difficulty which will become apparent during the course of this study is that of inferring process from form. One spatial pattern may be produced by a variety of different spatial processes (Harvey 1968; King 1962) and it must be part of the task to determine the possible range of the variety. Ways of differentiating between alternative hypotheses about the same spatial form will be examined (p. 88) but often one must look to non-spatial evidence to corroborate or disprove theories about spatial processes. As an example of the difficulty the distribution of sites can be considered. It will be shown that the form of many locational patterns is comparable to a Poisson distribution. This suggests that the settlements are located as a random and independent process. Much locational theory suggests quite the opposite.

> It is known that the probability of a store locating in any area is conditional upon a number of factors, not the least important of which is the relative location of other stores. Therefore, a simple model such as the Poisson law hardly is suggested by theory, and while it may serve as a convenient first approximation of the location pattern, it reduces to simplicity a situation which already has been acknowledged as a complex one. Besides, it is almost certain that other probability models could be found which would fit the observed facts equally well, and unless there is theory to guide us in our choice, one model may appear no better than the others [King 1969, 43].

The interpretation of random patterns will be discussed in section 4.1.

One approach that will continually be used to model spatial patterns is to use random or stochastic processes. This method has been widely found to be useful in modelling human behaviour and it has already begun to be used in archaeology (Isaac 1972, 178; Thomas 1972). Its use for examining spatial patterns should perhaps be explained. We expect non-random spatial patterns because we know that individual behaviour is not random but is constrained and determined by, for example, kinship factors in the exchange of goods and physical factors in the location of sites. However, it will be found that non-random behaviour is often not apparent in the spatial patterns. Many of the observed archaeological patterns have a form which is similar to patterns produced by a random process. If the form of the pattern is similar to the end result of a random process, this does not necessarily mean that the process which produced the observed pattern was random. It is possible, however, that, given a 'satellite view', aggregate human behaviour is often best simulated by a random process, or by very simple models incorporating a strong random element. This view has been put forward by Curry (1964; 1967) and developed by, for example, Cliff and Ord (1973; 1974). According to Curry, 'every decision may be optimal from a particular point of view and yet the resulting actions as a whole may appear as random. Lack of information, social ties, and so on will change an economic optimising solution but not the randomness formulation' (1964, 138). It is possible to consider behaviour as rational when all the constraints of a decision are known, and this is the level at which social anthropologists are able to work in studying human interaction (for example Barnes 1972). However, especially in a dynamic framework, there is such a large number of decisions being taken, rarely coincident in time and being separately motivated under differing circumstances and degrees of information, that comprehension of rationality on a wide scale is impossible. Thus, 'men, motivated by various ideas, act so that from the point of view of the locational structure as a whole their actions appear as random' (Curry 1964, 145–6).

It is perhaps helpful to compare this notion of random aggregate behaviour with that of entropy in Information Theory (Harvey 1969, 462; Wilson 1970). If a system contains n elements and it behaves in such a way that if the value of one element in the system is known all the other values can be predicted, then such a system is highly organised. In a similar system the values of $n - 1$ elements might be known, but the value of the nth element still cannot be predicted. Such a system is disorganised and is in a state of high entropy. In certain situations there may be a variety of choices available for any action so that the aggregate pattern of actions shows little order and provides little information about the actions. This is comparable to the notion of randomness discussed above. Information 'may be regarded as the measure of the amount of organisation (as opposed to randomness), in the system' (Klir and Valach 1967, 58). 'The results of an unrestrained random process can be defined as showing zero order. Order is achieved by placing constraints on the freedom of choice of action. This variety of available choice may be called entropy and is the complement of the degree of ordering' (Curry 1964, 144).

1.2 *Statistical introduction*

It would not be possible in a book of this length to give even an introduction to basic statistical theory, or to the use of the more common statistical techniques in general, without overwhelming the rest of the text. There is of course no need to do so, as there are many textbooks on the subject. For a straightforward introduction to the theoretical aspects we recommend Lindgren (first edition 1960 or second edition 1968, page references will refer to the first edition), while for a more practical approach Davies (third edition 1961) or Davies and Goldsmith (1972) is recommended. Where possible, these works will be quoted as source material for particular aspects of statistical theory or technique.

1.2.1 *Notation*

A certain amount of mathematical notation is needed in the presentation of techniques. Most of the symbols should be familiar – a few of the less common are given below; this section can of course be skipped by those familiar with them.

(i) *Subscripts*: are lower case letters, or numbers, slightly below a symbol, and indicating that that symbol represents a particular item out of a set. For example, in section 4.3 the symbol 'p' is used to denote the predicted proportion of the distance between two major towns at which a minor town is situated. There are several (n) roads, each with its own particular value of p, and these are denoted by p_1 for the first road, p_2 for the second and so on up to p_n for the nth. The expression p_i is commonly used for an unspecified ith proportion. Double or multiple subscripts can be used – for example in section 4.3 p_{1i} means the ith proportion if hypothesis 1 is true, and p_{2i} means the ith proportion if hypothesis 2 is true.

(ii) Σ *and* Π (sigma *and* pi): it is often necessary to express a multiple sum, for example in section 3.1 the average nearest-neighbour distance is calculated by summing r_1, r_2 up to r_n and dividing by n. This can be written as $\frac{1}{n}(r_1 + r_2 + \ldots + r_n)$ but it is simpler and shorter to write it as $\frac{1}{n}\sum_{i-1}^{n} r_i$; the 'range' of the subscript i (from 1 to n) means that one starts summing at r_1, and finishes at r_n. Where the range is obvious from the context, the expression can safely be shortened to $\frac{1}{n}\Sigma r$, and further to $\bar{r}$ ('r-bar').

Multiple products (e.g. $r_1 \times r_2 \times \ldots \times r_n$) are also used. The standard mathematical shorthand for this is $\prod_{i=1}^{n} r_i$, or just Πr.

(iii) *Factorials*: a special case of the multiple product is the factorial. Written as $n!$, it is the product $1 \times 2 \times 3 \times \ldots \times n$. An important piece of notation related to the factorial is the *binomial coefficient*, written as $\binom{n}{r}$, and standing for $\dfrac{n!}{r! \times (n-r)!}$. It will be used extensively in chapter 6. Two important properties of the binomial coefficient are that $\binom{n}{r} = \binom{n}{n-r}$ and $\binom{n}{0} = 1$.

(iv) *Estimates*: an estimate of an unknown parameter is often denoted by a '^' or 'hat'. For example, in section 3.2 the parameter λ (lambda) has to be estimated from the site density, and this estimate is written as $\hat{\lambda}$.

1.2.2. *Distribution functions*

The important concepts of random variable and distribution function are discussed by Lindgren (pp. 31–90). ('Distribution' in this sense is *not* the same as the 'distribution' of a distribution map.) Suppose a variable x (for example, a squared nearest-neighbour distance as in section 3.2, p. 47) can take as its value any one of a set of real numbers, and that the probability (P) of x being less than or equal to a certain value, say ω (omega) is written as $P(x \leqslant \omega)$.

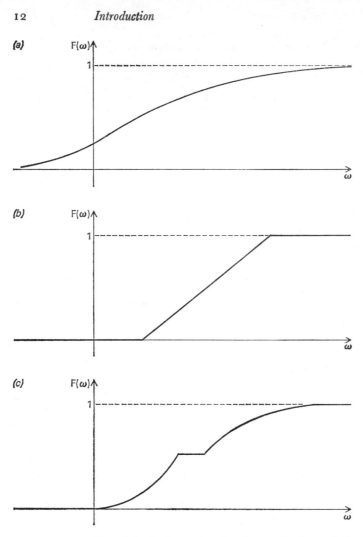

Fig.1.6 (*a–c*). Examples of various sorts of cumulative distribution functions. For explanation of symbols see text.

Then the function $F(\omega) = P(x \leqslant \omega)$ is a cumulative distribution function (cdf). A function of this sort will clearly increase (or stay the same) as the value of ω increases, and it will never be less than 0 or greater than 1 (because there cannot be a probability less than 0 or greater than 1). A few simple examples are shown in fig.1.6. A related function is the density function $f(\omega)$, which is in fact the derivative of the cdf, i.e. from the example just mentioned $f(\omega) = \dfrac{d}{d\omega} F(\omega) = \dfrac{d}{d\omega} P(x \leqslant \omega)$. It has the property that if the graph of $f(x)$ against x is drawn, the area to the left of the value $x = \omega$ and beneath the curve is equal to $F(\omega)$ (the shaded area of fig.1.7). Also the probability of

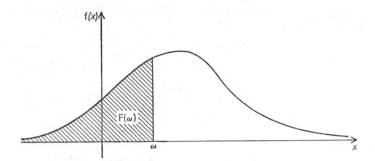

Fig.1.7. Example of density function showing relationship between it and the associated cumulative density function. For explanation of symbols see text.

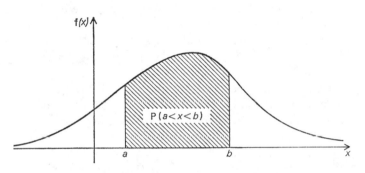

Fig.1.8. Example of a density function, showing probability interpretation of the area beneath the curve.

x falling between two values a and b, $P(a < x < b)$, equals the area beneath the curve between the values a and b (fig.1.8). The value of ω for which $F(\omega) = \alpha\%$ is known as the alpha-percentile of the distribution.

Also in section 3.2 (p. 47), *conditional* cdfs and density functions are used. They are distinguished by a short vertical line between the variable, in this case ω, and the condition (c). For example, $f(\omega | 0 \leqslant \omega \leqslant c)$ is the density function of ω on the condition that it must not be less than 0 nor greater than c.

Sometimes the variable can only take one of a finite (strictly speaking, countable) number of different values (for example, the number of sites in a grid-square can only be a whole number not exceeding the total number of sites). Such variables are called *discrete*, and their distributions are *discrete distributions*. They are characterised by the probabilities associated with the possible values the variable could take, which are written as $p_k = P(x = x_k)$ where x_k is one of the possible values x_0, x_1, x_2, etc.

The distributions most commonly used in this book are:

(i) The Normal distribution, $f(x) = \dfrac{1}{\sigma\sqrt{(2\pi)}} \exp\left\{-\dfrac{(x-\mu)^2}{2\sigma^2}\right\}$

(Lindgren, p. 88).

(ii) The (negative) exponential distribution, $f(x) = \lambda \exp(-\lambda x)$, $x > 0$, (Lindgren, p. 82) which are both continuous distributions, and

(iii) The Poisson distribution, $p_k = \exp(-m) \times m^k/m!$ (Lindgren, p. 76).

(iv) The negative binomial distribution, $p_k = \dfrac{(r+k-1)!}{k!(r-1)!}p^r q^k$,

where $q = 1 - p$, (Lindgren, p. 142) which are both discrete distributions.

Of these four distributions, two – the negative exponential and the Poisson – each have one parameter (λ and m respectively) which determine their shape, while two – the Normal and the negative binomial – have two parameters each (μ (mu), σ (sigma), and p, r respectively).

If one is considering two (or more) variables, it may be that the conditional distribution of one, given the value of the other, is independent of that value (Lindgren, p. 103). In other words, the value of the second variable may tell us nothing about the value of the first. In such circumstances, the variables are said to be *independent*. Many statistical tests are based on the assumption that the variables concerned are independent, and will not otherwise be valid.

If two variables are not independent, one may be interested in the degree of relationship or 'coherence' between them. The most common measure of coherence is the correlation coefficient, usually denoted by ρ (rho). It can take any value from -1 to $+1$: if it is zero the variables are said to be 'uncorrelated', while a value of $+1$ indicates perfect positive correlation and -1 perfect negative correlation. Uncorrelated variables need not necessarily be independent, but independent variables are always uncorrelated (see section 5.1).

Suppose we have a random sample $\mathbf{x} = x_1, x_2, \ldots, x_n$ from a distribution with density function $f(x)$, which is determined by a single parameter θ (theta), and can therefore be written as $f(x, \theta)$. The density function will take a separate value for each of the $x_i - f(x_1, \theta)$, etc. Multiplying all these together gives us a new function $L(\theta) = \prod\limits_{i=1}^{n} f(x_i, \theta)$ which is known as the *likelihood function* (Lindgren, p. 222). This can be used to estimate the parameter θ: *the maximum likelihood estimate* of θ being that value which maximises the likelihood function $L(\theta)$. However, we shall be more interested in comparing likelihood functions for different values of θ (see next section).

1.2.3 *Statistical tests*

Suppose we have a hypothesis (often called a *null* hypothesis if it is a particularly simple one) about a certain situation, which we wish to test by reference to a certain set of data. For example, in section 3.1 we use the hypothesis that a point-pattern is random in order to study a distribution pattern of sites. In such a situation there are two sorts of mistake one can make – (i) falsely rejecting a true hypothesis (called a type I error) and (ii) falsely accepting an untrue hypothesis (called a type II error). In devising a statistical test we have to agree on an acceptable chance of making a type I error – it might be a very small chance if the implications of rejecting the hypothesis are far-reaching, or it might be larger if we are using the hypothesis as an 'Aunt Sally' and are not committed to it. This chance is called the *significance level* of the test – commonly used values are 5 % and 1 %, but any value can be used. The test will then be to reject the hypothesis if some statistic based on the data (known as a *test statistic*) exceeds a *critical value* which depends on the test being used and on the significance level chosen. If, having performed the test, we say that 'the result is significant at the 5 % level' we mean that, if the null hypothesis were true, the probability of obtaining a set of data no more favourable to the hypothesis than our actual set of data, is 5 % or less.

As a simple example, suppose we take a sample of n observations from a Normal distribution with known variance 1 but unknown mean, and that our null hypothesis is that the mean $\theta = 0$. We choose 5 % as our significance level, which (via tables of the Normal distribution) tells us to reject the null hypothesis if the mean of our observations is outside the range $-1.96/\sqrt{n}$ to $+1.96/\sqrt{n}$ (the critical values). We calculate the mean (our test statistic), find that its value lies outside this range and say that it differs significantly from zero, at the 5 % level.

A rather different situation occurs if we have two hypotheses and wish to choose between them. This can be done (as in section 4.3) by calculating the likelihood function (or its greatest value) under each hypothesis and dividing one by the other to form a *likelihood ratio* (LR). There will be a critical value of this ratio, below which one hypothesis will be accepted and above which the other (see p. 82).

The topic of hypothesis testing is covered much more fully by Lindgren (pp. 232–67).

A particular case is the situation when the null hypothesis specifies the form of the parent distribution of which our data is a sample – for example, that our data are a random sample from a Poisson distribution. In such cases a *goodness-of-fit* test is often used. The well-known χ^2 (chi-squared) test (Cochran, 1952) is one such, but there are many others. Such tests are usually employed when the possible alternative to the hypothesis is not well defined. Lindgren (p. 296) points out a disconcerting feature of goodness-of-fit tests – that if the sample is large enough then the null hypothesis would almost certainly be rejected, since the true state of the situation, while perhaps very close to our null hypothesis, is probably not *exactly* as specified in the null hypothesis. The question to be asked may then be 'is the difference practically significant?' rather than 'is it statistically significant?'.

2
Archaeological distribution maps:

*a quantified approach and
associated problems*

It has been said that this study is an attempt to apply more rigorous
quantitative techniques to the analysis of archaeological distributions.
In this section the construction and simple examination of such distribution maps will be examined, and some of the many associated
problems posed by archaeological evidence in this respect will be
pointed out.

Any map is, in a sense, an attempt at quantification. It provides the
empirical evidence on which some theory can be built. But such a map
can be totally misleading due to the uneven way archaeological information survives and is collected. Included on the map, or in the discussion of the map, should be some attempt to assess its reliability.
Some of the ways of doing this will be discussed in this section. As well
as including information about the degree of distortion in the map, it is
also possible to include a much greater amount of quantified data than
is usually thought worthwhile. A major advance, for example, would
be to obtain some idea of the relative amount of the mapped variable at
each site or in each area. The percentage of a pottery type and the
relative amount of stone axes from different sources are instances of this.
With such information, much more detailed spatial trends can be
identified and examined. Some of the types of data which are worth
collecting will be discussed for two types of distributions: site and
artifact distributions.

2.1 *Site distributions*

Data on the altitude, aspect, local environment etc. of sites are often
collected and of value. One type of additional information which could
be collected about such distributions and which would lead to a much
better understanding about settlement patterns is some estimate of the
size of each site. It will be shown (p. 69) that one of the more interesting
characteristics of site relationships is their hierarchical organisation. By

ranking sites according to some criterion such as size, the spatial
relationship of settlements of different rank can be examined. As a
result of an interest in site size, Salway, Hallam and Bromwich (1970)
were able to identify a trend, in the first to fourth centuries A.D. in the
Fenlands, of increasing agglomeration into larger settlement clusters.

Deetz (1967, 11) has defined an archaeological site as 'a spatial
concentration of material evidence of human activity'. In certain cases,
however, it may prove difficult to define what is meant by a site on the
ground. Chang (1972) has listed some of the types of site which may be
encountered.

> An isolated house, granary, storage pit, or a continuous area
> incorporating a number of houses, granaries, and/or pits.
> A deposit of rubbish and other occupational debris distributed in a
> continuous area and deposited over a period of time during which
> no significant changes occurred – often delineated above and
> below by depositional disconformities.
> A burial in isolation.
> A workshop or work area in isolation.
> A kill site and/or butchering site in isolation.
> An isolated hearth.
> An overnight camp or one of short duration.
> A continuous area with all or a number of the above [*ibid.*, 9].

Although some of these sites are easy to delineate on the ground, others
are less so. In a surface survey of the Fenlands (Salway *et al.* 1970), an
individual site was described as 'a scatter of ploughed domestic debris,
often over an area of dark occupation soil' (*ibid.*, 49). These patches
varied in size from about 15 m long to an area 122 by 91.5 m, and were
assumed to indicate a farmyard, building or settlement. Groups of these
sites often represented a number of farms which overlapped in time.
Some difficulty, however, was found in deciding how close habitation
traces had to be before they could be described as one settlement. This
is a problem which may often occur in analysing crop marks. In the
Fenlands an arbitrary limit was chosen. Sites separated by less than
152.4 m were grouped into a settlement. These settlements often seemed
to be grouped into clusters. A rather different approach was used to
define settlement 'complexes' from these clusters. A quantitative
analysis of the distances between settlements showed that 'neighbouring
settlements lie between 500' [152.4 m] and 1500' [457.2 m] of each
other, more frequently than one would expect if they showed random
scatter, giving a unimodal curve' (*ibid.*). Settlements less than 457.2 m
apart were therefore grouped into complexes.

Another difficulty in defining the size of a site and the spatial
relationship between sites is that of the contemporaneity of the components. Was all of a large site occupied at one period? Are the sites
mapped in a distribution study precisely contemporaneous? Without
stratigraphical evidence it is often difficult to demonstrate such con-

temporaneity given the broad chronological divisions with which archaeologists are forced to work. It may also be difficult to determine whether a site was temporarily or permanently inhabited. Similarly 'a pile of industrial waste accumulated by ten flint knappers in one day and a pile accumulated by one flint knapper in ten days would be very difficult, if not impossible, to distinguish' (Chang 1972, 10). Chronological imprecision is more marked in earlier periods than in late, but it is a great restriction for the analysis of between-site relationships.

Perhaps the most serious problem associated with site distributions is the way they have been distorted by erosion, destruction and differences in fieldwork intensity (Taylor, C. 1971). The archaeologist has to work with an incomplete map, and he can rarely put much reliance on the picture such a map gives. The survival and destruction of sites is related to a large number of factors. For example, many sites must lie under expanses of modern urban sprawl. Ancient and modern settlement may be attracted by similar characteristics of the environment so the destruction and covering of sites in this way may be of extreme importance. Much depends also on the type and history of agriculture in an area, and the use of the subsoil for industrial purposes. In an important study, Benson and Miles (1974) have examined the effects of gravel extraction, suburban expansion, roads and modern agricultural methods on distributions of crop marks at a localised level in the upper Thames valley. 'It is obvious . . . that in the south and middle part of our area relatively little remains that is unaffected by suburban spread or gravel pits' (*ibid.*, 77).

The degree of intensity of research also varies considerably in different areas. This depends on, for example, the location and intents of active research institutes and the regional availability of funds. Intensity of research is also related to advances in air photography and, for example, the construction of motorways (Fowler 1969). Similarly, the numerous settlements found in the mountainous areas of Scandinavia 'were previously little known but came to light in recent years during systematic investigations in connection with water regulation, giving a completely new picture of finds and settlements in those regions' (Stjernquist 1966, 15). It may often be possible to assess the effects of site survival and fieldwork intensity on distributions. Kruk (1973) was able to produce a map of the degree of intensity of research in different parts of his study area. In the light of this, the map of archaeological finds is easier to interpret. It is in such studies of small areas that the effect of the history of recovery can best be examined. In certain cases it may prove possible to reconstruct distributions by weighting different areas according to the intensity of research and the resulting likelihood of sites having been recovered.

One of the main approaches to archaeological settlement studies is to map sites on different soil types or ecological zones (chapter 7). Even when it can be reliably shown that such soil maps represent the pattern contemporaneous with the sites and that they are not themselves the result of man's interference nor of climatic change, a relationship with the site distribution does not entail a direct causal connection. A number of environmental variables such as soil texture, fertility and woodland cover may be related to one soil type and it may be any one of these or none of them which has attracted human settlement. For example, a colonising settlement may choose a location because it is well situated for defense. Daughter settlements may prefer to locate near the mother settlement for social reasons. The whole cluster of settlements may be on one soil type although there is no causal connection.

As far as patterning within sites is concerned, the collection of more detailed quantified information may well prove to be of value (Clarke 1972). Detailed distributions of surface material may suggest functionally different areas. This may help in the excavation strategy, or, if excavation is not to be carried out, may allow comparison with similar excavated sites. Redman and Watson (1970) have made a detailed study of surface collections from two mounds in Turkey (Cayönü and Girik-i-Haciyan) to examine whether 'surface and subsurface artifact distributions are related so that a description of the first will allow a prediction of the second' (*ibid.*, 280). It could be shown that there was a high relationship at these sites between the distribution of surface material and subsurface excavated material.

2.2. *Artifact distributions*

Artifact distributions are affected by fieldwork intensity and survival conditions in much the same way as sites. In both cases blank areas on the map are difficult to interpret. These may not mean that the artifacts or sites did not occur there, but only that they have not been found there. For artifact distributions the problem can to some extent be alleviated by showing 'negatives' – that is contemporaneous sites where the artifact in question has not been found. This is a method used, for example, by Jope (1963). Similarly, in a study of the distribution of neolithic axe-hammers the pattern of finds from one source could be compared and contrasted with axe-hammers from other sources (p. 107). In a study of fine metalwork of the late pre-Roman Iron Age in southern England, Spratling (1972) examined the reliability of his distributional data by plotting all known finds and then, separately, all those finds made by 'chance' – that is omitting finds from excavations. Both maps are very similar and it appears that excavation has made no difference to the picture of distributions of objects. If it be said that the factors determining the pattern of excavation are different from those affecting single 'chance' finds (which is perhaps not wholly justifiable),

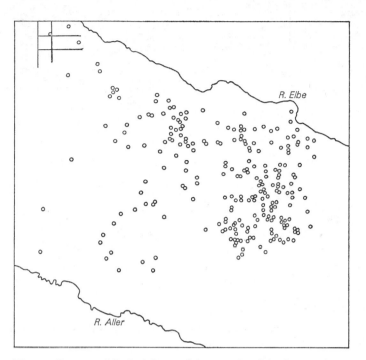

Fig.2.1. Pattern of finds (1820–79) in a study of the Bronze Age in north Germany. The section of a lattice shows the size of quadrat used in the analysis (see text). Information from Laux 1971.

then this approach provides some indication of the reliability of the distributions.

In fact, it is often possible to gauge the impact of fieldwork on artifact distributions. In Laux's (1971) study of part of the Tumulus grave Bronze Age in north Germany, the pattern of finds made at different time periods between 1820 and 1964 by museums and private collectors is shown. He concludes from this (*ibid.*, 29) that each part of his study area was at some time well investigated so that there are no gaps in the pattern of research. It is therefore possible to conclude that if an artifact type is not found in an area it was not likely to have been used there.

The factors influencing the recovery of artifacts at different periods in Laux's study vary considerably. It is of interest to see whether the varying influence of these different factors has a great impact on the overall pattern of artifact retrieval. This is tested by using the V coefficient of spatial association which is to be discussed below (section 6.1, p. 203). We can ask whether the patterns of finds at different phases vary significantly in the area between the Elbe and Aller rivers (figs.2.1 and 2.2). If we compare the pattern of finds made in the period

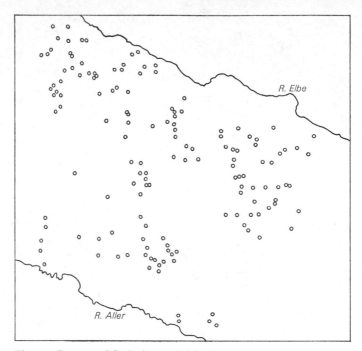

Fig.2.2. Pattern of finds (1921–64) in the same study as fig.2.1.

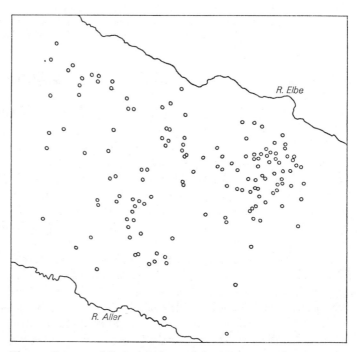

Fig.2.3. Pattern of finds (1876–1920) in the same study as fig.2.1.

from 1820 to 1879 with that in the period 1921 to 1964, we find there is significant association between the two patterns at $p = 0.01$ (table 2.1). In other words, there is a probability (p) of less than 1 in 100 that the observed degree of association could have occurred 'by chance'.

Table 2.1. *The relationship between the pattern of finds made in north Germany in 1820–79 and 1921–64*

| | | 1820–79 | | |
		Present	Absent	Total
1921– 64	Present	56	52	108
	Absent	57	175	232
	Total	113	227	340

$V = 0.28$; significant at $p = 0.01$

This association was considered at the scale of the squares in fig.2.1. If, however, we join all adjacent four squares to produce a larger quadrat, the V coefficient of association is increased (table 2.2).

Table 2.2. *The relationship between the pattern of finds made in north Germany in 1820–79 and 1921–64 at a broader scale*

| | | 1820–79 | | |
		Present	Absent	Total
1921– 64	Present	40	12	52
	Absent	12	19	31
	Total	52	31	83

$V = 0.39$; significant at $p = 0.01$

There is thus greater similarity between the two distributions at a less detailed scale. With greater detail, variation is noticeable. For example, there are more late finds to the northwest and south, and more early finds to the northeast. It is of great importance that, in general, the effect of differential survival and fieldwork depends to a considerable extent on the scale at which the pattern is studied.

If we compare two more recent periods (1876–1920 and 1921–64), we find an even higher degree of association at the smaller scale (figs.2.2 and 2.3, and table 2.3).

There is thus less difference between the two later periods than between the earliest and latest. On the whole it seems that, although the factors influencing the recovery of artifacts change through time, the overall pattern of finds does not in this case vary significantly.

Table 2.3.   *The relationship between the pattern of finds made in north Germany in 1876–1920 and 1921–64*

		1921–64		
		Present	Absent	Total
1876–	Present	42	9	51
1920	Absent	9	21	30
	Total	51	30	81

$V = 0.52$; significant at $p = 0.01$

Some of the additional quantitative information which might be included in artifact distribution studies is an indication of the context of the find. For example, the maps produced by Bergmann (1970) of the distributions of early Bronze Age finds in northwest Germany give different symbols for occurrences in graves, hoards, settlements or as single finds. The context of deposition shows interesting spatial patterning (Hodder 1975). The early Bronze Age spearheads from Scandinavia and north Germany studied by Jacob-Friesen (1967) occur in hoards in some areas and in graves in others (see p. 169). Such differences might be taken to indicate social variation.

For artifacts from a known source or which are clearly defined, an important type of information which can be collected is the percentage of the artifacts in the total assemblage of items. For example, the percentage of an obsidian or a pottery type (cf. Peacock 1969*b*) may be counted. Trends in the spatial variation of these percentages may yield information about trade and exchange patterns (Renfrew 1969; 1972*b*). The problems associated with the collection and analysis of such data are to be discussed in section 5.2, but some of the more immediate advantages may be mentioned here. In a study of the distribution of Romano-British pottery in the south and west of England (Hodder 1974*d*) detailed data were collected for the percentages of pottery types at a large number of sites. It was hoped that this would yield information about marketing processes or would at least indicate what additional knowledge could be obtained. In fig.2.4 is shown the distribution in the southwest of late Romano-British fine wares such as mortaria and the other good quality products of the Oxford and New Forest kilns. Contemporaneous sites where such pottery is absent are indicated,

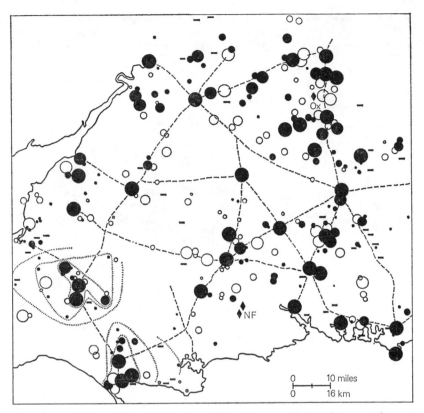

Fig.2.4. The distribution of late Romano-British fine ware in southwest England. The New Forest (NF) and Oxford (Ox) kilns (◆) are indicated. ○, Assemblages with fine wares and coarse-ware rims, bases and decorated pieces; ●, assemblages also containing coarse-ware body sherds. The size of the circle for each site reflects the percentage of fine pottery in the total assemblage.
Dashed lines = roads; horizontal bars = sites without fine pottery; dotted lines = contours suggesting concentrations around important centres. Source: Hodder 1974*d*.

and the size of circle for each site reflects the percentage of fine pottery in the total assemblage. One of the major problems in analysing such distributions results from the common practice of keeping much or all of the fine in preference to the other wares and so greatly increasing its percentage. To try and overcome this problem the sites in fig.2.4 have been divided according to whether only the interesting sherds have been kept – that is fine wares and coarse-ware rims, bases and decorated pieces (open circles in fig.2.4) – or whether they also have coarse-ware body sherds (filled circles in fig.2.4). This may appear extremely arbitrary since different amounts of body sherds have been retained in

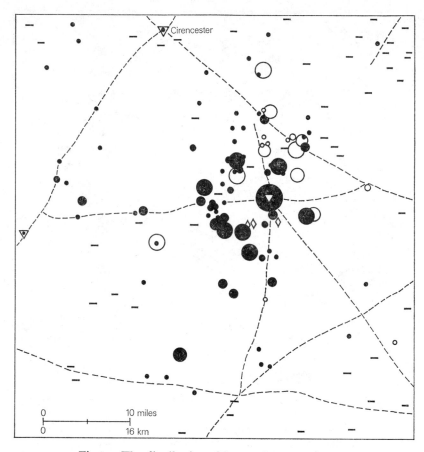

Fig.2.5. The distribution of Savernake ware. ▽, Walled towns;
◇, Savernake kilns; dashed lines = roads; horizontal bars =
sites without the pottery type. ○, collections of rims, bases
and decorated sherds; ●, assemblages including many
coarse-ware body sherds without decoration. Source: Hodder
1974*d*.

different collections. In practice, however, the presence of unremarkable
body sherds was found to be a good indicator of a fairly complete
collection. The resulting distribution map shows that in the late third
and fourth centuries finer wares were only found in large percentages
(20 % to 25 %) in the towns and in sites on or near the roads (see also
Swan 1973, 123–4). These sites with high percentages of fine pottery
are not all one class of important site, such as villas, but include small
rural settlements such as Durrington. Their main point of similarity,
therefore, may be suggested as being propinquity to the main roads.
However, by producing a detailed map, it is clear that, in fact, few sites

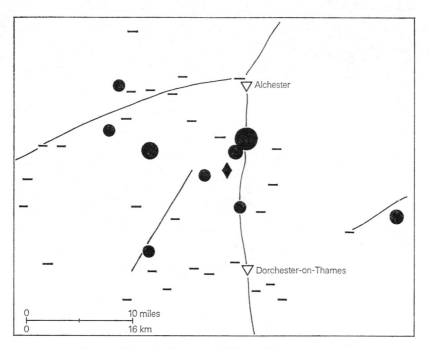

Fig.2.6. The distribution of 'Churchill orange' coarse-ware jars produced in the Oxford kilns. ▽, Walled towns; ◆, kilns; continuous lines = roads; horizontal bars = sites without the pottery type. Source: Hodder 1974*d*.

have been studied away from the roads. The apparent clustering on the roads may be fortuitous.

Further analyses of Romano-British coarse pottery were able to identify two types of marketing mechanisms. The first type is exemplified by fig.2.5, in which less reliable (small) samples are again shown as open circles (Hodder 1974*b*). The kilns producing this Savernake pottery are near a walled town and the main concentration of high percentages of pottery is in a localised area around the town and kilns, with some westward extension along the main roads. The overall pattern of finds is widespread, but by showing percentages and contemporaneous sites without the pottery type more information is available. It could be suggested (*ibid.*) that the main marketing of the products was through the central walled town. In fig.2.6, on the other hand, some coarse-ware products of the Oxford kilns occur around the kilns but not in the areas around the nearby walled towns (Hodder 1974*d*). The kiln production is on a larger scale than in the previous example and marketing seems to have been able to take place without reliance on a major market town. Similar studies of other Romano-British coarse pottery types were able to give further support for these

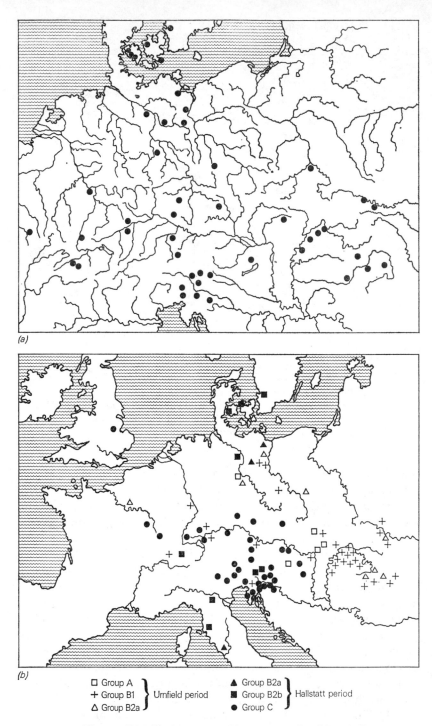

(a)

(b)

□ Group A ⎫
+ Group B1 ⎬ Urnfield period
△ Group B2a ⎭

▲ Group B2a ⎫
■ Group B2b ⎬ Hallstatt period
● Group C ⎭

Fig.2.7. Distribution maps of bronze vessels with cruciform handle fittings. (a) after Sprockhoff; (b) after von Merhart. Source: Stjernquist 1966.

two types of marketing mechanism. In spite of the difficulties in analysing such material (p. 104), detailed study would seem to be worthwhile.

In the above discussion artifacts from a known source have been considered. In studying the distributions of types of artifact an important factor is the way the artifact type has been defined. Some artifacts, such as simple flat axes, are less capable of detailed definition than others which are highly decorated and complex, such as decorated pottery or Iron Age fibulae. Different researchers may wish to define an artifact type in different ways. Defining a type according to functional traits may produce rather different results in spatial studies from the same artifacts defined by stylistic traits. The effect of the definition of an artifact type on distributional studies is of some importance and has been examined in a study of middle Bronze Age palstaves (section 5.2).

Azoury and Hodson (1972) have examined the influence of using different trait lists on the typological clustering of artifacts. Spatial patterning was not considered. Stjernquist (1966, 18–21) has provided a further example of the problem. She compared Sprockhoff's (1930) and von Merhart's maps of bronze vessels with cruciform handle fittings. Sprockhoff's map shows no differentiation between the various examples, but von Merhart distinguishes localised groups of vessels which have a chronological significance. As Stjernquist (1966, 18) stated 'the interpretation of the chronologically differentiated map as regards the place of manufacture and the lines of communication will be totally different depending on whether von Merhart's map or Sprockhoff's is followed.'

It appears, then, that there are some serious problems associated with the analysis of archaeological distribution maps. These problems can usually be taken into account in a spatial study and it would often seem possible to construct maps of erosion, destruction and fieldwork intensity against which the maps of archaeological finds can be compared. The varying reliability of archaeological samples can often be indicated on a map by the use of different types of symbols. The more quantified information which is on a map or which pertains to spatial patterning the better that map can be discussed and interpreted. This is already apparent from the above discussion and will become clearer in the more detailed analyses in the following chapters.

3
Point pattern analysis

This chapter is concerned with the analysis of distributions of points, whether these points be artifacts within a site, artifacts scattered over an area, or archaeological sites. Although the methods involved are becoming increasingly more used in archaeology they were developed in plant ecology and geography. In all these fields 'the study of spatial patterns starts from the assumption of randomness' (Ord 1972), and it is first necessary to define what is meant by this term. If an area is divided up into cells (*quadrats*) and points are allocated to the area at random, then we mean that every quadrat has an equal and independent chance of receiving a point, and every point in turn has an equal and independent chance of occurring in any one quadrat. The probability that a quadrat will contain exactly x points is given by the Poisson function (King 1969, 42).

This theoretical random process can be used as a norm against which a particular pattern may be examined and measured. Stimulating generalisations about spatial pattern can then often be made. But fitting probability distributions such as the Poisson to the data really amounts to fitting *a priori* models which have no necessary theoretical validity and to which it is difficult to give a real-world interpretation (Harvey 1969, 381). However, it will be shown below (p. 53) that the random process model can perhaps be given a theoretical interpretation. The general approach followed here is to search maps of points for some order or structure.

> In terms of map pattern, pure chance means that each map location has an equal probability of receiving a symbol. Since it is highly unlikely that geographic distributions, particularly locational patterns involving human decisions, are the result of equally probable events, it is expected that most map patterns reflect some system or order. It is for this reason that map patterns are examined for evidence of a spatial process [Dacey 1964, 559].

For example, three types of distribution are shown in fig.3.1 (*a–c*). Most maps will have patterns intermediate between these extreme

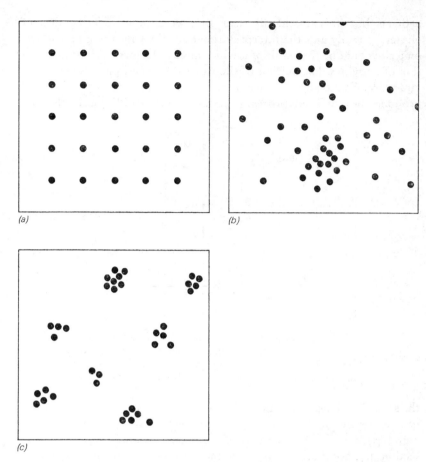

Fig.3.1. Possible patterns of points on maps. (*a*) Points regularly spaced on a grid or network; (*b*) points scattered at random; (*c*) points grouped in clusters. Source: Davis 1973.

values, and the problem is to determine where the pattern lies within the spectrum of possible distributions. For example, the distribution of points in fig.3.2 might be considered random by many people. It is not, because the map was first divided into regular cells and one point then placed at random within each cell. The distribution therefore has both random and regular aspects (Davis 1973, 301). As Stanislawski (1973) has pointed out, the identification of a structured pattern does not mean that anything has been explained. The identification is simply an aid in the interpretation of the spatial process which produced the pattern.

Techniques for distinguishing non-random patterns have recently come to be widely applied in archaeology. For example, the distribution of artifacts within a site can be used to define localisations of activities. It may be possible to identify non-random clusters of artifacts but it is not at all clear that the simple identification of clustering really aids the interpretation of a site. Clustering of artifacts on a site could be the result of a wide range of factors, such as localisation of activities, localisation of the discard of tools, periodic cleaning and reorganisation of a site, wind and water disturbance, or differential erosion. These different processes are unlikely to be distinguishable from

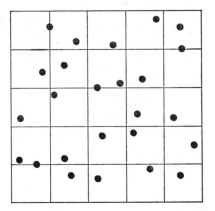

Fig.3.2. An apparently random pattern created by assigning one point to a random location within a regular pattern of cells. The distribution of points is more uniform than expected for a completely random pattern. Source: Davis 1973.

the spatial patterns alone and by the simple methods of analysis usually used. (For the application of more complex methods see sections 3.2 and 4.4.) The simpler methods of point pattern analysis, discussed in section 3.1, are more valuable for the analysis of distributions of sites, because here the identification of non-random uniformity of spacing can usually be explained readily in terms of competition between sites (see section 4.2). However, studies of both within-site and between-site patterns have been carried out by archaeologists. For example, Whallon has examined the distribution of flint debitage, plant and animal remains on occupation floors in the cave site of Guila Naquitz in the valley of Oaxaca, Mexico (Whallon 1973). He has also searched for spatial patterning in the distribution of tool types on a Protomagdalenian occupation floor at the Abri Pataud in southwestern France (Whallon 1974). Dacey (1973) has used the methods to analyse tool type distributions because 'a defect with a visual approach is the difficulty of insuring that other analysts can replicate the assessments and, thereby, the inferences they support' (*ibid.*, 320). Hill (1966) has also examined the pattern of objects within a site. 'Non-random distributions of ceramic design elements, pottery types, firepit types, storage pits, "chopper" types and animal bone indicated discrete *localisations* within the pueblo (which could not be explained in terms of functionally specific areas)' (*ibid.*, 17). It was considered of interest that only the female items showed spatial clustering while the spacing of male items appeared random. Longacre and Deetz have suggested that in a matrilineal and/or matrilocal society ceramic training involves a woman teaching her daughter or other local lineage and/or residence group mates. Some spatial clustering of stylistic elements on pottery is therefore to be expected, although Stanislawski (1973) has claimed that there is no evidence of such patterning as yet, and that clustering of stylistic elements may result from a wide range of factors.

For wider distributions of artifacts Thomas (1972) in his discussion of Great Basin socio-economic patterns has suggested that for autumn activities 'in the archaeological record, artifacts would be deposited primarily in the piñon [nut] harvesting areas and those zones connected with seed sowing and hunting. The harvesting, winter village and rabbit-driving implements are in a clumped distribution, while hunting artifacts tend to be randomly distributed over piñon–juniper and upper sagebrush–grass zones' (*ibid.*, 681). The theoretical distributions of the artifacts could be simulated and compared with the observed patterns.

The tests have also been used to examine the distribution of archaeological sites. Examples are the studies of Iron Age hillforts in Wales (Pierson-Jones 1973) and of hillforts in Cornwall (Hodder 1971; Newcomb 1970). Identification of a non-random pattern was the first stage in the examination of the spacing of Romano-British walled towns (Hodder and Hassall 1971; Hodder 1972). Peebles (1973) has used similar techniques to identify clustering of mound sites in Alabama. Changes in settlement patterns over time (related to a supposed climatic deterioration) have been studied by Washburn (1974), using nearest-neighbour methods on data from a surface survey of Pueblo sites on the middle Rio Puerco of the East, New Mexico.

3.1 *Methods of point pattern analysis*

Tests for randomness can be divided into quadrat methods and distance methods. These and some alternatives will be briefly discussed in this section. In the case of quadrat methods the area is divided up by a uniform grid of squares or rectangles, and the number of observations in each quadrat of the grid is recorded. Although it is theoretically possible to use a grid of triangles or hexagons, they do not seem to have been used in practice. Tests for non-random patterns have been devised, based on the property that for a random pattern the numbers of quadrats containing 0, 1, 2, ... etc. points are determined by the Poisson function (Greig-Smith 1964, 61). The numbers of quadrats containing 0, 1, 2, ... etc. points can be counted, and this observed frequency distribution can be directly compared with the Poisson distribution corresponding to the same density of points, by means of a goodness-of-fit test and the χ^2 statistic (*ibid.*; Davis 1973, 305). Alternatively a test can be based on the property of the Poisson distribution that its mean and variance are equal. For a random distribution of points, the variance/mean ratio (V/m) is equal to one: for a regular distribution it is less than one and for a clustered distribution more than one. The significance of departures of the observed ratio from a value of one can be tested by comparing the index of dispersion, $(V/m) \times (n-1)$, where n is the number of quadrats, with the χ^2 statistic for $n-1$ degrees of freedom (Greig-Smith 1964, 63). The use of these tests in an archaeological context has been suggested by Whallon (1973). The variance/mean ratio test has been used by Dacey (1973) in his study of the distribution of tool types at the Sole Divshon site in the Avdat area. Carinated scrapers were found to have a random pattern although this was not the case for end scrapers and burins. Thomas (1972, 698–9) has used the variance/mean ratio to examine the distributions of artifacts over an area. 'The artifacts of a winter village should be in a clumped distribution, for they would not be expected to be randomly strewn across the landscape' (*ibid.*, 698). On the other hand, 'projectile points lost while pursuing deer in the upper sagebrush–grass zone of the Reese river valley are expected to fall in a Poisson distribution' (*ibid.*, 699). These expectations and their variance/mean ratios are reproduced in fig.3.3. An additional method for studying point patterns which uses quadrats is that which tests for spatial autocorrelation. A discussion of this is left until section 5.5.

 A further approach using quadrats allows the search for structured pattern to be carried out at different scales. Greig-Smith (1952; 1964) uses a method in which each side of the imposed grid of contiguous quadrats has a number of quadrats which is a power of 2, e.g. 16 × 16, 32 × 64. The number of points in each quadrat is first counted. Adjacent pairs of quadrats are then combined to give oblong two-quadrat 'blocks' which are twice as big and half as numerous as the original quadrats (Pielou 1969, 104). Adjacent two-quadrat blocks are next combined to give square four-quadrat blocks. In this way a sequence of block sizes is obtained in which the block area is doubled at each step. The sum of squares (S) for each block size is then calculated. For block size j, this value is

$$S_j = \frac{1}{j} \Sigma N_{j(i)}^2 \tag{3.1}$$

where $N_{j(i)}$ is the number of points in the ith block of j grid squares, and the values of N^2 are summed over all such blocks. From this the variance of 'mean square between blocks' (M) is calculated as

$$M_j = (S_j - S_{2j})/D_j \tag{3.2}$$

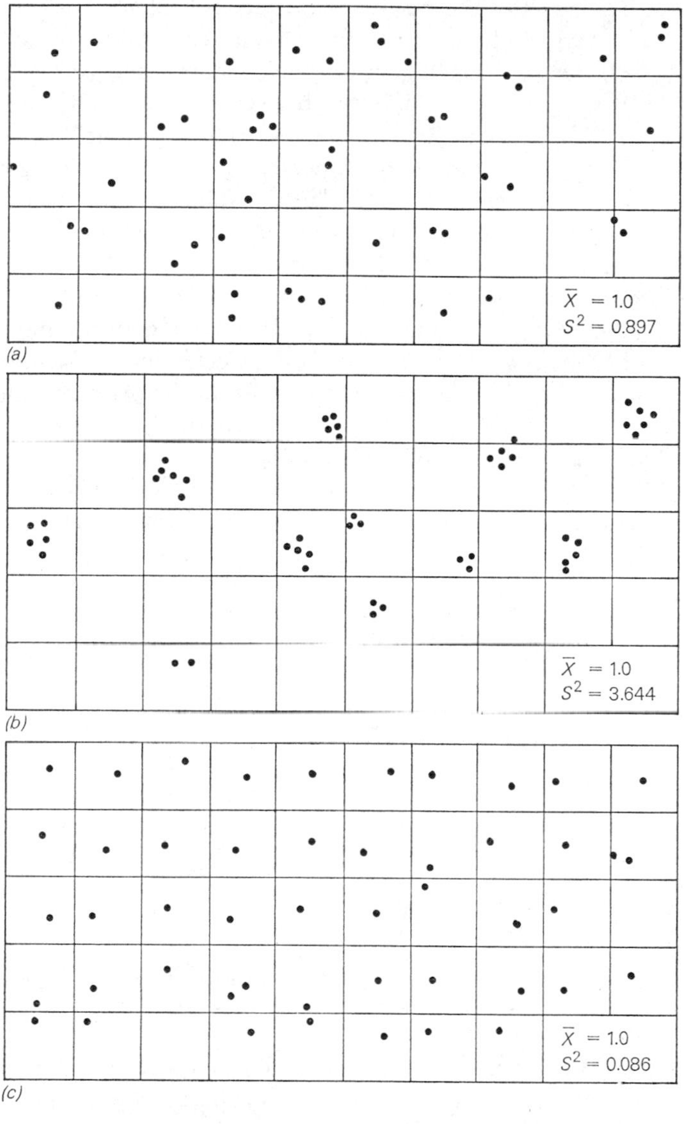

Fig.3.3. Simulated point distributions within a grid system. Each example contains 48 points. Means ($\bar{X}$) and variances (S^2) are shown. (*a*) Random distribution (variance/mean ratio of 0.90); (*b*) clumped distribution (ratio of 3.64); (*c*) dispersed distribution (ratio of 0.09). Source: Thomas 1972.

where the number of degrees of freedom (D_j) is defined as

$$D_j = T/2j \tag{3.3}$$

T being the total number of quadrats in the grid.

If a graph of the mean square for each block size is drawn, block sizes at which there is a tendency to clustering will show as peaks in the graph, because moving to the next larger block size (i.e. from '*j*' to '*2j*') reduces the variability between blocks. The significance of observed peaks can be tested by converting the calculated variance for a given block size into a variance/mean ratio by dividing by the mean number of items per block of that size (Greig-Smith 1964, 87; Whallon 1973), and applying the variance/mean ratio test described above. However, Whallon has suggested that a subjective appraisal of 'significance' may be more appropriate in some circumstances.

The main advantage of tests based on quadrat methods is that archaeological information is often collected in this form. For example, on a palaeolithic site the numbers of artifacts per excavation unit may be known, but often not the exact location of each artifact. There are, however, a number of problems associated with the use of quadrats. The first of these is that the results are seriously affected by the size of quadrat used. This may be illustrated from fig.3.4, which shows a

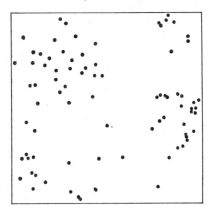

Fig.3.4. Patches of higher density imposed on a general distribution at lower density. Source: Greig-Smith 1964.

slightly clustered pattern (Greig-Smith 1964, 56). A relatively small quadrat will clearly tend to be unoccupied more often in such a distribution than in one with the same density of points randomly distributed. There will, therefore, be evidence of a non-random pattern. With an even smaller quadrat, which is so small that even when within a cluster of points it is usually unoccupied, a different result emerges. Unless a very large number of samples is taken, the pattern will appear random. If a large quadrat is used, such that it generally includes one or several high density patches, the grouping together of points will tend to affect only their distribution within the quadrat and not the number it contains. The distribution will thus tend to appear random. These conclusions have been checked on artificial distributions by Greig-

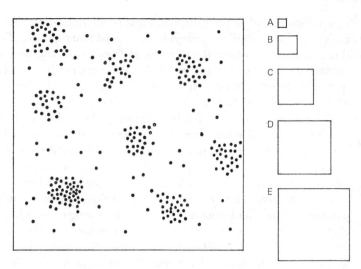

Fig.3.5. Relations between sampling quadrats and pattern.
Sampling with smaller quadrats (A and B) suggests slight
clustering, with intermediate quadrats (C) strong clustering,
and with large quadrats (D and E) regularity. Sources:
Kershaw 1964; Haggett 1965.

Smith (1952). The presence and scale of clustering that can be identified depend to a considerable extent on the size of quadrat used. This is
also clear from fig.3.5.

A further problem is the shape of the quadrat used. Ord (1972)
suggests that the effect of this is less marked than that of the size of the
quadrat (cf. King 1969, 109). In certain cases, however, the shape of
quadrat used may be of importance. For example, Stiteler and Patil
(1971) have shown that for a pattern of points located at the vertices of
a square lattice, sampling with long thin rectangular quadrats (the
shape of many excavation trenches) may yield a distribution of quadrat
counts with a variance/mean ratio of greater than one, which would
usually be taken as evidence of clustering, rather than regularity. This
may be a rather extreme situation, but it is worth bearing in mind.

Archaeological distributions are often of a small number of points
and this provides a further difficulty in the use of quadrat methods. The
variance/mean ratio test, for example, appears to behave erratically
when the mean is very small (Greig-Smith 1964, 70). Under this
condition the results must be interpreted with caution. The χ^2 goodness-
of-fit test will not be effective if the number of quadrats is small or the
density low. Because this test is only approximate and does not hold
sufficiently accurately for 'small' expected values (i.e. when the predicted number of quadrats containing a certain number of points each
is small), then if the number of quadrats predicted by the Poisson model
to have (for example) k points each is less than five, this group must be

merged with another (for example, those predicted to have $k - 1$ points each) and so on, until all groups have at least five quadrats. Sometimes this can greatly reduce the degrees of freedom of the test, and may obscure deviations from the predicted Poisson distribution. It may be preferable to use a test that does not suffer from this disadvantage, such as the Kolmogorov–Smirnov test (see section 7.1.2).

The advantage of the third test discussed above, in which the size of quadrat is gradually increased, is that the scale of pattern which can be determined is not limited to one quadrat size. However, since the block size is doubled at each step, there is no means of knowing what the form of the mean square/block size graph would have been if blocks of intermediate sizes had been used as well. Obviously no examination of pattern can be made below the minimum size of quadrat used. If elongated clusters occur in the point distribution then the quadrat grid must be orientated so that the long axes of the rectangular blocks formed in the analysis at least roughly correspond to the long axes of the spatial clusters being sought.

Perhaps the most severe restriction on the use of the mean square/ block size method is that imposed by the necessity of having a square or rectangular grid. The number of quadrats along each side of this square or rectangle must be some power of 2 (4, 8, 16, 32, 64 etc.). If the grid is rectangular, one axis must be twice the other (for example 8×16, 64×128). It is rare that an excavated area or surveyed area will conform to these limits, although Whallon (1973) suggests leaving aside a few minor, peripheral areas, and/or adding a few imaginary or 'dummy' quadrats to the area being analysed.

Pielou (1969, 105) has some further criticisms of this method. One of these is that the mean square/block size graph sometimes has a saw-toothed shape because oblong blocks consistently give mean squares less than those of the square blocks on either side of them in the sequence of sizes. A second criticism is illustrated by fig.3.6, in which a clustered pattern and its reverse are shown. These two have very similar mean square/block size graphs.

Because of the very severe problems associated with the use of quadrat methods, the more sensitive tests based on distance measures are more appropriate for most archaeological data. A useful test for the archaeologist is that supplied by Clark and Evans (1954). The basic data consist of the distances from each point to the point nearest to it (its 'nearest neighbour'). These distances are usually denoted by r. Suppose there are n points to be studied in an area of A units. Then the density of points, ρ, is given by

$$\rho = (n - 1)/A \qquad (3.4)$$

and the mean nearest-neighbour distance, $\bar{r}_0$, is given by

$$\bar{r}_0 = \Sigma r/n \qquad (3.5)$$

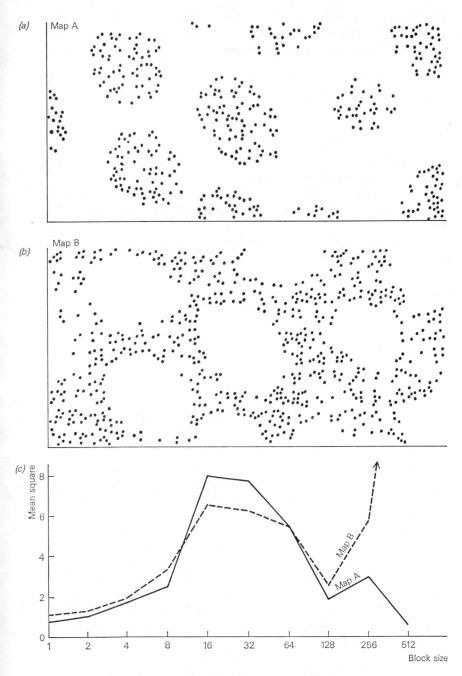

Fig.3.6. A cluster pattern (*a*) and its reverse (*b*) give very similar graphs of mean square versus block size. Source: Pielou 1969.

Clark and Evans (*ibid.*) showed that for a random distribution of points the expected mean nearest neighbour distance $(\bar{r}_e)$ depends only on the density of the points, and is in fact given by

$$\bar{r}_e = 1/(2\sqrt{\rho}). \tag{3.6}$$

The 'randomness' of the observed distribution is indicated by the ratio R, where

$$R = \bar{r}_o/\bar{r}_e. \tag{3.7}$$

For a random distribution $R = 1$, while for an aggregated (clustered) distribution R is less than 1, approaching zero in extreme cases, and for a regular distribution R is greater than 1, reaching as high as 2.1491 in the extreme case of a uniform arrangement of points on a triangular lattice.

One would often wish to go further and test whether the observed value $(\bar{r}_o)$ differs significantly from the expected value $(\bar{r}_e)$. The correct distribution for testing this difference is the Pearson type III distribution (Hodder 1971), but when n is large (over 100) the Normal distribution can be used as an adequate approximation. The standard error (σ) of $\bar{r}_e$ is

$$\sigma(\bar{r}_e) = 0.26136/\sqrt{(n\rho)} \tag{3.8}$$

and the test statistic is

$$C = (\bar{r}_o - \bar{r}_e)/\sigma(\bar{r}_e) \tag{3.9}$$

which can be compared with the standard Normal distribution at various significance levels. For example, the 5 % level of significance is reached when $C = 1.96$ and the 1 % level when $C = 2.58$. In many archaeological examples n will not be so large, and either the exact test or alternatively a test making use of a χ^2 statistic (Dacey 1963; King 1969, 100–1) should be used. Whallon (1974), in an application in archaeology, found that the χ^2 statistics were more conservative in their detection of spatial clustering than the Clark and Evans R statistic. They are, however, easier to use than tests based on the Pearson type III distribution.

Washburn (1974) has suggested that a comparison of the median nearest-neighbour distance, $\bar{r}_m$, with its expected value $\bar{r}_e$, may be more useful in some archaeological situations, particularly those with a few very large nearest-neighbour distances. In an appendix she gives the derivation (due to Holland) of $\bar{r}_e$ as

$$\bar{r}_e = (ln\ 2/\pi\rho)^{1/2}. \tag{3.10}$$

The ratio $R = \bar{r}_m/\bar{r}_e$ is shown to run from 0 (maximum clustering) through 1 (random pattern) to 2.29 (uniform pattern on a hexagonal lattice). A significance test for the difference between the observed value of R and the value for a random pattern is given, as is an analysis of variance test for comparing the median nearest-neighbour distances of two or more point patterns.

An important expansion of nearest-neighbour analysis is to include measurements to 2nd, 3rd ... nth nearest-neighbour (Greig-Smith 1964, 74; King 1959, 100). This is important because it allows determination of pattern at more than the most detailed scale. Dacey and Tung (1962) have discussed a method in which the area around each point is divided into k equal-sized sectors and the mean distance to nearest neighbour in each sector calculated and compared with expected values for theoretical patterns. They suggest this method may be efficient for detecting non-randomness in the direction of uniform spacing.

Tests based on Clark and Evans' R statistic, or on quadrat methods measure only the intensity of a pattern (i.e. the extent to which density varies). Also of interest is the grain of a pattern (the rate at which the density varies). Statistics which are influenced by both intensity and grain include that of Holgate (1965) and Pielou's (1959) and Mountford's (1961) 'a' test. Methods based on 'random pairs' (Cottam and Curtis 1949) and a 'wandering quarter' (Catana 1963) have also been developed.

It is important to mention some of the limitations of nearest-neighbour analysis. One of these is that it is often difficult to delimit the size of the area to be analysed. In certain cases natural boundaries may exist to the study area. More often, however, some boundary will have to be chosen. For the Clark and Evans test, for example, the R value will indicate random, regular or clustered distributions according to how much surrounding area is included in the analysis. An isolated cluster of settlements may be regularly spaced within the cluster, but as more surrounding area is included the pattern appears more clumped. Thus we can often determine pattern *within* a region, but to examine the pattern *throughout* a region is more difficult (Hsu and Tiedmann 1968). Getis (1964) admits that the boundaries often have to be subjectively determined in accordance with the aims of the study. Much the same conclusion is reached by Kariel (1970, 128).

However, the fact that a study area has boundaries, whether these be natural ones such as coasts or imposed lines, causes additional problems in the use of nearest-neighbour analysis. Clark and Evans have noted that 'the presence of a boundary beyond which measurements cannot be made will tend to make the value of $\Sigma r/n$ greater than would be obtained if an infinite area were involved' (Clark and Evans 1954). This boundary effect has been shown (Hodder 1971) to be considerable in cases where many of the sites involved are near the coast. The effect of imposing a boundary is shown in fig.3.7. The study area is represented by the inner square and onto this area a number of points have

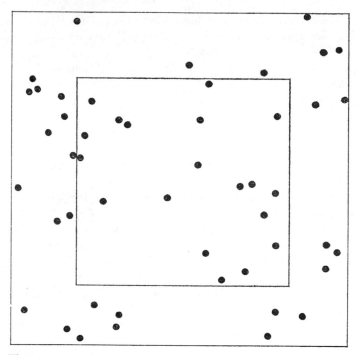

Fig.3.7. The effect of imposing a boundary on a study area.
For explanation see text.

been located at random, using co-ordinates derived from random
number tables. The R value for the Clark and Evans test, however, is
1.25 indicating a movement towards a uniform pattern. If, however, a
surrounding band is attached containing points randomly placed at the
same density, the R value for the central study area can be recalculated.
In this second case the nearest neighbours of some of the points in the
study area are in the surrounding band. The resulting R value is 1.09
which is close to expectation under the null hypothesis of a random
pattern. Three further trials in which the point pattern in the surrounding band is again simulated produce R values of 1.05, 1.04 and
1.04. It is clear, then, that the presence of a boundary has a marked
effect on the results of the analysis. If the sampling area is rectangular
in shape and contains a fairly large number of points, and if one can
assume that a similar picture would hold for other sampling fields, one
can repeat the same set of points top and bottom and at the sides.
Precise conditions for this to be a satisfactory technique still need to
be developed (Coleman, personal communication). Another solution
to the problem of edge effects is to limit the analysis within the total
distribution so that measurements can be made to points outside the
study area (Hodder and Hassall 1971). Alternatively, 'for most practical
applications, measurements from i should be recorded only to those j

neighbours which are closer to i than i is to the boundary' (Dacey 1963). In this way the value of n is decreased.

Another aspect of the application of nearest-neighbour analysis in archaeology is discussed by Diggle in the appendix.

Two further points may be mentioned. The first of these is that a repeated pattern of two or more closely spaced points occurring some distance from one another would yield a low value of R suggesting a clustered pattern, even when the overall arrangement may appear dispersed (Getis 1964). This problem can be alleviated by using measures to more than first nearest neighbours. The second point results from the pattern of towns in North Dakota shown in fig.3.8.

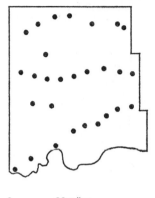

0   20 miles

0   32 km

Fig.3.8. The distribution of modern towns in North Dakota. Source: King 1962.

This distribution proved to have an R value of 1.11 which was not found to be significantly different from the expected value in a random arrangement (King 1962). However, the pattern does not give a visual impression of being random. The settlements are located along three major transportation axes which have an approximate east–west orientation. It is probable that the Dacey and Tung approach mentioned above (p. 41) would identify the pattern as non-random, but a further example will be given in section 3.2 of cases in which a pattern found to be random by simple nearest-neighbour analysis is in fact structured in some way. It may be advisable, therefore, to analyse any one distribution with a number of different tests. In any case the value of $R = 1$ is a convenient and useful origin from which to measure tendencies towards aggregation or uniform spacing.

3.2 *Some applications of nearest-neighbour analysis in archaeology*

Whallon (1974) has used the Clark and Evans test and the χ^2 statistic to examine the distributions of arc-ended endscrapers, worked bone

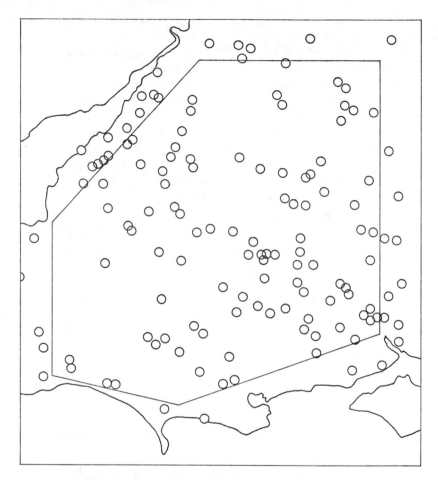

Fig.3.9. The univallate hillforts in the south and west of England.

and antler, retouched blades, and partially backed blades on a Protomagdalenian occupation floor at the Abri Pataud. All four distributions
were found to be significantly clustered using a 5 % level of significance.
Peebles (1973) has used the Clark and Evans test to identify clustering
in the distribution of mound sites in Alabama. The 'border-effect'
problem was overcome by determining that 'for the points under
consideration, any point that is nearer the border of the area than it is
to its nearest neighbour must be eliminated from the analysis' (*ibid.*).

A further study is presented here of hillforts in the Wiltshire area.
Detailed maps of the hillforts have been constructed (figs.3.9 and 3.10),
and the internal acreage measured from detailed O.S. maps. The forts
are classified according to whether they are univallate or multivallate.
An area has been chosen for the analysis so that the nearest-neighbour
distance from any fort is less than or equal to the distance from that fort

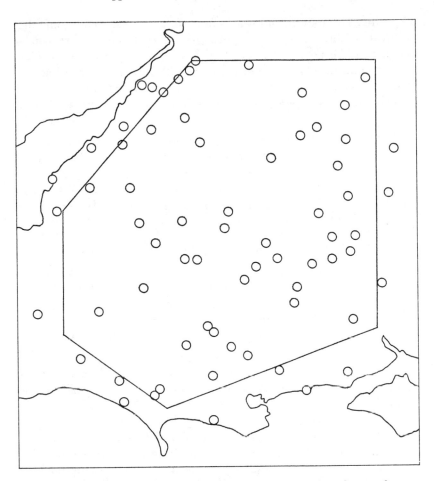

Fig.3.10. The multivallate hillforts in the south and west of England.

to the coast, in order to avoid edge effects. Straight line distances to nearest neighbour have been measured. The results of the application of the Clark and Evans test on all the hillforts in the study are given in table 3.1. This shows that the total pattern is not significantly different from a pattern produced by a random process.

The interpretation of the overall pattern will be left until later (section 4.1), but this example may serve to show that a random pattern may sometimes be broken down to identify underlying structure. In table 3.1 the sites have been grouped into various size categories of univallate and multivallate forts. As with the total pattern most of these various categories of hillfort are randomly spaced. No structured pattern is discernible. The multivallate forts, on the other hand, show a significant departure from randomness in the direction of uniformity of spacing. This movement towards uniformity is greater when only the multivallate forts of more than 12 acres internal acreage are considered. Cunliffe (1971*a*) has given a visual impression of the regular spacing of major hillforts at one period in Wiltshire. By considering one class of site, and so removing some of the disturbance to the pattern, it appears that some degree of ordering, in this case competition between

Table 3.1.   *Nearest-neighbour analysis of southwestern hillforts*

	A	n	ρ	$\bar{r}_e$	$\bar{r}_o$	R
All hillforts	266	148	0.556	0.672	0.683	1.017
All hillforts $\geqslant$ 13 acres	266	49	0.180	1.177	1.140	0.968
All univallate forts	266	97	0.361	0.833	0.751	0.903
Univallate $\geqslant$ 12 acres	266	31	0.113	1.488	1.329	0.893
Univallate $\geqslant$ 8 acres	266	48	0.177	1.189	1.248	1.050
All multivallate forts	266	51	0.188	1.153	1.341	1.162*
Multivallate $\geqslant$ 12 acres	266	24	0.086	1.7	2.138	1.257*

* = significant difference between $\bar{r}_o$ and $\bar{r}_e$ at $p = 0.05$.
Units of measurement are centimetres ($\times 0.05$) on the maps (figs.3.9, 3.10).

sites, is recognisable in the aggregate random pattern. The identification of this ordering in the pattern indicates that the degree of contemporaneity and competitive relationship between these sites would be worth examining in greater detail.

The distribution of Mayan ceremonial sites (data provided by N. Hammond) is also analysed in detail. Surveys of varying intensity have been carried out in three parts of the area covered by the analysis. These three subsets of the total distribution have been used for the following analysis (Hodder and Orton 1974). The boundary around the sites has been assessed by drawing perpendiculars at the mid-points between peripheral sites in each subset, and the nearest site outside the subset. Connecting these perpendiculars gave an area enclosing the sites in each subset.

In all three cases, using the Clark and Evans test, the pattern is not significantly different from a random pattern of the same density. However, C, the standard normal variate, shows a movement towards a significant departure from random (in the direction of uniform spacing) as the density of sites increases. Thus subset 3 has the lowest density (0.0012 per km²) and the least significant departure from random ($C = 0.495$), while subset 1 has the highest density (0.0030 per km²) and the most significant departure from random in the direction of a uniform distribution ($C = 0.92$). This covariation between increasing density and increasingly significant departures from random could easily be due to chance. However, it is thought worthwhile to examine further whether in the higher densities of Mayan ceremonial sites any uniformity or competition in the pattern can be detected.

In many populations of, for example, plants or sites there may be competition, as seen in a uniformity of distribution, in the areas of highest density, even though the overall pattern appears random or aggregated when methods such as that of Clark and Evans are applied. But localised uniformity can be detected if only the short distances between sites are compared with the short distances between sites which could be expected in a random distribution. The closer two sites are to each other, the more intensely will they compete with each other so that there may be a lower limit to the distances between sites.

To detect competition in higher densities a method similar to that used by Pielou (1962) is used. The distance from each site to its nearest neighbour is calculated but those greater than 14 km are ignored as only close neighbours are being studied. Thus a truncated frequency distribution of nearest-neighbour distances is obtained.

Table 3.2.   *Basic data*

	Subset 1	Subset 2	Subset 3	Others	All
Area (km²)	4680	5002	10 608	3616	23 906
n (all)	16	9	14	9	48
n' (≤14 km only)	15	6	6	9	36

It is necessary to fit a curve of form

$$f(\omega|0 \leqslant \omega \leqslant c) = \lambda e^{-\lambda\omega}/(1 - e^{-\lambda c}) \tag{3.11}$$

to the truncated sample, where $\omega = r^2$ (r = nearest-neighbour distance), $c = 196$ (c = the constant, the chosen upper limit of ω), and λ is to be estimated. In this case λ is estimated from the site density (untruncated observations), using the formula

$$\hat{\lambda} = n\pi/A, \tag{3.12}$$

which for all areas together gives $\hat{\lambda} = 0.00636$, $\hat{\lambda}c = 1.236$ and $1 - e^{-\hat{\lambda}c} = 0.7095$. The nearest-neighbour distances between 0 and 14 are divided into equal classes or cells and the number of sites falling in each class is compared with the number that would be expected to fall in that class if the distribution was random. The distances for all the

Mayan sites are divided into seven equal classes, the boundary values being found by

$$\omega_r = \frac{-1}{\hat{\lambda}} \log\left(1 - \frac{r}{i}\left(1 - e^{-\lambda c}\right)\right) \tag{3.13}$$

when $0 < r < i$. The observed and expected number of sites in each class are shown in table 3.3.

Table 3.3. *Mayan ceremonial sites*

Cell	1	2	3	4	5	6	7
Boundaries	0– 4.0	4.5– 5.5	6.0– 7.5	8.0– 9.0	9.5– 10.5	11–12	12.5– 14.0
No. of observations	0	4	4	5	11	9	3
Expected no.	$5\frac{1}{7}$	$5\frac{1}{7}$	$5\frac{1}{7}$	$5\frac{1}{7}$	$5\frac{1}{7}$	$5\frac{1}{7}$	$5\frac{1}{7}$

Interest is centred on whether competition occurs at higher densities, and an exact binomial test (preferable to Pielou's approximate Normal test) gives the probability of having no observations in the first cell, given a random distribution of sites, of about 0.4 %. There is thus significant evidence for competition.

If the same method is applied to the three subsets in turn the results shown in tables 3.4–3.6 are obtained.

Table 3.4. *Subset 1*

Cell	1	2	3	4	Total
Boundaries	0– 4.5	5.0– 7.0	7.5 10.0	10.5– 14.0	0–14
No. of observations	0	2	5	8	15
Expected no.	$3\frac{3}{4}$	$3\frac{3}{4}$	$3\frac{3}{4}$	$3\frac{3}{4}$	15

Probability of 0 in first cell = 0.013

Table 3.5. *Subset 2*

Cell	1	2	3	Total
Boundaries	0–6.5	7.0–10.5	11.0–15.0	0–15.0
No. of observations	0	4	3	7
Expected no.	$2\frac{1}{3}$	$2\frac{1}{3}$	$2\frac{1}{3}$	7

Probability of 0 in first cell = 0.059

Table 3.6. *Subset 3*

Cell	1	2	3	Total
Boundaries	0–7.5	8.0–11.0	11.5–14.0	0–14.0
No. of observations	4	2	0	6
Expected no.	2	2	2	6

Deviations from the expected pattern are not significant, but, as in subset 2, the sample is very small

From this evidence we can see the competition at high density (subset 1), and medium density (subset 2) but not at low density (subset 3). The pattern of sites using the Clark and Evans test proved to be random. It does seem, however, that localised competition does occur so that the closer together sites are located, the more intensely do they compete, resulting in a lower limit to the distances between sites.

It is clear from table 3.3 that the theoretical curve (equation 3.11) would give a very bad fit to the observations. This impression is reinforced by fig.3.11 which compares the observed cumulative frequency distribution of nearest-neighbour distances with the cumulative form of equation 3.11, i.e.

$$F(\omega | 0 \leqslant \omega \leqslant c) = \frac{1 - e^{-\lambda\omega}}{1 - e^{-\lambda c}}, \tag{3.14}$$

which is plotted as a thick solid line in fig.3.11. The fit is particularly bad around $\omega = 80$. Since it might be thought that this lack of fit stems

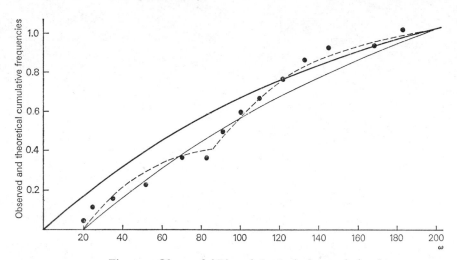

Fig.3.11. Observed (●) and theoretical cumulative frequency distributions for ω. Thick solid line = theoretical untruncated distribution; thin solid line = theoretical truncated distribution; dashed line = specially fitted 'double' distribution.

from the lack of distances below $r = 4.5$ ($\omega = 20$), a doubly truncated curve

$$f(\omega|\omega_a \leqslant \omega \leqslant c) = \frac{\lambda e^{-\lambda(\omega - \omega_a)}}{1 - e^{-\lambda(c - \omega_a)}} \qquad (3.15)$$

or

$$F(\omega|\omega_a \leqslant \omega \leqslant c) = \frac{1 - e^{-\lambda(\omega - \omega_a)}}{1 - e^{-\lambda(c - \omega_a)}} \qquad (3.16)$$

was fitted with the lower cut-off (ω_a) at 20. The density was re-estimated using Pielou's equation

$$\bar{\omega}/c = \frac{1}{c\lambda} - \frac{e^{-c\lambda}}{1 - e^{-c\lambda}} \qquad (3.17)$$

and the resulting cumulative curve is plotted in fig.3.11 as a thin solid line. It fits the deviations better than the origin curve for $\omega < 110$, but it is worse at higher values of ω. Of the 14 data points, the first three lie above this curve, the next four below it and the final seven above it again, strongly suggesting a systematic departure from the fitted curve, in the form of a 'kink' in the region of $\omega = 80$ to 90. The answer seems to be to fit two curves, one for $\omega \leqslant 90$ and one for $\omega > 90$. First a curve of the above form (equation 3.15) with $\omega_a = 20$ and $c = 90$ is fitted to the first six data points, and scaled to give a value for the probability (P) of 0.4 at $\omega = 90$. When extrapolated, it reaches a value of $P = 0.47$ at $c = 196$. A further curve of the same form, with

$\omega_a = 85$ and $c = 196$, is superimposed on the extrapolated curve and fitted to the remaining data points. The resulting 'kinked' curve, shown as a dashed line (fig.3.11), fits the observations well at all values. One might infer from the shape of this curve that there are two 'populations' of nearest-neighbour distances, one consisting of all the distances of 9 km or less plus one or two above this limit (say 17 in all) and the other consisting of all (19) other distances. In archaeological terms, this could be interpreted as two groups of centres, one with a minimum spacing of 9 km and one with a minimum spacing of 4.5 km.

The fitting of special *ad hoc* curves in this way is not recommended unless the deviations of the data points from the 'simple' curve exhibit a strong systematic pattern, as they do here.

3.3 *Some additional approaches*

Two further approaches for examining spatial patterns which have not been used in archaeology should be briefly mentioned. Medvedkov (1967) has discussed an approach to settlement patterns derived from the statistical theory of information. 'Regularity of spacing is the "signal", and we can consider disturbances produced by local geographic features as "noise"' (*ibid.*, 165). He used the entropy measure to examine the amount of uniformity and randomness in settlement patterns. 'Entropy helps to measure disorder in settlement patterns. Then random and uniform components in such patterns are effectively separated and measured' (*ibid.*). When the pattern tends towards regularity of spacing he sees a decrease in entropy so that a greater amount of information is available within it. This may prove a useful approach for archaeological distributions

A common situation in archaeological distribution maps is a linear arrangement of settlements. For example Romano-British settlements are regularly spaced along the Roman roads and Branigan (1967) has noted the apparently regular arrangement of Romano-British sites down the river valleys in the Chilterns, one site occurring every 2.4 to 3.2 km. There are a number of statistics which can be used to test for randomness in the arrangement of points along a line. These are outlined by King (1969, 98; see also Pinder and Witherick 1975).

Archaeologists are often interested in estimating population size from the size of excavated settlements and houses, and various methods and formulae have been proposed (e.g. Leblanc 1971; Naroll 1962). Constant figures or formulae for the settlement area needed per person seem to fit available data less well than regression models of the form, Area $= a \times$ population^b. (For the definition of a and b see section 5.1.) Wiessner (1974) has fitted such a model to data from !Kung Bushman camps (fig.3.12). The result suggests that while there is a figure of 5.9 m^2 per person in camps with a population of 10, 10.2 m^2 per person

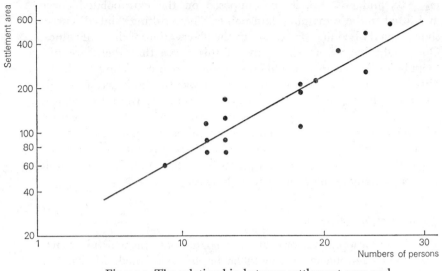

Fig.3.12. The relationship between settlement area and
population of Bushmen camps. Area = $a \times$ population^b
plotted on double logarithmic paper. $a = -0.23 \pm 0.68$;
$b = 1.96$; $r = 0.91$.

is found in camps of 25. Wiessner also discusses the variation of the
b value which describes the slope of the line in fig. 3.12 with different
types of site and different types of society – it will vary considerably
depending on whether hunter–gatherer camps, settled villages or
urban areas are being considered.

4
Some models for settlement patterns

In the previous chapter some techniques were outlined for determining structured patterning in archaeological distributions. In the case of distributions of sites, what models are available for interpreting the different types of pattern – random, regular or clustered? Some of these models are to be discussed in this section, although one cannot hope to cover the field exhaustively.

4.1 Random patterns

Consider a situation in which a distribution of sites has been examined by a number of tests and found to be not significantly different from a random pattern. It is not immediately clear how this should be interpreted because we know that sites are not located such that any point in an area has an equal and independent chance of being chosen. In general, as has been shown (p. 30), it may be suggested that a random distribution is one in which there is no structured patterning. 'To say that a distribution is random, in a non-technical sense, is to say that the pattern has no discernible order and that its cause is undeterminable' (Dacey 1964, 559). It is the non-randomness which provides information about the distribution.

The general lack of order in a random pattern may be considered to derive from two main sources. The distribution of hillforts in south-west England examined in the previous section will be taken as an example. The first factor is that the aggregate pattern of hillfort locations at any one time may have been random. This is in the spirit of the 'random spatial economy' discussed by Curry (p. 9). In locating a settlement, a wide range of variables had to be taken into account, such as the distance to water, the type of soil and vegetation cover, the location of other settlements, defence, the distance to suitable building materials, and the proximity of routes or roads and markets. Differing reactions to this range of factors may have resulted in an aggregate random pattern. Although this may be true of certain classes of hillforts it is not the case with all of them as has been shown (p. 46).

The second, and perhaps most important, factor to have affected the distribution of hillforts is the pattern of site survival and fieldwork. Again, there are a large number of variables to be considered. Perhaps of greatest importance in the case of the hillforts is that the modern distribution represents a palimpsest of distributions of different dates. Also it is possible that all the sites classified as hillforts do not represent one category of site. Some may have been more stock enclosures than villages. Regional variation in site survival must also be considered, with upland, massively constructed forts, surviving better than small lowland examples. Some areas of Britain have been subject to much more detailed study, and this is a general problem in the analysis of archaeological distributions. We have already seen (p. 24) that, although the factors influencing the recovery of archaeological material in one area may change through time, the overall pattern of finds may in certain cases not vary significantly. Major fieldwork effects which have been made apparent in some areas of southern England by, for example, gravel digging, air photography, and motorway construction, can usually be taken into account when considering archaeological patterns. These major effects are likely to produce a structured pattern whose structure can be interpreted accordingly. In other cases there is clearly a great variety of factors influencing site survival and recovery. It is possible that the overall effect of these factors may help to produce a random pattern of sites. Dacey and Tung (1962) have shown that as the 'random disturbance' of a pattern of points increases, so any trace of that pattern may be lost (King 1969, 103–7). 'Skellam (1952) has pointed out that if random elimination of individuals occurs in a randomly distributed population, the distribution remains random, and, more important, if individuals are eliminated randomly from a non-randomly distributed population, a random distribution will eventually be produced when the density is sufficiently reduced' (Greig-Smith 1964, 217). It is possible therefore that, in the case of the hillforts, the varied disturbances of the distribution may have helped to produce a random pattern.

The identification of a random pattern does not preclude the possibility that the pattern may have been generated by random disturbances of some other spatial pattern. In certain cases some idea of the structure behind a disturbed pattern may be obtained (cf. p. 46).

4.2 *Uniform patterns*

There has been great interest in uniform patterns on the part of geographers and archaeologists because, unless sites are located on some regularly spaced environmental or physical feature, the uniform arrangement indicates some degree of competition between sites. The nature and extent of this competition is something to be examined and explained. Most of the available interpretative models have been developed for modern or recent societies. However, it will be found that these can often be made more general and applied to prehistoric situations.

Two components of settlement patterns, their horizontal and hierarchical organisation, will be examined before considering the development of settlement patterns through time. However, an initial generalisation of some importance must be made. This is that even in the simplest societies, certain sections demand products or services that they do not provide for themselves. This is evidenced in the neolithic by the widespread movement of stone axes, obsidian and some fine pottery (Peacock 1969a). Service centres are often necessary for the circulation and exchange of these products. Throughout the following discussion the term 'service centre' or 'central place' will be used in the broadest way to include centres for the exchange of food, craft, and specialised products, as well as centres providing administrative, military or religious services.

4.2.1 *Horizontal relationships*

Consider a hypothetical situation in which a small island is evenly spread with dispersed habitation. One service centre providing type A services and three providing type B services are to be placed on the island (fig.4.1). Where will they locate? Bunge (1966) suggests that the one A type centre will always go to the centre (given no need for external coastal contact). Such a position is not only more efficient for the dispersed population whose longest travelling distance to the centre is minimised, but by being centrally located those providing the

Fig.4.1. Possible distributions of type B services in a hypothetical situation. Source: Bunge 1966.

services in centre A can be sure of the maximum possible contact. The B type centres may also locate at the centre if multipurpose trips are relevant to the discussion. If the services are all available in the same centre then 'a person coming to town for one purpose is likely, by the proximity of additional services, to use some of these services as well' (Morrill 1970, 62). For the population this arrangement minimises the

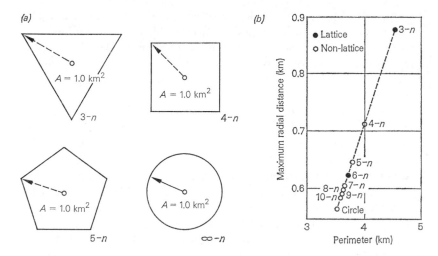

Fig.4.2. Efficiency of alternative types of regular polygons in relation to distance from centres and perimeter length.
(*a*) Different shaped regions with an area (*A*) of 1.0 km², and with three or more edges (3–*n*, 4–*n* etc.) are shown. (*b*) Shows that, as the number of edges around a region of constant size decreases, the region's perimeter and the maximum radial distance increase. Source: Haggett 1965.

total trip distance to obtain both types of service. If multipurpose trips are not relevant to the type of service provision being considered, then the three B type centres might be expected to partition the area between them.

The first instance serves to illustrate that the agglomeration of services is an important effort-minimising characteristic of settlement patterns.

A second characteristic which also relates to effort-minimisation concerns the shape of the area served by a centre. The area within easiest reach of a centre, assuming a flat featureless plain, is circular in shape. If a number of service centres and their service areas are to be packed into a region, how can they most efficiently be organised? Haggett (1965, 49) has shown that the hexagon is the service area shape which allows the greatest amount of packing into an area and which at the same time minimises movement to or from the boundary and minimises boundary length. Figure 4.2 shows that for a given area the maximum distance to the boundary is less for the hexagon than for the square or triangle and the total boundary length **is** also least. There have been few studies which seek to determine whether hexagonal shapes of service area exist in reality. Haggett's (1965, 50–1) examination of 100 Brazilian counties, however, 'suggests that criticism of the hexagonal system as over-theoretical may have been too hasty'

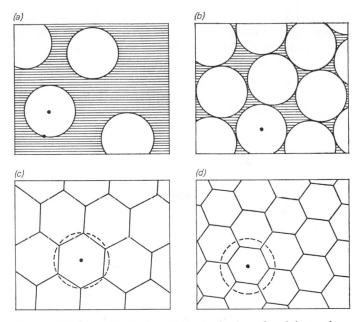

Fig.4.3. Packing of centres in the colonisation of a plain to give hexagonal territories. Sources: Haggett 1965; Lösch 1954.

(*ibid.*, 51). In such a pattern of packed hexagons (fig.4.3) the service centres have a triangular arrangement. 'If the land is to be served by a perfectly uniform net of central places, so that there are neither too many nor too few places of this type, and so that there is no unsupplied part, then the neighbouring central places must be equidistant from one another. This is the case, however, only if the places lie at the corners of equilateral triangles' (Christaller 1933, 63).

Because, in early society, travel to and from a market centre is on foot or by cart, we find some interesting regularities in the location of these local service centres. It appears that in such rural societies the maximum distance to market which is usually preferred is in the range of 3-7 km. Above this distance, the effort involved in getting to market outweighs the advantages gained. But below 3-7 km – that is about 10 km between markets – the markets are so close together that the population cannot ensure enough trade for each market to continue. Thus there is an average figure of 10 km which combines movement minimisation with simple market economics to provide the most efficient distance between local markets.

There is considerable evidence for this figure. For example, a twelfth-century law forbade the setting up of markets within 6⅔ miles of each other (Humbert de Romans). Also, in East Anglia, 'the *maximum* range of influence of the medieval market was about 6 miles [10 km] ... The actual market area, however, rarely reached this limit' (Dickinson 1932, 22). Dickinson in fact found that circles of 6.5 km radius around each market gave the best compromise between circle overlap and land cover. Again, an important study by Brush and Bracey (1955) compared the distribution of centres in rural southern England – from Somerset to Oxfordshire and Hampshire – and in southwestern Wisconsin. In spite of marked differences of population density and economic functions between the two areas, the distances between members of the hierarchical tiers were remarkably similar. Higher order centres were 33 km apart, lower order centres 13–16 km apart, and the smallest service centres 6–10 km apart from each other and from centres of higher order. Brush and Bracey stressed that they were only considering the rural service functions of the centres, and suggested that the present pattern in the two areas is based largely on the situation prior to modern transport.

> During medieval times there were market towns in southern England, spaced at intervals of four to six miles [6–10 km], that served as rudimentary trade centres, accessible by cart roads from the rural villages within an hour's journey ... In the early nineteenth century, before the coming of railways and automotive vehicles, hamlets also developed in Wisconsin at intervals of five to six miles and served as rudimentary trade centres for the farmers living a journey-hour away by wagon roads [*ibid.*, 568].

Further evidence for the spacing of markets has been provided by work in west Africa, where, as indeed may often have been the case in the past, they tend to be periodic. For example, in the belt of Yorubaland in southwest Nigeria in which a regular pattern can be observed, 'the periodic markets are distributed fairly evenly at an average distance of 7.2 miles [11.4 km] from each other' (Hodder 1963, 103). A further study of markets in ten areas in west Africa showed that the average distance from a given market to the nearest adjacent market regardless of its day of meeting is 8.8 km, with a range from 5 to 15.1 km in the 10 areas (R. H. T. Smith 1969). These figures provided by Smith give the average minimum distance rather than the average distance to all adjacent markets that has been considered so far.

Thus there is much evidence that rural local markets are often separated by distances averaging approximately 10 km, serving an area of 3–7 km radius. No claim is made here for a universal 'law', since individual measurements may vary for a variety of local reasons. It is, however, possible to suggest a model that states that it is reasonable to assume that approximately these distances will lead to the most efficient and effort-minimising arrangement of settlements in those rural societies in which other overriding factors, such as difficult terrain, or very low population density, are not at work.

It is of interest, therefore, that Hodder (1972) was able to suggest that the service centres of the lowest level in Roman Britain might be

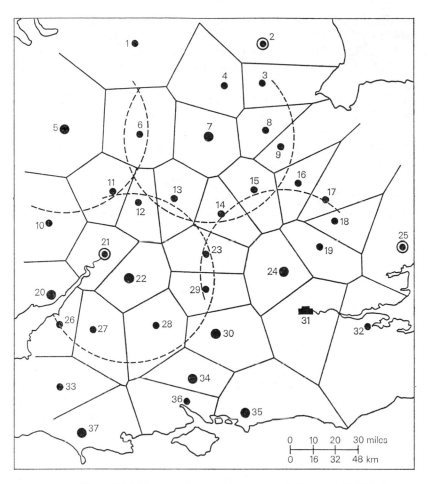

Fig.4.4. Thiessen polygons drawn around Romano-British
walled towns. Arcs of circles (dashed lines) have also been drawn
around some of the major centres (cantonal capitals) to show
the regular placing of the lesser walled towns (smaller filled
circles) in relation to the cantonal capitals (larger filled circles).
⊙ = Colonia. For number references see Hodder and
Hassall 1971. Source: Hodder and Hassall 1971.

spaced about 10.5 km apart. Drury (1972, 8) has noted that the
Romano-British nucleated settlements providing artisan and trading
functions in Essex were so placed that no point in the countryside lay
more than about 6–10 km from one of them.

A useful technique for determining the service areas of centres is to
use Thiessen polygons. These are shown in fig.4.4 constructed around
Romano-British walled towns. They are produced simply by drawing
perpendiculars at the mid-points between towns. Given the observed

distribution of points, these polygons can be seen as defining the areas which could most efficiently be served by the walled towns, if factors such as ease of access were uniform, and assuming that movement minimisation was an important factor. In doing this they allow suggestions as to the shape and size of service areas. These suggestions can be tested by reference to actual artifact distributions (p. 188). The lines of the Thiessen polygons have sometimes been suggested as running along features such as rivers which may have acted as boundaries (Cunliffe 1971a). A number of applications of Thiessen polygons have been made in archaeology (p. 187), but they should only be constructed around contemporaneous centres. A rather limiting assumption, which will be examined later (p. 188), is that Thiessen polygons give equal weight to centres of different size. Large centres are not shown with relatively larger service areas.

4.2.2 *Hierarchial relationships*

'It is a common observation that there are fewer larger places than smaller ones in a region and that the larger centres provide a greater number and variety of goods than the small places do' (Garner 1967, 322). Such hierarchies exist because for certain activities or services there is not sufficient demand to support their functioning at the local level. These more specialist services are therefore provided by the larger centres spaced at greater intervals. In classical Christalleran central place theory, central places fall into a hierarchy comprising discrete groups of centres (Berry and Pred 1961, 4). Centres of each higher order group perform all the functions of lower order centres plus a group of central functions that differentiates them from the lower order. The importance of this for archaeological artifact distributions will be examined in section 5.6. The spatial arrangement of these different hierarchical levels can take on a number of forms. Three main types were suggested by Christaller (1933), and these are shown in fig.4.5. In the first, second-level centres are arranged according to the marketing principle and are best situated for access to three larger centres. The second arrangement is according to the transport principle in which, due to the importance of lines of communication, centres are placed at the midpoints of the roads linking larger centres. They are thus dependent on two larger centres rather than three. The existence of roads in Roman Britain was of extreme importance for the economic landscape and some similarities with the transport principle were found in the arrangement of the main towns (Hodder and Hassall 1971; Hodder 1972). We shall see, however, that the approach used was rather naïve (section 4.3). The third pattern of centres follows the administrative principle in which secondary centres are wholly within the area of larger centres. Vance (1970, 163) has discussed the arrangement of centres in a feudal system in these terms.

In market economies in which there is not sufficient demand or purchasing power within a service area for the service centre to function continuously, periodic markets may be found in which the markets are open on certain days in the week. Traders are thus able to move from market to market in a cycle of market days in order to obtain a sufficiently large custom (Berry 1967).

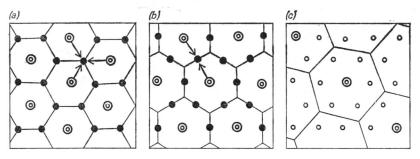

Fig.4.5. The distribution of centres according to (*a*) the market, (*b*) the transport and (*c*) the administrative principles of Christaller. Sources: Haggett 1965; Lösch 1954.

Central place theory has been used in the analysis and interpretation of archaeological sites of the Early Dynastic I period on the Diyālā Plains, Iraq (*c.* 2800 B.C.) (Johnson 1972). 'Most central place studies have concentrated on hexagonal distributions, although rhomboidal patterns have been noted. The roughly parallel paths of major watercourses in the Diyālā were apparently responsible for the rhomboidal distribution which seems to occur there. Thus for present purposes, Christaller's distributions have been adapted to a rhomboidal pattern' (*ibid.*, 771). The distribution followed the transport principle, and five hierarchical levels were suggested based on the size of the settlements.

The relationships between settlements were suggested in a 'proposed lattice'. The derivation of this lattice is shown in fig.4.6. This is Johnson's figure 2.

Figure 2A presents the model lattice. Fig. 2B indicates sites which due to their truncated complementary regions might be expected to be smaller than predicted by the model. Fig. 2C illustrates the locations of observed sites relative to site locations predicted by the model. Fig. 2D indicates deviation of observed from predicted site size in terms of the five level hierarchy. Filled circles represent an accurate size class prediction. A half-filled circle indicates that a site is larger than predicted. 'Most reasonable' connectivity lines are retained. Fig. 2E introduces deviations in relative site to site distance from that predicted by the model. Additional connectivity lines (dashed) are added on a subjective basis. Fig. 2F represents the proposed lattice [Johnson 1972, 773].

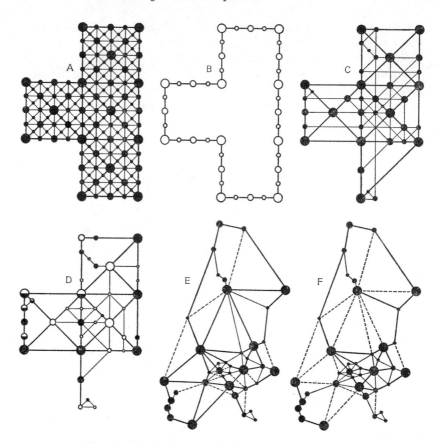

Fig.4.6. The derivation of Johnson's proposed settlement
lattice. For explanation see text. Source: Johnson 1972.

As Johnson points out this is not a rigorous procedure. Since the relationship between settlements in the proposed lattice has been derived
in this rather subjective way, the value of comparing the lattice with the
theoretical model (the approach followed by Johnson) is not easy to see.
This is especially the case since it is particularly easy to find structure in
a random distribution if the analysis is not rigorous (p. 6). In fact in
certain areas the proposed lattice and the model did show a significant
difference (*ibid.*, 776–7). However, Johnson was able to suggest that in
many instances larger sites tended to have an associated ring of smaller
sites in a manner similar to that predicted by Christaller's (1933)
transport principle. This is a hypothesis capable of being tested by, for
example, examining the relative amounts of imported raw material at
the sites. Sites at higher levels in the hierarchy might be expected to
have been important for the redistribution of these materials to smaller
centres and thus to contain larger quantities.

A modification of the classical central place model may be discussed which has relevance to archaeological material. In Christaller's view a particular range of services is provided to tributary areas of constant size regardless of the hierarchical rank of the service centre. Kolb and Brunner (1946), on the other hand, have suggested that the size of the tributary area to which one range of goods is provided will vary with the size of the service centre (fig.4.7). 'The aggregate of all services

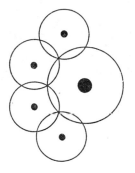

Fig.4.7. An alternative pattern of spatial organisation. Source: Hodder 1972.

provided by the higher centre attracts people from a greater distance and reduces the lower centres' areas even in those primary and secondary services in which they duplicate the higher centre' (Brush 1953, 392). Thus 'the smaller centres are not likely to develop as close to large centres as they are to one another' (*ibid.*, 393). As Morrill (1970, 69) has pointed out, this model corresponds rather better than does Christaller's to the empirical evidence. For example, the tributary areas around rural service centres in southwestern Wisconsin were identified by examining the direction of greatest traffic flow (Brush 1953). This showed quite clearly both that larger centres had larger service areas than smaller centres, and that the smaller centres were distributed around the larger centres in a pattern corresponding to the present model (fig.4.7). A similar pattern of settlements has been noted by Bracey (1956) in rural southern England.

There are elements within the pattern of Romano-British walled towns which suggests that this might be an applicable model. For example, the mean distance between the smaller walled towns (34.6 km) is considerably less than that between the smaller walled towns and the major centres (51.5 km). In effect, the smaller centres are simply located as far away as the larger centres as possible.

Figure 4.8 is an attempt to interpret part of the observed locational pattern in terms of the present modified theory of central places. On to the distributional pattern of walled towns have been imposed circles of

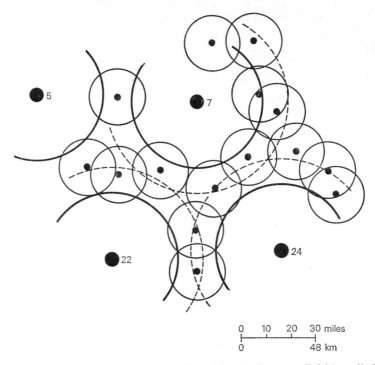

Fig.4.8. Service areas predicted for the Romano-British walled centres. Source: Hodder 1972.

two constant sizes, corresponding to the two hierarchical levels represented (continuous lines). The two levels are the major centres (cantonal capitals) and the lesser walled towns. Broken arcs of constant radius are also constructed around the major centres. The diameters of the circles have been chosen to give the best possible compromise between minimum overlap and maximum surface coverage.

It may be possible to test predictions about the size of service areas by examining the pattern of artifacts distributed through the centres. This possibility will be examined in greater detail in section 5.6, but in a discussion of the pattern in fig.4.8 Hodder (1972) found there was insufficient evidence at the moment to test the fit of the model in this case.

The concept of a hierarchy of centres serving areas of different sizes in some interlocking spatial pattern is of general importance to the archaeologist. Chang (1972) has shown, for a hypothetical situation (fig.4.9), that hierarchical structure may be of great complexity and related to different facets of life within the same society. In general it may be useful to distinguish network or non-centralised relationships between settlements from hierarchical or centralised relationships.

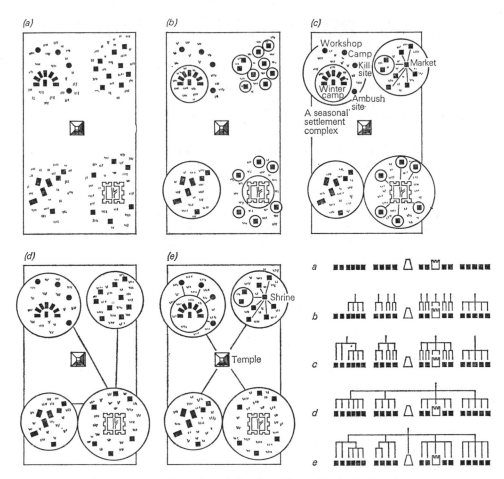

Fig.4.9. The articulation of sites into hierarchical relationships.
(*a*) Archaeological ruins whose contemporaneity has been
established; (*b*) spheres of domestic activity; (*c*) local networks;
(*d*) political networks; (*e*) religious networks; (*f*) hierarchies of
the inter-relationships in *a* to *e*. Source: Chang 1972.

Sahlins (1965) has outlined a similar broad division between reciprocal
and redistributive patterns of exchange. Dalton (1969) has suggested
that most primitive economies without centralised polity are small,
partly in relation to modern society. But by this he also means that in
the economy of the Tiv, the Nuer or the Trobriand Islanders, for
example,

> most (but not all) resource, goods and service transactions take
> place within a small geographical area and within a community
> of persons numbered in the hundreds of thousands. It is true that
> external trade is common and, as with the Kula, sometimes is
> carried out over long distances. Typically, however, it is inter-
> mittent, petty in amount, or confined to very few goods. It is rare

(except in peasant economies) for foreign trade transactions to be frequent, quantitatively important or essential to livelihood [*ibid.*, 72].

Relatively small numbers of goods and services are produced or acquired, and economic relationships are closely tied up with neighbourhood, religious, kinship and political contacts.

Primitive economies which are part of centralised political authority, on the other hand, 'have socio-economic transactions in addition to those found within the local community and between local communities. These are of two principal sorts, transactions between the political centre and its local constituencies, and external trade transactions between the political centre and foreigners' (*ibid.*, 73). Unlike the non-centralised economies, the elite is therefore localised at nodal centres which articulate the internal and external movement of goods and services (fig.4.10). Tribute in the form of ordinary subsistence

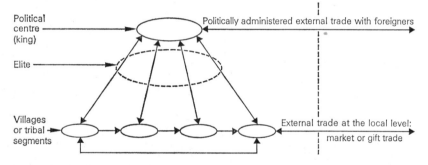

Fig.4.10. Socio-economic transactions in the primitive economy within a centralised political system. Source: Dalton 1969.

goods, labour, military service and luxuries reserved for elite usage may move up the hierarchy, the local constituents receiving in turn military protection, juridicial services, and emergency subsistence in time of local famine or disaster. Although there seems to be little evidence of the spatial arrangement of centres in such a hierarchical system, the underlying necessity for accessibility and control may result in spatial organisations broadly comparable to those already discussed.

There have been a number of attempts by archaeologists to examine the spatial pattern of a centralised or hierarchical system. Renfrew (1972*a*, 392), for example, has discussed the Minoan settlements on Crete in these terms. Hodder (1975) has attempted to show that the distribution of artifacts in the late pre-Roman Iron Age in southern England is orientated around the central oppida and the localised areas of wealth as indicated by the finds of rich burials and imported luxury goods. Struever and Houart (1972) have discussed the relationship between sites within the so-called Hopewell Interaction Sphere, which

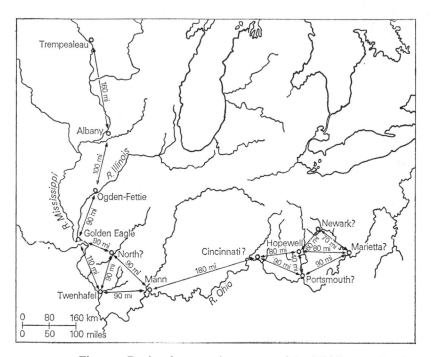

Fig.4.11. Regional transaction centres of the Middle Woodland period in the Midwest–Riverine area. Source: Struever and Houart 1972.

is made up of Middle Woodland period traits scattered over Ohio, Illinois, Michigan, Wisconsin and elsewhere. The main artifact similarities over this area are in status-objects. Struever and Houart were able to suggest that, among the mound sites in the area, those that are bigger, more complex and have Interaction-Sphere goods in greater numbers functioned as regional transaction centres (fig.4.11). In at least one localised area around such a centre a hierarchy of sites could be defined down which the Interaction-Sphere goods flowed (fig.4.12). The definition of hierarchical levels was based on, for example, the size, similarity of construction and location, and distance between sites. It would certainly seem possible that archaeological sites can be divided into hierarchical levels by using multivariate lists of traits.

Hierarchical relationships within genealogies may also sometimes have a corresponding spatial patterning. For example, in fig 4.13 the spatial expression of the Tiv lineage segments is shown.

> The father or founder of segment a was a brother of the founder of segment b. Each is a minimal segment today, and each has its own territory. The two segments taken together are all descended from 1, and are known by his name – the children of 1. In the

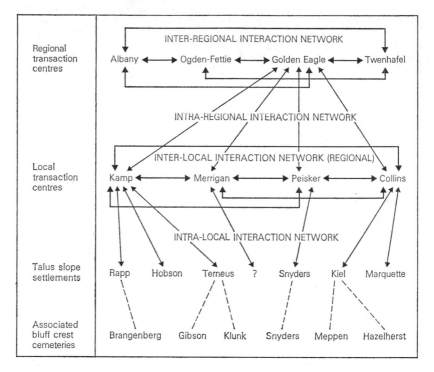

Fig.4.12. A hierarchy of interaction networks illustrated by specific Illinois Middle Woodland sites believed to exemplify the various settlement types involved. Source: Struever and Houart 1972.

same way, the territory of lineage 1, made up as it is of the combined minimal territories a and b, combines with the territory of lineage 2, made up of the combined minimal territories of c and d, to form territory A, occupied by lineage segment A, all descended from a single ancestor 'A'. This process is extended indefinitely right up to the apex of the genealogy, back in time to the founder who begot the entire people, and outwards in space to the edges of Tivland. The entire 800,000 Tiv form a single 'lineage' (*nongo*) and a single land called *Tar Tiv*. The geographical position of territories follows the genealogical division into lineages [Bohannan 1954, 3].

In certain cases it may be possible for the archaeologist to examine the relationships between centres by studying the links which connect them. For example, Hammond (1972) has determined the relative centrality and accessibility of plazas in the ceremonial centre at Lubaantun from the connections between them. Dicks (1972) has identified the relative importance of roads in Roman Britain by examining their pattern of connections centred on London (figs.4.14 and 4.15). The methods employed in this analysis of the Roman roads

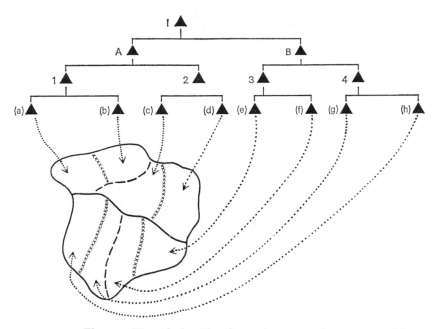

Fig.4.13. The relationship of genealogy to territory suggested by Bohannan for the Tiv. Different boundaries between territories are shown. Source: Bohannan 1954.

have already been fully discussed by Langton (1972), Hindle (1972) and Hutchinson (1972).

4.2.3 *The rank-size rule*

In classical central place theory it is assumed that the hierarchical levels are clearly distinct. In modern examples a hierarchy can usually be identified (Garner 1967, 325; Berry and Pred 1961, 6). However, Vining (1953) has suggested that variation within each level tends to blur any clear-cut steps which might otherwise have been visible. In fact a continuum of centres is often found so that 'in practice, more or less arbitrary divisions have to be made' (Haggett 1965, 124).

The continuum formed by the relationship between rank and size has been found empirically to show some regularity. If the settlements in an area are ranked in decreasing size from 1 to n, then the rank–size rule states that

$$S_n = S_1(n)^{-1} \qquad (4.1)$$

where S_n is the size of the nth ranked settlement (Haggett 1965, 101). Haggett (1972) has suggested that the Romano-British walled town rank–size relationship (Pounds 1969) fits this rule. If the relationship is written as

$$\log S_n = \log S_1 - b \log n \qquad (4.2)$$

Fig.4.14. Roman road network centred on London. Roads are broken where alternative routes to London are estimated to be of equal length. Source: Dicks 1972.

the parameters of the model may be obtained by the 'least squares method' (Blalock 1960). (For a discussion of equations of this form and the *b* parameter see section 5.1.) A group of Welsh hillforts (Pierson-Jones 1973) for which the acreages are known may be analysed in this way, with the result that

$$S_n = 17.54(n)^{-0.8421} \tag{4.3}$$

Comparative studies may be able to determine the reasons for variation of the parameter *b* (−1 in equation 4.1). The relationship between the rank and size of the hillforts is shown in fig.4.16. It is clear that although the model (equation 4.3) gives a good fit to most of the data, this is not the case for the smaller range of forts. A similar lack of fit for small settlements has been found in other studies (Haggett 1965, 107).

Berry (1961) has made a wide-ranging study of the relationship between rank and size in modern societies. He found two major types of relationship, the one corresponding to the rank–size rule, and the other being a 'primate' relationship in which there are deficiencies of intermediate sizes so that one or two very large settlements dominate the distribution. Simon (1955) has suggested that the rank–size rule

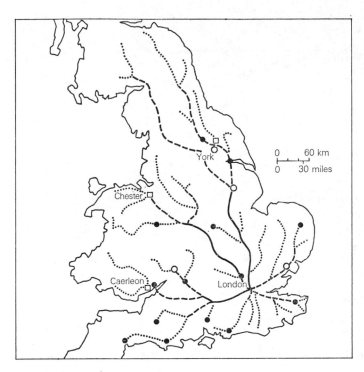

Fig.4.15. The network ordered with reference to London, showing coloniae (○), cantonal capitals (●), and fortresses (□). Dotted lines = second order routes; dashed lines = third order routes; and solid lines = fourth order routes. Source: Dicks 1972.

represents a condition of entropy in which the forces affecting the distribution are many and act randomly. This relationship is found in more complex societies, or in a settlement pattern of some age in which, over time, many forces have had effect. In the case of the 'primate' relationship fewer forces have produced inhomogeneities in the system. Berry suggested that this form of rank–size relationship is found more often when the country is small, has had a shorter period of settlement development, has a simpler economic and political life, or has had a lower degree of economic development.

Cliff, Haggett and Ord (1974, summarised in Cliff and Ord 1974) have obtained a model from Whitworth's (1934) work. Whitworth took a line of unit length cut at $(n-1)$ points located at random (random splitting) into n segments; he gave the relationship between the resulting size shares. A threshold minimum share size (Cohen 1966) may also be introduced into the model. Cliff, Haggett and Ord (1974) have tested the goodness-of-fit of the rank–size rule and this model with some real data. In most cases the random splitting process with a minimum share size gave the best fit to the data.

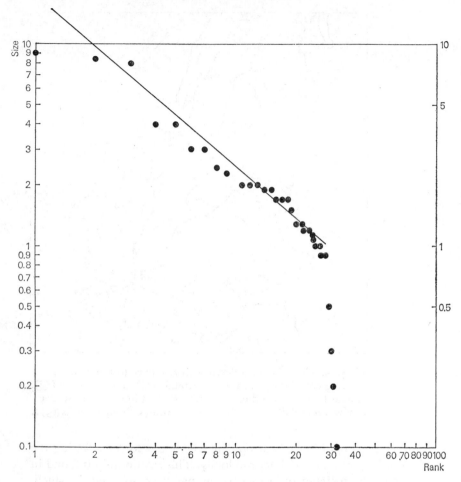

Fig.4.16. The rank-size rule applied to Welsh hillforts. The scales are logarithmic.

Curry (1964) argues that 'the rank–size rule can be regarded as the outcome of constrained, spatially random processes which allocate people to cities with attention concentrated on the "contagiousness" of numbers of people attracting further people' (Cliff and Ord 1974).

This is clearly an area in which it would be worthwhile to examine the fit of a model to archaeological data. Variation in the rank–size relationship in different regions, with different types of site and over the great time-span offered by archaeological material, may be noticeable and of interest. As was found in the study by Berry (1961), this variation might relate to differences between the social organisation of societies.

However, application of such methods in archaeology must take account of the problems discussed in section 2.1. In particular, it is often difficult to define the exact size of sites, their exact contemporaneity, and to be certain that sites of different sizes have been equally preserved. It is only in cases in which such problems can be overcome that application of, for example, the rank–size rule is appropriate.

4.3 *The development of uniform patterns through time*

It has already been shown that a relationship between site density and site regularity may sometimes exist (p. 49). This may also have a chronological significance. In time, increased population may lead to increased site density, greater competition between sites for land, and therefore greater uniformity in spacing (cf. Hudson 1969).

There are a number of specific models about the development of central place patterns and the emergence of a hierarchy of settlements. For example, Godlund (1956) has suggested that secondary centres emerge at the boundaries between service areas of larger centres (fig.4.17). It is in these areas that there is less competition and more

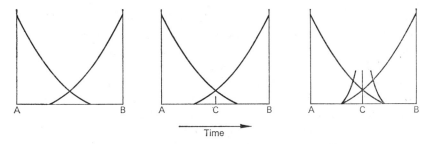

Time

Fig.4.17. Godlund's model for the growth of second-level centres. Source: Godlund 1956.

local demand because of distance from the main centres (Abler, Adams and Gould 1971). Empirical support for such a development has been provided by Carter (1955) and Godlund (1956).

Marshall (1964) has criticised this model because it assumes that interstitial centres emerge later than the main centres. 'Real chronology is disregarded and, in fact, reversed' (*ibid.*, 7). Perhaps more realistic would be to begin with the smaller centres and allow certain of these to develop into regional service centres. In fact it seems likely that both processes occur (as well as others) to differing degrees in different circumstances. For the emergence of regional centres, two alternative hypotheses may be mentioned. The first of these is that they grow up through internal demand. Change is endogenic (Vance 1970, 141) requiring the internal growth of population and income. The process is comparable to that suggested in early work on the development of market centres, a theory reviewed by Berry (1967). This hypothesis

> starts with an agrarian society in which surpluses develop, per-
> mitting a basic form of division of labour to emerge from the
> propensity of individuals to barter the surpluses, and leads to the
> establishment of a specialist group of artificers (smiths, carpenters,
> wheelwrights) located in a village central to the farmers they
> serve and with whom they exchange. The village becomes the most
> convenient site for trade between the cultivators, too, and assumes
> the status of a periodic market [*ibid.*, 108].

Further specialisation leads to inter-regional trade.

Although such a process may often occur, the initial impulse to the growth of centres is often outside contact and trade (Pirenne 1936). This external impulse may take a number of forms which can be considered in three groups. The first is the impact of long-distance trade for the emergence of regional centres and markets (Hodder and Ukwu 1969, 29; Jackson 1971, 31–2). Vance (1970), on the basis of medieval European and early American examples, has suggested that important service centres may grow up through close external ties in long distance trade (fig.4.18). Such centres may act as collecting points for the syphoning off of goods from internal networks and the articulation of these goods with external centres. They may also act as nodes for the redistribution of imports to surrounding areas (Rowlands 1973). Thus externally orientated trade at such centres involves local organisation and exchange mechanisms. For example, in pre-European sub-Saharan west Africa large states arose with a strong commercial power based on the trade flowing along the trans-Saharan caravan routes. 'In these northern savanna lands arose a succession of often powerful indigenous states whose very life lay in their ability to trade across the Sahara with the Mediterranean world' (Hodder and Harris 1967, 4). Most of this trade was in luxury items. 'Gold, slaves, ivory, ostrich feathers and hides moved northward across the Sahara in return for salt and luxury items' (Hodder 1967, 223). The later European contact in west Africa was, before the late nineteenth century, almost exclusively in the form of coastal trading bases. This was because the hinterland trade was adequately organised by the African states. The main European interest was slaves and these were provided in large numbers by indigenous African states at or near the coast which acted as middlemen for European traders (Hodder and Harris 1967, 6). These states thus articulated the externally orientated trade. A similar development may be suggested for the late Iron Age in Britain (Hodder 1975). Strabo's *Geography*, the finds of imported amphorae and the development of a trade in slaves indicate widespread trade in luxury items controlled at political centres. The growth of oppida in Britain may be seen as a response to external contact.

A similar model may be relevant for the development of centralised

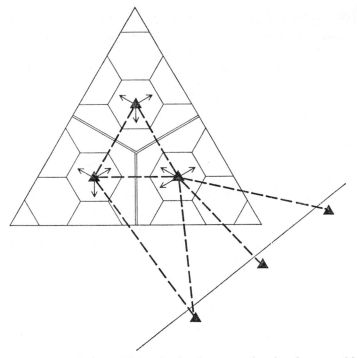

Fig.4.18. A model for the development of regional centres (▲).
These grow up through external ties (dashed lines) in long-
distance trade.

societies in a more general sense. For non-chief societies 'the path to
chief type political organisation seems to lie in the realm of an adequate
resource base, economic surplus, and the development of trade. . . .
Such change is also associated with the emergence of social stratifica-
tion' (Cohen and Schlegel 1968, 145). 'The basis for the rise of chief-
tainships and their most distinctive economic features appears to be
regional specialisation in goods. Chiefs arise to distribute the gains from
the market or the increase in production that has resulted from trade'
(Bessac 1968; see also Lewis 1968). It seems possible that the development and differentiation of political and social divisions may often be
partly related to the co-ordination of trading activities (Rowlands
1973, 594).

The second and third types of external contact concern the development of markets. The particular relevance of this will be made clear
below in an archaeological example, but some preliminary points are
perhaps appropriate. By the term market is meant the 'market place'
(Firth 1967a; Neale 1957) in which exchange is fairly free from insti-
tutional kinship obligations. It should be emphasised that market place
exchange may occur without the use of money and certainly without the
use of coinage as we know it (Bohannan and Dalton 1962; Kluckhohn

1962; Reader 1964). Also, early markets, which are often periodic, may, apart from being centres of exchange, perform equally, or more, important functions as social or administrative centres (Benet 1957, 198; Bohannan and Dalton 1962). It is often in the market place that social and kinship ties are maintained and that political or administrative announcements are made.

The second instance of external contact occurs at the boundaries between ecological zones where the differing products of adjacent areas can be most easily exchanged. Active exchange of this sort may well lead to the growth of markets as local service centres. (Hodder 1965, 99; Meillassoux 1962; Vansina 1962, 194).

The boundaries between tribal groups provide a third area in which external exchange may occur. It is in these contact areas that there is likely to be any great need for exchange especially when there is some cultural or ecological variety between the groups. Sahlins (1965) has defined a zone of intertribal exchange on the tribal periphery where barter or haggling may occur, as opposed to gift or reciprocal exchange within the tribal area. 'It is particularly in the peripheral areas of exchange, where personal contacts are required but not constrained by moral obligations to be "fair", that the need for trade can overcome tendencies towards intergroup hostility and stimulate wider social and cultural integration' (Rowlands 1971). It is in such areas that a market system is likely to emerge (Benet 1957; Hodder 1965; Menger 1892). Such markets often need to be placed in contact areas to provide a neutral point for exchange between warring tribes (Benet 1957, 199; Hodder and Ukwu 1969, 130; Vansina 1962, 194). Also 'fairs were most often held on boundaries in neutral lands where rival tribes could meet to trade. In ancient Italy, for example, one of the most important fairs was held on a boundary which separated Etruscan from Sabine lands. In Greece, markets were held on boundaries under the protection of gods of the Agora' (Berry 1967, 101). It is partly for this reason that fairs and markets are often located in the open countryside rather than in settlements. An example of this tribal contact area marketing is provided by the traditional markets in Yorubaland in western Nigeria. The 8-day periodic markets (i.e. those occurring every eighth day) are larger and more important than other traditional markets and can be seen to cluster in fairly definite groupings.

> One possible explanation for the groupings of 8-day markets may lie in the fact that with the exception of the lagoon-side markets they all lie at the junction of different groups or sub-groups of the Yoruba-speaking people. . . . It is probable that these 8-day market groupings represent the original foci of the market network in their location at junction zones between the Egba and Ijebu; between the Ibadan and Oyo (proper) Yoruba; and between the Ife-Elesha, Ekiti and Ondo Yoruba [Hodder and Ukwu 1969, 64].

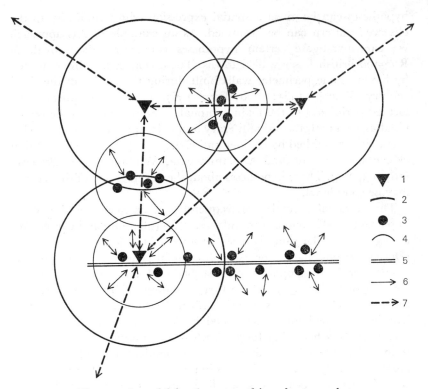

Fig.4.19. A model for the external impulse to market development. 1, Tribal centre–central market; 2 (heavy line), tribal area; 3, local market centre; 4 (thin-lined circles), market area; 5, ecological boundary; 6, local market movements; 7, close contact in external trade.

The external impulse to market development is represented in diagrammatic form in fig.4.19. Markets occur at the contact zones between tribes, at ecological boundaries, and at tribal centres. While local exchange at these markets may initially be concerned with food-stuffs (Benet 1957, 194; Douglas 1962), active exchange may encourage specialised craft industries to develop since it provides a known and reliable market for products such as cloth and pottery (Jackson 1971; Middleton 1962). These craft products will thus be distributed in the market areas around the market centres, reflecting the areas of inter-action with the markets.

In the preceding discussion a number of models have been mentioned concerning the development of a pattern of nodal centres over time. Given an archaeological distribution of sites known to have functioned as service centres, how can we differentiate between the various models and decide which or which combination is most appropriate? An advantage of making hypotheses about spatial patterns is that the hypotheses can be given a spatial expression whose similarity to the observed pattern can be examined. As an example of this approach we can investigate certain hypotheses concerning the growth of Romano-British lesser walled towns. These centres are differentiated by having stone perimeter walls built during the course of the third century (Wacher 1964; 1966; Frere 1967, 249). They appear to be located peripheral to the main cantonal capitals which can be recognised as such with the aid of literary and epigraphic evidence. The list of sites is as published by Hodder and Hassall (1971), with the addition of the more recent find at Bannaventa, Whilton lodge (*Britannia* (1972) **3**, 325). Three hypotheses about the development of the pattern may be considered.

The cantonal capitals are frequently on or near the site of an important pre-Roman centre (Silchester, Verulamium and Cirencester for example). The same is true for some of the lesser walled towns (Dorchester-on-Thames for example) but in general it seems possible to consider the development of the secondary level as a response to the location of major centres. The first hypothesis about the growth of these second-level centres is derived from Godlund's model (fig.4.17). The lesser walled towns developed half-way between larger centres because it was here that there was least competition from them. In terms of military, administrative and political control there was greatest need for additional centres in these areas. We have seen that by constructing Thiessen polygons, lines are drawn midway between centres. In fig.4.20 Thiessen polygons have been drawn around the cantonal capitals, and according to the proposed hypothesis, the lesser walled towns should be clustered along them. Figure 4.20 shows that this is generally the case.

A second hypothesis can be suggested. It has been assumed that the service area around a cantonal capital can be reconstructed regardless of its size. Lines half-way between the centres thus indicate the boundaries of the service areas. It will be shown (section 5.6) that larger centres tend to have relatively larger service areas than smaller centres. The boundaries of service areas around centres of different sizes can be constructed using Reilly's breaking-point formula (p. 188). The boundaries for the service areas of the cantonal capitals are shown in fig.4.20, the size of each major centre being taken as the area enclosed within its walls.

The second hypothesis for the location of the lesser walled towns may thus be seen to reflect normal distance-decay factors. Second-level towns would develop in these locations if the size of the cantonal capitals reflected their importance in the early Roman period in Britain, and if the development of towns was the result of the need to provide services to a dispersed population. In the first hypothesis, on the other hand, some additional factors might be supposed to be involved. We

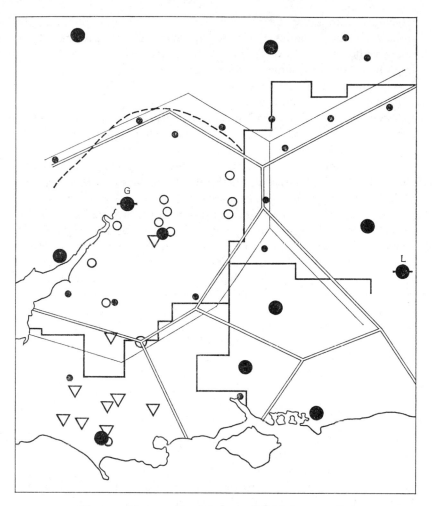

Fig.4.20. The growth of Romano-British lesser walled towns.
○, Corinium school of mosaics; ▽, Durotrigian school of
mosaics; ●, cantonal capitals – major centres; -●-, London (L)
and the 'colonia' at Gloucester (G); ●, lesser walled towns.
Double lines = Thiessen polygons around major centres;
single line = service area around major centres as predicted by
gravity models; single heavy line = boundary between Iron
Age coin distributions.

have seen that the point half-way between two major centres might not
be the true boundary between two service areas. For such a regular
mid-point location some form of control, perhaps by the military, might
be assumed. For example, Webster (1966) has stressed the influence
exerted by forts of the Julio-Claudian period (A.D. 43–69) outside
which settlements of traders and camp followers arose. These sometimes

developed into independent townships after the withdrawal of the military in the seventies of the first century. A large number of the lesser walled towns have origins of this form. Thus, while the first hypothesis stresses military and/or administrative control, the second lays emphasis on the normal economic servicing of an area.

It may be possible to test whether the second hypothesis does relate to servicing factors by examining artifact distributions. If a service is provided by the major centres to the area predicted by the hypothesis, then it is reasonable to suppose that the predicted service area corresponds to the actual one. An example of the type of service provided by the major centres alone is given by Smith (D. J., 1969). His examination of fourth century mosaics in rich villas led to the conclusion that there is a 'tendency for certain subjects and themes to appear more or less localised' so that groups of related mosaics can be identified. 'Each group is characterised by features which are not found, or are found significantly less often or in a significantly different form, elsewhere' (*ibid.*, 95). Smith suggests that this indicates 'schools' of mosaicists with their workshops at, for example, Cirencester and Dorchester (Dorset). The distribution of mosaics from the latter two schools is shown in fig.4.20. Although the mosaic types are in general confined to the predicted service areas there is not sufficient evidence to be able to say that the area predicted by the second hypothesis fits any better than that predicted by the Theissen polygons.

A third hypothesis is that the lesser walled towns are market centres which developed at the boundaries between tribal areas in the way outlined above. The tribal areas in the immediately pre-Roman period may be suggested by the distribution of late Iron Age inscribed coins (see however Hodder 1975). To obtain the boundaries between these coin areas, a grid was placed over the distributions of coin find spots and a smoothed density map obtained (section 5.4). The boundary between two coin areas is defined as the grid line on either side of which the density of find spots is the same. However, this is not a very satisfactory procedure since the boundary line depends very much on the size of grid quadrat used, on the relative amount of coins produced in each area, and on the relative length of time during which the different coin types which have been mapped were being produced. Nevertheless the method allows an approximation to the tribal boundaries which has been shown to have some validity by the distribution of Romano-Celtic temples (Hodder 1975). There seems to be some evidence that these temples were located on tribal boundaries and their distribution is similar to the boundaries predicted in fig.4.20. Since no coin types are found north of the Dobunnic area, the boundary at this point (dashed in fig.4.20) has had to be constructed from the distribution of Dobunnic coins alone.

Three different hypotheses about the emergence of the lesser walled

towns have been suggested. By comparing the observed distribution of
lesser walled towns with their locations predicted by each hypothesis,
it was hoped to be possible to identify which hypothesis is correct or is of
greatest importance. It is clear from fig.4.20 that the lesser walled
towns are not placed closer to one predicted line than to another. It
does not seem possible to differentiate between the three hypotheses.

Table 4.1.   *The locations of Romano-British lesser walled towns on the roads.*
Predicted distances (p_1, p_2) from the first-named cantonal capitals, to the lesser walled
towns, according to the first and second hypotheses and actual observed distances (x)
are given. These distances are also expressed as proportions of the total distances
between the major towns. Observed distances are in centimetres on the Ordnance
Survey Map of Roman Britain

	Road	Town	Total distance	Distances			Proportions		
				p_1	p_2	x	p_1	p_2	x
1.	Cirencester to St Albans	Alchester	11.7	5.8	6.1	6.0	0.5	0.52	0.51
2.	Cirencester to Silchester	Mildenhall	8.6	4.3	5.1	4.1	0.5	0.59	0.48
3.	Cirencester to Dorchester	Bath	13.4	6.7	8.8	4.6	0.5	0.66	0.34
3a.	Cirencester to Dorchester	Ilchester	13.4	6.7	8.8	9.4	0.5	0.66	0.70
4.	Cirencester to Leicester	Chesterton	11.8	5.9	7.1	6.7	0.5	0.60	0.57
5.	Cirencester to Wroxeter	Droitwich	13.6	6.8	7.3	7.2	0.5	0.54	0.53
6.	Cirencester to Wroxeter	Kenchester	14.7	7.4	7.9	7.6	0.5	0.54	0.52
7.	St Albans to Leicester	Towcester	12.4	6.2	7.2	6.0	0.5	0.58	0.48

A simpler approach is to consider the one-dimensional case of the
location of the towns on the main roads which link the cantonal
capitals. This allows us to consider only a limited number of the sites
since not all the lesser walled towns are on one of these arterial roads.
The towns used are shown in table 4.1, which also contains the total
distance between each pair of cantonal capitals along the roads. The
distance from the first-named cantonal capital in each pair to the lesser
walled town on the road is also indicated. For Bath and Ilchester,
which are both on the road between Cirencester and Dorchester
(Dorset), the predicted locations are the same. The predicted locations
are obtained from hypotheses one and two. Table 4.1 also shows the
predicted and observed distances between the first-named cantonal

capitals and the lesser walled towns as a proportion of the total distance. Thus hypothesis 1 predicts that the towns should be half-way along the roads – that is a proportion of 0.50. An examination of the table shows that neither hypothesis is obviously a better fit.

To examine the relative claims of rival hypotheses more objectively, one can use a likelihood ratio (LR) test. We suppose that each hypothesis predicts, not a completely determined location for an intermediate town – since if it does, then in our example both hypotheses are 'wrong' and there is no more to be said – but a probability density centred in some way on the 'most favoured location' of that hypothesis. The probability densities are functions of the parameters of the hypothesis – in this case of the predicted proportions p_1 and p_2 – and can be denoted by $f(x, p_1)$ and $f(x, p_2)$ where x represents the observed proportions (see table 4.1). The likelihood ratio, given by

$$\lambda = f(x, p_1)/f(x, p_2), \tag{4.4}$$

is then a measure of the extent to which the evidence (x) supports hypothesis 1 against hypothesis 2. The greater the value of λ, the greater the evidence in favour of hypothesis 1. Interpretations of the LR may vary: if, for example, one had strong *a priori* reasons to support hypothesis 2, one would require a high value of λ to convince one that hypothesis 1 was the better of the two, while if one's initial beliefs supported hypothesis 1, one might find further support in even a relatively low value of λ.

In this particular example we approached the LR with an open mind, i.e. with the view that a LR greater than 1 would be evidence in favour of hypothesis 1, a value of less than 1 would favour hypothesis 2, and that a value greater than about 10 or less than 0.1 would constitute strong evidence. At this stage one must choose a density function $f(x, p)$, to represent the probability of the intermediate town being situated at a proportion x of the distance between the two main towns, when the predicted proportion is p. It seems desirable that this density function should possess the following properties:

(i) it should be positive for $0 < x < 1$, and the area beneath it should equal 1, i.e. the intermediate town must exist and must lie between the main towns;

(ii) it should decrease to zero as x decreases to 0 or increases to 1, i.e. the probability of the intermediate town being very close to a main town should be very small;

(iii) it should be greatest when $x = p$, i.e. the predicted value should be the 'most likely' value.

The simplest family of probability densities fulfilling these conditions are of the form

$$f(x, p) = k[x^p(1 - x)^{1-p}]^c. \tag{4.5}$$

The constant c can be chosen to 'sharpen' or 'flatten' the shape of the function, while the value of k is calculated so that the area beneath the curve should equal 1 (see fig.4.21).

With a density of this form, the LR for one road becomes

$$\lambda = \left(\frac{k_1}{k_2}\right)\left(\frac{x^{p_1}(1 - x)^{1-p_1}}{x^{p_2}(1 - x)^{1-p_2}}\right)^c \tag{4.6}$$

and for all roads together,

$$\lambda = \prod_{i=1}^n \left(\frac{k_{1i}}{k_{2i}}\right)\left(\frac{x_i}{1 - x_i}\right)^{c(p_{1i}-p_{2i})}. \tag{4.7}$$

Using a value of $c = 1$, the overall LR, taking Bath as the intermediate town on road 3, was about 1.2, while when Ilchester was chosen, the LR was 0.95. If road 3 was omitted, the LR was 1.06. In other words, if Bath is included, hypothesis 1 is roughly 20 % 'more likely' than hypothesis 2, while if Ilchester is taken, 1 is about 5 % 'less likely' than 2.

However, the value of $c = 1$ does not discriminate well between rival hypotheses, and a higher value of c is now favoured. It seems desirable that the function should show a concave curve on either side of the 'most likely' value of p, and that the slope of the curve at $x = 0$ and $x = 1$ should be zero. This will be so if cp is greater than 1 and $c(1 - p)$ is greater than 1. Since in practice it appears unlikely that values of p of less than 0.25 or more than 0.75 will commonly occur, a value of $c = 4$ should be sufficient to ensure that this condition is satisfied. Figure 4.21 shows the shapes of the curves which seem to be indicated for $c = 4$, with $p = \frac{1}{2}$ and $\frac{1}{4}$.

Repeating the above calculations with the new value of $c = 4$ instead of $c = 1$ gives an overall LR of about 2.2 (with Bath as the intermediate town) or 0.85 (Ilchester as the intermediate town). Thus, even with a more discriminating test there is no strong evidence in favour of either hypothesis against the other.

In this example we have used two arbitrarily chosen density functions from a whole family of possible functions of the form of equation 4.5, all of which satisfy the conditions laid down. The first, ($c = 1$), was chosen as being the simplest, while the second ($c = 4$) was chosen as likely to satisfy a desirable but not necessary extra condition. It is clear that by choosing higher values of c we could increase the apparent significance of the likelihood ratio. A less *ad hoc* way of choosing c is needed, which in turn implies the need for further investigation into the sources and likely sizes of departures from the theoretical Thiessen polygon and gravity models.

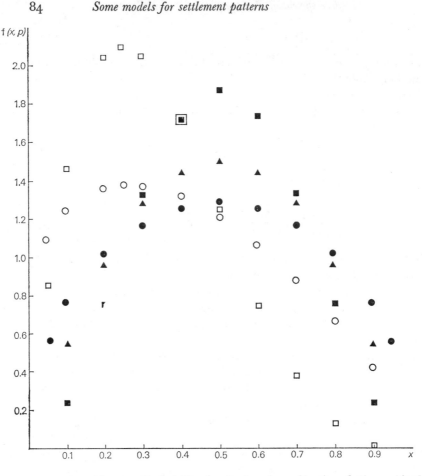

Fig.4.21. Probability density functions, $f(x, p) = [x^p(1-x)^{1-p}]^c$.
$\bigcirc$, $\bullet$, $c = 1$; $\blacktriangle$, $c = 2$; $\square$, $\blacksquare$, $c = 4$. Solid symbols,
$p = \frac{1}{2}$; open symbols, $p = \frac{1}{4}$.

It is often the case that archaeological evidence is not detailed
enough to allow successful testing between alternative hypotheses
(cf. section 5.3). In the present case we have tried to differentiate
between different hypotheses which were considered in isolation. The
actual situation is likely to have been much more complex. For example,
the initial site location may have been related to military factors, while
the pattern of development of certain military forts into lesser walled
towns may have been due to economic servicing and other factors. A
further complication is the importance of the historical development of
a site. Dorchester-on-Thames, for example, continued from a pre-
existing centre. Because of the great complexity of interlocking factors
determining site location, and because the alternative hypotheses
considered do not have markedly distinct spatial expressions, distri-

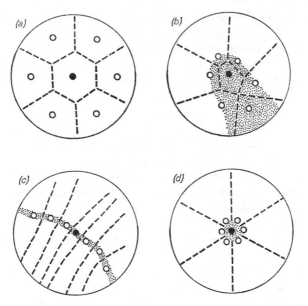

Fig.4.22. Sequence of settlement patterns associated with an increasingly localised resource (stippled areas). Source: Haggett 1965.

butional studies do not lead to a detailed understanding of the process of town development. The general approach outlined here, however, provides a more rigorous examination of hypotheses about spatial processes.

4.4. *Clustered patterns*

Clustering of archaeological sites may result from a variety of different causes apart from the effects of uneven fieldwork and site survival. One of these is clustering due to the localisation of resources. In the previous section it has been assumed that settlements locate uniformly on a featureless plain (fig.4.22a). However, a simple rural village needs agricultural land, water, building materials, fuel etc., all of which are resources in some degree localised. Some idea of the effects of such localisations is given in fig.4.22 for zones such as a preferred soil type (b), a linear resource such as a river (c), and a point resource such as a well or geological outcrop (d). Variety in the response to resource localisation is evidenced in a study by Ellison and Harriss (1972) of settlement and land use in southern England.

Agglomeration of sites may also occur around a more important site such as a major town or religious centre. Population is attracted to such nodes in order to, for example, obtain protection, or to be able to take advantage of the greater range of functions and activities available.

Some archaeological examples are the clustering of Romano-British villas around towns such as Ilchester and Bath, and the agglomeration of Bronze Age barrows around Stonehenge and related monuments. An alternative process is that the existence of clusters of settlements encourages the development of centres within them in order to, for example, articulate local and widespread contacts, or to provide military protection.

An interesting regularity which may be investigated in archaeological situations where agglomeration around centres occurs, is that urban population density declines from the centre in a negative exponential way. Berry, Simmons and Tennant (1963) were able to point to almost 100 cases of this in various parts of the world over the last 150 years. It would be of great interest to see whether this empirical finding holds for the fall-off in density around important archaeological sites, especially since some regularities in changes of the fall-off gradient through time have been noticed (*ibid.*).

Settlement agglomeration may also be due to the temporal stages in the spread of settlement. Hudson (1969) has suggested a theory for the spread of settlement (cf. Greig-Smith 1964, 216). An initial stage is that of colonisation of an area by individual settlements or small groups of settlements. The spacing of these colonisers may appear random. A second stage of spread from these initial centres then occurs as population increases. There is a tendency to move short distances outwards from the initial colonies. Such a process may be aided by movement into the area from elsewhere, but the resulting pattern is one of clusters of settlements, which may be placed at random. A final stage in the development of the settlement pattern is a movement towards regularity of spacing due to increased overall density and pressure on the environment, a stage for which Hudson (*loc. cit.*) was able to give empirical support.

Wood (1971) has suggested that, for prehistoric settlement processes, this model of the generation of clusters by a contagious process of spread could be examined by fitting probability distributions to frequency information based on quadrat counts. Indeed plant ecologists and geographers have made use of a number of 'contagious' models in which each occurrence (of a settlement for example) increases the probability of further occurrences nearby (King 1969, 45). These models include the Neyman type A, and the negative binomial. The hypothetical spatial process which lies behind the negative binomial and which may be termed true contagion or generalised Poisson (Cliff and Ord 1973) has the following form. The clusters of points in the study area are defined as having a Poisson distribution, with each cluster containing one or more points. The number of points in each cluster follows a generalising distribution. If the generalising distribution is logarithmic, the generalised distribution is written as Poisson ∧

logarithmic, which is equivalent to the negative binomial, while Poisson ∧ Poisson yields the Neyman type A (Cliff and Ord 1973). Bartlett (1960, 15) showed that if you assume a circular Normal distribution of offspring around a centre, then the negative binomial provides a *useful approximation* to the distribution of the number of offspring in randomly placed quadrats of *small* size. "Insofar as the existence of a cluster means that an object is "more likely" to have other similar objects nearby, we say that these processes represent "true contagion"' (Cliff and Ord 1973). A strict assumption is that the clusters are 'sufficiently well spaced from one another for it to be impossible for a quadrat of the size selected to include more than one cluster' (Harvey 1968; see also Skellam 1958). Thus the size of quadrat used must be about the same as the size of the clusters. According to Diggle (personal communication) the reason for insisting that the clusters are sufficiently well spaced from one another is that a tacit assumption of the derivation of the negative binomial as a true contagious distribution is that if one member of a cluster lies within a quadrat, then so do all other members of the same cluster. This can at best be an approximation, unless all members of a cluster are assumed to occupy the same point. The degree of approximation will in practice be a function of how small is the 'within cluster' dispersion, relative to the mean separation distance between clusters, and the quadrat size.

This model for the generation of clusters of settlement has also been discussed by Anscombe (1950, 360). 'If colonies or groups of individuals are distributed randomly over an area ... so that the number of colonies observed in samples of fixed area ... has a Poisson distribution, we obtain a negative binomial distribution for the total count if the numbers of individuals in the colonies are distributed independently in a logarithmic distribution.' Harvey (1968) has suggested that the spatial diffusion of information is basically of the same form.

However, the negative binomial distribution will also give a good fit to clusters which have been arrived at by a different spatial process. Clusters of settlement can be derived when the allocation of settlements is a random process (simple Poisson) but the mean density of that process varies from place to place according to some specified law. If we assume that the mean density is itself a random variable, then if this mean density follows a gamma distribution, the compound distribution is Poisson ∧ gamma, which is the negative binomial. Likewise, Poisson ∧ Poisson yields the Neyman type A (Cliff and Ord 1973). This compound Poisson or apparent contagion process simply implies random inhomogeneity in the density of the population. Harvey (1968) has also discussed this model in relation to the diffusion of innovations. In this case, with the compound model, inferences are being made about regional variation in the susceptibility of a population to accepting information. This might result, for example, from varying density of the population through which information is being diffused, or from spatial inhomogeneity in the cultural characteristics of the population accepting the information.

It is important to note that the very different spatial processes of true and apparent contagion can both yield either the same negative binomial or the same Neyman type A distribution and this difficulty has been widely discussed (Harvey 1968; Wood 1971). However, an approximate procedure for the negative binomial which can be used to distinguish between the real and apparent contagion processes, and which is based on the variations of the parameters of the negative binomial model with changes in the quadrat size, has been developed by Cliff and Ord (1973; see also Dacey 1967).

Suppose that a study area has been partitioned into quadrats and a 'good fit' of the negative binomial to the frequency distribution of items in the quadrats has been found by using (for example) a χ^2 test. Further suppose that the parameters of the negative binomial distribution are k_1 and p_1, the subscript 1 indicating that single quadrats are being considered. If blocks of s original quadrats are combined into new larger quadrats, the resulting frequency distribution of items in the new quadrats is still negative binomial, but with parameters k_s and p_s. Cliff and Ord found that (under certain assumptions), if the original negative binomial distribution had been generated by a 'true contagion' situation then the parameters for the original and new quadrats were related by the formulae

$$k_s = sk_1 \tag{4.8}$$

and $p_s = p_1$,

whereas, if it had been generated by a 'spurious contagion' situation, the relationships would be

$$k_s = k_1$$

and $$p_s = \frac{1}{1 + s \left(\dfrac{1 - p_1}{p_1} \right)}. \tag{4.9}$$

'Thus by calculating estimates for p and k for different sized lattices, we can see which of the models appears to be nearer the truth.' This is only an approximate method of analysis because we cannot be certain that the quadrats combined to form larger quadrats have the same value [for the mean density] initially in the compound Poisson model. However, the procedure would seem to provide a reasonable check' (Cliff and Ord 1973).

Cliff and Ord have used this method to analyse a modern settlement

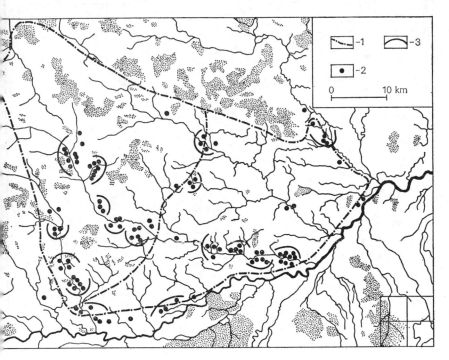

Fig.4.23. Distribution of Banderamik sites in a localised region
(1) in the Polish loess zone: 2, the sites; 3, some hypothetical
boundaries of settlement micro-regions suggested by Kruk.
Source: Kruk 1973.

pattern in Japan which had been suggested to be one of nucleated
villages. The apparent contagion (compound Poisson) version of the
negative binomial model was found to give a better fit to these data than
the generalised model. 'This would seem to argue for a pattern of
colonisation essentially random (Poissonian), but with varying propen-
sities to settle in different parts of the region (because of different land
quality, for example)' (*ibid.*).

This method for distinguishing between the apparent and true
contagion versions of the negative binomial model has obvious importance in archaeology. Settlement and artifact distributions (whether
over a wide area or within one site) frequently exhibit some degree of
clustering. It is usually difficult to understand the process which produced these clusters since regional variations in site occurrence, survival
and retrieval result from a wide range of inter-related variables. As an
initial example of the application of the method to archaeological data,
distribution maps were studied (Hodder 1975) of the early neolithic in
a small area of the south Polish loess zone (Kruk 1973). This is an area
of intense archaeological activity and the impact of survey and excavation strategies on the site distributions has been assessed by Kruk.

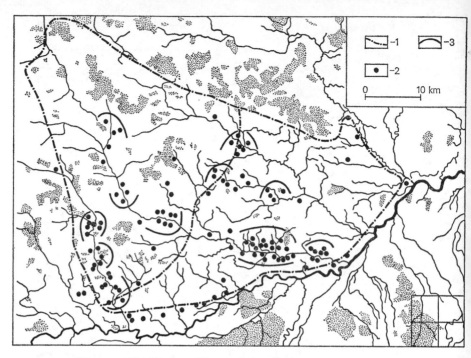

Fig.4.24. Distribution of Lengyel sites in the same area
as fig.4.23. 1–3 as in fig.4.23. Source: Kruk 1973.

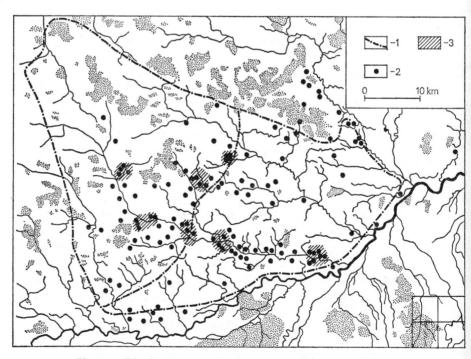

Fig.4.25. Distribution of TRB sites in the same area as fig.4.23.
1 and 2 as in fig.4.23. 3, some regions of dense settlement.
Source: Kruk 1973.

Table 4.2. *Maximum likelihood estimates of parameters k_s and p_s for the lattices from the Polish Bandkeramik sites, and derived estimates of parameters k_1 and p_1 for the original lattice*

Lattice no.	s	$\hat{k}_s$	$\hat{p}_s$	True contagion		Spurious contagion	
				$\hat{k}_1$	$\hat{p}_1$	$\hat{k}_1$	$\hat{p}_1$
1	1	0.235	0.195	0.235	0.195	0.235	0.195
2	2	0.518	0.211	0.259	0.211	0.518	0.348
3	2	0.381	0.164	0.190	0.164	0.381	0.282
4	3	0.659	0.190	0.220	0.190	0.659	0.413
5	6	1.087	0.153	0.181	0.153	1.087	0.520
6	4	1.340	0.255	0.335	0.255	1.340	0.604
7	4	0.807	0.172	0.202	0.172	0.807	0.454
8	4	0.701	0.100	0.175	0.100	0.701	0.432
9	8	1.57	0.167	0.196	0.167	1.57	0.615
Overall				0.221	0.185	0.811	0.429

Distributions of sites in the Bandkeramik, Lengyel and TRB (funnel-necked beaker) phases are available for study.

In order to fit the negative binomial to the distribution of Bandkeramik sites, the map of sites was partitioned by a grid of the size shown in figs. 4.23 to 4.25. So that changes in the parameters of the model could be examined as the quadrat size increased, adjacent cells of the base lattice were combined in various combinations to produce new quadrats. The value of s in tables 4.2 to 4.6 indicates the number of adjacent quadrats which were combined to form one quadrat in the new lattice. The negative binomial was then fitted by maximum likelihood to the observed frequency distribution of settlements in the quadrats for each lattice.

The estimates so obtained for the Bandkeramik, Lengyel and TRB data are shown in tables 4.2, 4.4 and 4.6 respectively. The estimates for k_1 and p_1 under true contagion are obtained from $\hat{k}_s$ and $\hat{p}_s$ by equations 4.8, while the estimates for k_1 and p_1 under apparent or 'spurious contagion' are obtained by equation 4.9. The 'overall' estimates denoted by $\hat{\hat{k}}_1$ and $\hat{\hat{p}}_1$ are simple averages of the values obtained for each lattice: a maximum likelihood estimate based on information from all lattices would probably be better but was not available. The goodness-of-fit between the observed and expected frequency distributions (the expected values were obtained by interpolation from Williamson and Bretherton 1963), (a) using the values of $\hat{k}_s$ and $\hat{p}_s$ initially estimated from each lattice, (b) using values for k_s and p_s based on the overall estimates $\hat{\hat{k}}_1$ and $\hat{\hat{p}}_1$ from the true contagion model, and (c) using values for k_s and p_s similarly derived from the spurious contagion model, was

Table 4.3. *Fitting the negative binomial to Polish Bandkeramik sites; (a) individual lattice's estimates of k and p, (b) overall estimates of k and p derived from the true contagion model, (c) overall estimates of k and p derived from the spurious contagion model*

Observed and expected values (a)

Sites/ quad- rat	1 O	1 E	2 O	2 E	3 O	3 E	4 O	4 E	5 O	5 E	6 O	6 E	7 O	7 E	8 O
0	66	69.6	23	21.4	25	23.0	11	9.3	2	1.9	4	4.1	7	6.1	7
1	11	11.1	5	8.5	6	7.6	5	5.3	2	1.8	5	4.0	2	4.0	2
2	4	5.2	5	5.1	4	4.5	2	3.6	2	1.6	2	3.4	3	2.9	2
3	4	3.2	3	3.4	2	3.0	2	2.7	—	1.4	2	2.8	1	2.2	2
4	3	2.0	4	2.4	2	2.1	4	2.1	2	1.2	3	2.2	3	1.7	2
5	3	1.3	1	1.7	—	1.6	2	1.6	1	1.0	—	1.7	1	1.4	1
6	2	0.86	3	1.2	4	1.2	1	1.2	—	0.88	1	1.3	—	1.1	2
7	2	0.67	3	0.91	2	0.91	1	0.99	1	0.75	2	1.0	2	0.8	—
8	—	0.48	—	0.67	—	0.72	1	0.77	1	0.65	—	0.79	—	0.7	—
9	1	0.38	1	0.53	3	0.58	1	0.62	1	0.54	3	0.60	3	0.5	2
10	—	—	—	—	—	—	—	—	—	—	2	0.46	—	0.4	1
11	—	—	—	—	—	—	—	—	—	—	—	—	—	0.4	—
12	—	—	—	—	—	—	—	—	—	—	—	—	2	0.3	—
χ^2	5.68		4.8		4.9		2.7		—		—		—		—

Note: Totals do not always sum to total number of quadrats, because higher values have been omitted.

Table 4.4. *Maximum likelihood estimates of parameters k_s and p_s for the lattices from the Polish Lengyel sites, and derived estimates of parameters k_1 and p_1 for the original lattice*

Lattice no.	s	$\hat{k}_s$	$\hat{p}_s$	True contagion $\hat{k}_1$	$\hat{p}_1$	Spurious contagion $\hat{k}_1$	$\hat{p}_1$
1	1	0.414	0.269	0.414	0.269	0.414	0.269
2	2	0.719	0.244	0.360	0.244	0.719	0.393
3	2	0.968	0.301	0.434	0.301	0.968	0.463
4	3	1.062	0.239	0.354	0.239	1.062	0.485
5	4	1.282	0.222	0.320	0.222	1.282	0.533
6	4	1.355	0.251	0.339	0.251	1.355	0.573
7	4	1.541	0.255	0.385	0.255	1.541	0.579
8	6	1.955	0.225	0.326	0.225	1.955	0.636
9	8	2.495	0.236	0.312	0.236	2.495	0.732
Overall				0.360	0.249	1.310	0.518

Table 4.3. (*continued*)

	Expected values (b) and (c)												Sites/
	1		2–3		4		5		6–8		9		quad-
	E(b)	E(c)	E(b)	E(c)	E(b)	E(c)	E(b)	E(c)	E(b)	E(c)	E(b)	E(c)	rat
64	66.2	48.2	22.8	16.7	10.4	8.7	1.7	2.7	5.4	5.4	0.49	1.6	0
86	11.8	22.3	8.1	10.1	5.7	5.6	1.8	1.9	3.9	3.7	0.88	1.2	1
94	5.8	11.5	4.8	6.5	3.7	4.1	1.7	1.6	3.0	2.8	0.98	1.0	2
95	3.6	6.2	3.2	4.3	2.8	3.0	1.6	1.3	2.3	2.2	1.01	0.83	3
91	2.3	3.4	2.3	3.1	2.0	2.3	1.4	1.1	1.8	1.8	0.98	0.72	4
86	1.6		1.6	2.2	1.6	1.8	1.2	0.95	1.5	1.4	0.92	0.66	5
79	1.2		1.2	1.5	—	1.4	1.0	0.8	1.2	1.2	0.85	0.60	6
72	0.83		0.91		—		0.88	0.7	—	1.0	0.77	0.54	7
65	0.61		0.67		—		—	0.6	—	0.8	0.68	0.48	8
59	0.46		0.50		—		—		—		0.60		9
51	—		—		—		—		—		0.53		10
45	—		—		—		—		—		—		11
	—		—		—		—		—		—		12
	1.88	18.2	2.99	6.3	2.74	2.79	0.79	0.19	1.94	1.13	—		χ^2

evaluated using χ^2 and/or the Kolmogorov–Smirnov statistic wherever the data were adequate (see tables 4.3, 4.5 and 4.7; also 4.8).

With regard to the Bandkeramik data, the left-hand part of table 4.3 shows a good fit to the negative binomial for each lattice individually. The right-hand side shows that the generalised model of true contagion (b) fits better than the compound model of spurious contagion (c).

It seems that the pattern of settlement may therefore be compared with a true contagious process. This may be due to clustering around the initial colonisers as in the model suggested by Hudson (1969). This is also clear if we compare the development of the settlement groupings into the Lengyel phase. Most groups show a marked tendency towards expansion outwards. The formation of groupings is, however, also the result of the functional inter-relationship of sites noticed by Kruk (1973). In view of the lack of any strong relationship between the settlement distribution and environmental factors, it seems that the main determinants of the pattern may be a process of contagious spread and a functional interdependence of settlements.

For the Lengyel distribution the negative binomial again fits each lattice's data individually (table 4.5). The generalised model of true

Table 4.5. *Fitting the negative binomial to Polish Lengyel sites; (a) individual lattice's estimates of k and p, (b) overall estimates of k and p derived from true contagion model, (c) overall estimates of k and p derived from the spurious contagion model*

Observed and expected values (a)

Sites/quadrat	Lattice No.											9
	1		2		3		4		5	6	7	8
	O	E	O	E	O	E	O	E	O	O	O	O
0	56	55.9	17	17.6	15	14.4	6	6.6	3	4	4	1
1	17	16.5	11	9.4	12	10.1	9	5.5	5	4	2	1
2	7	8.5	6	6.0	2	7.0	3	4.4	3	2	3	3
3	5	5.1	3	4.1	8	4.9	2	3.5	2	2	—	—
4	4	3.2	2	2.9	5	3.4	2	2.7	1	2	4	2
5	3	2.1	2	2.1	—	2.4	2	2.1	—	1	1	—
6	1	1.3	3	1.5	1	1.7	4	1.6	4	3	—	2
7	1	0.86	1	1.1	2	1.2	1	1.2	2	1	2	2
8	1	0.57	1	0.77	1	0.82	—	0.96	1	—	2	—
9	—	0.83	—	0.57	—	0.58	—	0.73	—	—	2	—
10	1	0.29	1	0.43	2	0.38	1	0.57	1	3	—	—
11	—	—		—		—		—	—	1	—	—
χ^2	0.83		1.26		6.8		3.68		—	—	—	—

Table 4.6. *Maximum likelihood estimates of parameters k_s and p_s for the lattices from the Polish TRB sites, and derived estimates of parameters k_1 and p_1 for the original lattice*

Lattice no.	s	$\hat{k}_s$	$\hat{p}_s$	True contagion		Spurious contagion	
				$\hat{k}_1$	$\hat{p}_1$	$\hat{k}_1$	$\hat{p}_1$
1	1	0.893	0.409	0.893	0.409	0.893	0.409
2	2	1.462	0.376	0.731	0.376	1.462	0.545
3	4	2.424	0.323	0.606	0.323	2.424	0.655
4	6	2.598	0.251	0.436	0.251	2.598	0.668
5	8	2.538	0.197	0.317	0.197	2.538	0.597
6	8	22.315	0.683	2.789	0.683	22.315	0.946
Overall				0.962	0.373	5.372	0.637
Excluding lattice 6				0.597	0.311	1.983	0.575

Table 4.5. (*continued*)

pected values (*b*) and (*c*)

(*b*)	E(*c*)	2–3 E(*b*)	E(*c*)	4 E(*b*)	E(*c*)	5–7 E(*b*)	E(*c*)	8 E(*b*)	E(*c*)	9 E(*b*)	E(*c*)	Sites/quadrat
3	40.7	17.6	12.1	7.1	5.6	3.2	3.2	0.8	1.35	0.2	0.7	0
6	25.3	9.5	10.3	5.6	5.4	3.7	3.2	1.3	1.5	0.5	0.9	1
o	14.2	6.1	7.7	4.5	4.6	3.2	2.9	1.6	1.45	0.7	0.9	2
7	7.6	4.2	5.6	3.5	3.7	2.8	2.6	1.6	1.4	0.8	0.8	3
o	3.9	2.9	3.9	2.7	2.9	2.3	2.3	1.6	1.25	0.9	0.8	4
-		2.1	2.7	2.0	2.3	1.8	1.8	1.4	1.15	1.0	0.7	5
-		—	1.8	1.6	1.8	1.5	1.5	1.3	1.0	0.9	0.7	6
-			—	—	1.4	1.2	1.2	1.1	0.9	0.8	0.6	7
-					—	—	1.0	1.0	0.8	0.7	0.6	8
-								0.8	0.7	0.6	0.5	9
-								0.7	0.6	0.6	0.5	10
-										0.5	0.4	11
78	14.2	1.27	5.1	3.86	9.5	—	—	—	—	—	—	χ^2

contagion (*b*) fits better than the compound model of spurious contagion (*c*). The contagious process suggested in this way is also apparent in the growth of the clusters, as discussed above.

The TRB results are rather different. For the first time, both models fit the data adequately, and there is in fact little to choose between them. This represents a distinct shift towards the spurious contagion model when compared with the Bandkeramik and Lengyel situations. The differences between the three periods are brought out in table 4.8. Although groupings of sites still occur, as suggested by Kruk in fig.4.25, the TRB pattern is becoming more like one in which sites are located by a random process (Poisson) with density variation according to, for example, the position of rivers and the pattern of site retrieval. There seems therefore to be some evidence for the sort of pattern of settlement development envisaged by Hudson. An initial stage of contagious growth leads to the expansion of clusters of settlement and finally to a more dispersed pattern of sites with local variation in density. As we have seen when discussing the simple Poisson model, in certain cases increased density will lead to increased uniformity in the spacing of sites.

Table 4.7. *Fitting the negative binomial to the Polish TRB sites: (a) individual lattice's estimates of k and p, (b) overall estimates of k and p derived from the true contagion model, (c) overall estimates of k and p derived from the spurious contagion model (estimates for (b) and (c) have been calculated omitting lattice 6)*

Observed and expected values (a)

Sites/ quadrat	1 O	1 E	2 O	2 E	3 O	3 E	4 O	4 E	5 O	6 O
0	44	42.0	11	11.0	2	1.6	—	0.54	—	—
1	21	22.7	11	10.2	2	2.5	2	1.0	—	—
2	11	12.9	8	7.9	5	2.9	2	1.3	3	—
3	12	7.5	6	5.7	—	2.9	1	1.4	3	—
4	3	4.4	3	3.9	2	2.6	—	1.5	—	1
5	—	2.6	—	2.7	3	2.3	2	1.4	1	1
6	2	1.5	3	1.8	1	1.9	1	1.3	1	—
7	3	0.86	3	1.2	4	1.6	1	1.2	—	2
8	—	0.48	1	0.80	—	1.2	2	1.0	—	2
9	—		—	0.51	1	1.0	—	0.89	1	1
10	—		1	0.33	1	0.77	—		1	1
χ^2		3.56		2.49						

Expected values (b) and (c)

Sites/ quadrat	1 E(b)	1 E(c)	2 E(b)	2 E(c)	3 E(b)	3 E(c)	4 E(b)	4 E(c)	5–6 E(b)	5–6 E(c)
0	47.7	32.0	11.8	8.0	1.5	1.6	0.2	0.6	—	0.3
1	19.7	26.9	10.0	9.4	2.4	2.3	0.6	0.9	0.2	0.4
2	10.8	17.2	7.4	8.4	2.8	2.6	1.0	1.1	0.3	0.6
3	6.4	9.7	5.4	6.6	2.9	2.6	1.2	1.2	0.5	0.6
4	4.0	5.1	3.9	4.9	2.6	2.4	1.4	1.2	0.6	0.7
5	—		2.8	3.5	2.3	2.1	1.4	1.2	0.8	0.7
6	—		2.0	2.4	2.0	1.8	1.4	1.15	0.8	0.7
7	—		1.4	1.6	1.6	1.6	1.3	1.1	0.9	0.7
8	—		—		1.3	1.3	1.2	1.0	0.9	0.6
9	—		—		—	1.1	1.1	0.9	0.9	0.6
10	—		—		—		0.9	0.8	0.8	0.6
χ^2	6.3	9.4	3.6	5.5	—		—		—	

Table 4.8. *Values of Kolmogorov–Smirnov statistic 'D' for (a) individual lattices, (b) true contagion model, (c) spurious contagion model (the (a), (b) and (c) of tables 4.2, 4.4 and 4.6) compared with significance levels of D*

(1) Bandkeramik

Lattice no.	(a)	(b)	(c)
1	0.050	0.030	0.184
2	0.050	0.061	0.131
3	0.059	0.078	0.172
4	0.054	0.089	0.078
6	0.104	0.088	0.061
7	0.100	0.088	0.068
8	0.050	0.118	0.092
5	0.050	0.095	0.092
9	0.079	0.092	0.133

(2) Lengyel

Lattice no.	(a)	(b)	(c)
1	0.027	0.031	0.160
2	0.024	0.034	0.102
3	0.062	0.091	0.095
4	0.091	0.071	0.166
5	N.A.	0.124	0.079
6	N.A.	0.083	0.067
7	N.A.	0.188	0.143
8	N.A.	0.162	0.101
9	N.A.	0.138	0.194

(3) TRB

Lattice no.	(a)	(b)	(c)
1	0.031	0.038	0.125
2	0.050	0.046	0.097
3	0.063	0.093	0.112
4	0.134	0.136	0.090
5	N.A.	0.207	0.144

Values of D at various significance levels

No. of cells	20%	10%	5%	1%
96	0.109	0.125	0.142	0.170
48	0.154	0.176	—	—
	—	—	—	—
32	0.19	—	—	—
24	0.21	—	—	—
	—	—	—	—
16	0.26	—	—	—
12	0.30	—	—	—

SUMMARY

(1) Bandkeramik:
(a) and (b) fit very well – no difference significant at 20% level; (c) fits badly – difference for lattice 1 significant at 1% level.

(2) Lengyel:
(a) and (b) fit very well – no difference significant at 20% level; (c) fits fairly badly – difference for lattice 1 significant at 5% level.

(3) TRB:
(a) fits very well – no difference significant at 20% level; (b) and (c) fit fairly well – (b) slightly better than (c).

5
The distribution of single artifact types

5.1 *Regression analysis*

A common type of quantitative information collected by the archaeologist is the percentage of, for example, pottery or obsidian from a known source at a number of excavated or surveyed sites. Information about two variables is therefore available – the percentage at each site and the distance of the site from the production centre. Recently a desire has been shown to identify and compare trends in the relationship between these two variables (Hogg 1971; Renfrew 1969; 1972*b*; cf. Edmonson 1961). A method appropriate for the examination of such trends is called regression analysis. Some possible types of relationship between the dependent or regressed variable (for example the percentage of pottery at a site), indicated by Y, and the independent or regressor variable (for example the distance from the site to the source), X, are shown in fig.5.1.

It is important to note that, if a trend in the relationship between the X and Y values can be identified, this covariation may result from one of a number of possible causes (Chorley and Kennedy 1971; Croxton 1953, 127–8).

1. The covariation may mean that X is the cause of Y. This can only be claimed if considerable knowledge is available about the processes involved. This is rarely the case with prehistoric data, and often all we can say is that Y changes in a predictable manner as X changes.

2. A third variable may be the cause of the changes in X and Y.

3. X may be the cause of Y indirectly via other variables.

4. The observed covariance between X and Y may have appeared by chance, due to the peculiarities of the archaeological data. If this is the case, then collection of new data or increasing the sample size should provide different patterns of covariation.

The simplest form of relationship between the two variables is a linear one, expressed by the equation

$$Y = a - bX + e \tag{5.1}$$

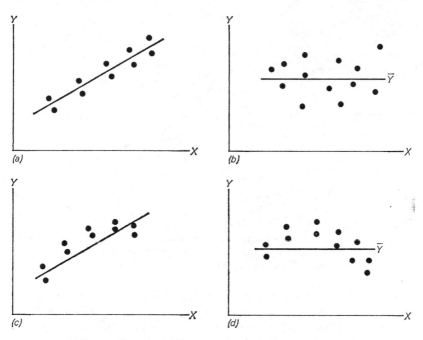

Fig.5.1. Some possible regression relationships between two
variables (*X* and *Y*). (*a*) Significant linear regression, no lack of
fit; (*b*) linear regression not significant, no lack of fit;
(*c*) significant linear regression, significant lack of fit; (*d*) linear
regression not significant, significant lack of fit. $\bar{Y}$ = mean of
dependent variable. Source: Davis 1973.

The terms *a* and *b* represent unknown constants determining the form
of the relationship: *a* giving the value of *Y* when *X* is zero and *b* giving
the rate at which *Y* decreases as *X* increases, higher values of *b* indicating a higher rate of decrease, and a zero value of *b* indicating that there
is no *linear* relationship between *X* and *Y*. There may, however, be
some other form of relationship (as in fig.5.1*d*). The 'error term', *e*,
expresses the fact that the relationship between *X* and *Y* is not exact,
but that *Y* has a random component to it. In this sort of situation it is
often assumed that the variable *X* is a non-random (or 'controlled')
variable, and that the error term *e* is an independent random variable
with zero mean and a variance that is independent of *X*. The latter
assumption is depicted in fig.5.2 – here in addition it is assumed that
the *e* possesses a Normal distribution.

The regression line can then be fitted by a relatively simple method,
such as the method of Least Squares (Davies 1961, 158) which minimises the sum of the squared deviations of each observed *Y* from the
fitted line. In practice it would be rare to find a controlled variable in
an archaeological situation – in other words both *X* and *Y* would be
random variables. Blalock (1960) points out that in such cases it is

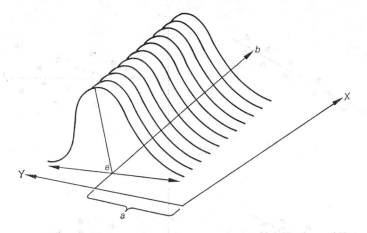

Fig.5.2. Components of the regression model $Y = a + bX + e$.
Error is assumed to be Normally distributed about the
regression line. Source: Davis 1973.

convenient to assume that for each value of Y the values of the Xs are
distributed normally, to produce a bivariate normal distribution. This
is important if tests of significance are to be applied. However, 'if one is
merely interested in point estimates rather than confidence intervals or
significance tests, he can estimate the population parameters of the
regression equation without having to assume bivariate normality'
(*ibid.*, 279).

If one or more of the above assumptions do not hold, the 'classical'
methods of regression analysis (including Least Squares) may not be the
best to use. The topic of regression analysis under less restrictive
assumptions has been much studied in the field of econometrics (see for
example Johnston 1963). One possible approach is to use Weighted
Least Squares (Draper and Smith 1966, 77). Such approaches generally
require some knowledge of the way in which the data depart from the
usual assumptions. In archaeological situations even that may not be
known, and circumstances may force the archaeologist to use simpler
methods.

One simple way of testing for association between two variables
X and Y which does not rely on these assumptions is to reduce the data
to a 'contingency table'. The ranges of X and Y values are divided into
groups. The number of observations for which the value of X falls in the
ith group of X-values and the value of Y falls in the jth group of
Y-values is denoted by r_{ij}. The two-way array of number r_{ij} form a
contingency table, and a null hypothesis of 'no association between
the variables' can be tested by a χ^2 goodness-of-fit test (Davies 1961,
288). The groupings of X and Y values must be such that the 'expected'
numbers in the cells of the array are large enough for a χ^2 test to be
applicable.

For the sort of data mentioned at the beginning of this section a straight-line model as in equation 5.1 is often not appropriate. For most distance-decay studies some form of curvilinear relationship is found. The forms of curve usually encountered (Taylor, P. J. 1971) can be described in terms of a straight line by transforming either one or both the variables by taking logarithms, and by varying an exponent of distance (the distance transformation, α). Thus the most common distance-decay functions met with in interaction data can be divided into single-log and double-log cases. In the single-log case, the curves have the general form

$$\log Y = a - bX^{\alpha} + e \qquad (5.2)$$

In the 'normal' form $\alpha = 2$, in the exponential it has a value of 1, and in the square root exponential a value of 0.5. In the double-log case the general form of the function is

$$\log Y = a - b \log X^{\alpha} + e \qquad (5.3)$$

In the log-normal model $\alpha = 2$, and in the 'pareto' model α has a value of 1. Alpha can be further varied between these values. Variation of the transformations simply alters the curvature of the regression line. This is shown in fig.5.3 where functions with the five different transformations mentioned above have been fitted to one set of data (cf. Taylor, P. J. 1971).

An important measure of the scatter of the Y values about the fitted regression line is the 'standard error about the regression' (Davies 1961, 159), sometimes referred to as the 'standard error of the estimate' (S.E. of E.) (Chorley and Kennedy 1971; Gregory 1963, 218).

Regression analysis is most useful when one variable is clearly the independent variable and the other is clearly the dependent one, as in the context discussed here in which distance is the independent variable. In some archaeological situations the two variables may be of equal status, and the use of regression analysis gives different results according to which variable is chosen (possibly quite arbitrarily) as the independent one. In such situations the linear correlation coefficient (r) can be used as a measure of the degree of inter-relation between variables. Values of r for a number of different relationships are shown in fig.5.4. It is important to remember that it is the *square* of the coefficient that expresses the degree of inter-relationship: for example a correlation coefficient of 0.7 between the two variables sounds large, but it means that slightly less than half the variation in one variable can be ascribed to the other. Figure 5.4f shows no correlation because the correlation coefficient is an expression of the linear relationship between two variables, and the circular relationship shown is not linear. Unfortunately tests of significance for r require that a number of

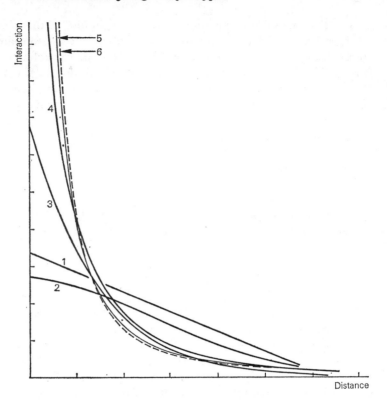

Fig.5.3. The effect of different transformations of interaction
and distance. 1, Variables untransformed; 2, 'normal' model;
3, exponential model; 4, square-root model; 5, log-normal
model; 6, 'pareto' model. Source: Hodder 1974*a*.

assumptions be made about the data (Blalock 1960, 303). These can
seldom be made for archaeological material. The effects of departures
from the assumptions have been discussed by Kowalski (1972). An
approach followed by Redman and Watson (1970) in their study of
surface collections from two mounds in Turkey is only to use the
correlation coefficient to one decimal place and to regard it as giving
a relative measure instead of a precise one with exact levels of significance. Similarly, in deciding which r values should be considered
significant 'in geologic studies, we often must rely on experience and
intuition to provide an answer' (Davis 1973, 335). This is clearly not a
rigorous approach and we shall see (p. 121) that correlation coefficients
obtained from random permutations of the data may provide useful
guidelines as to whether an observed correlation coefficient could
easily have been obtained by chance. Martin (1974) has discussed the
effect on ordinary Least Squares regression of spatial autocorrelation
among the observations for the independent variable (section 5.5).

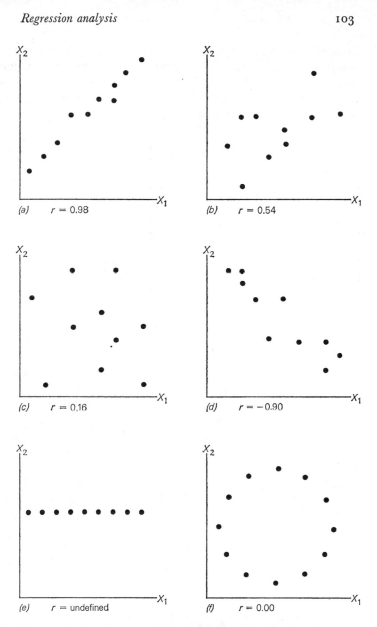

Fig.5.4. Scatter diagrams of two variables (X_1, X_2) showing different correlations (r). Source: Davis 1973.

Some further problems associated with the fitting of regression lines should be mentioned. For example, archaeological data are often very patchy and it is dangerous to determine trends through a scatter of points in which large gaps occur. In fig.5.5 it would be difficult to substantiate the fitting of a straight-line as opposed to a curvilinear or some other trend to these data. In fact there may be a lack of correlation in the main clump, but the existence of a few extreme values might give a high correlation (Blalock 1960, 290). Wherever possible, attempts should be made to fill in the gaps. Depending on the purpose of the study, it might be better to leave out extreme values.

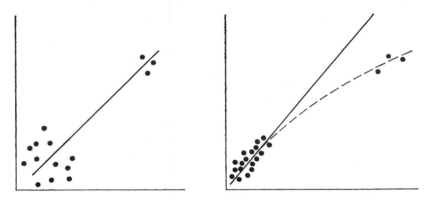

Figs.5.5. and 5.6. Some problems of curve fitting.

Alternatively, data points in a small area may indicate a straight-line relationship between the variables although distant samples suggest a curvilinear relationship (fig.5.6). In such a case further data points should be obtained or the study should be limited to the small area. It should be noted that a relationship found in one area may not be the same given a broader view. It is dangerous to generalise beyond the limits of one's data.

In many archaeological instances the Y or dependent variable will be a percentage value. In such cases the fitted regression line may predict values over 100 %. If the percentage count for a site or observation i is defined as p_i, then to obviate this problem some sort of transformation, such as the logit transformation, may be used (Martin, personal communication). Thus $r_i = \log_e [p_i/(100 - p_i)]$, and the r_i values may then be used in place of the raw percentages.

5.2 *Regression analysis in archaeology*

This account is concerned only with cases of the use of regression analysis in archaeology in which the independent variable is some distance measure. It is first important to realise the difficulties in using these techniques on archaeological data. The following discussion results from a number of studies carried out by one of us (I.H.) of the percentages of particular types of Romano-British pottery in collections from sites in southern England. The comments are, however, also of more general applicability. An initial problem results from regional differences in fieldwork. For example, any map of Romano-British pottery found in Wiltshire is likely to show a marked concentration around the Roman town at Mildenhall thanks to some very intensive field-walking collections by a few local enthusiasts. Other areas may remain comparatively blank. The spread of types outside the area chosen for a study cannot of course be gauged. Spatial variation in site survival has also occurred (Taylor 1972). For these reasons it is helpful when constructing distribution maps, to show 'negatives' – that is contemporary sites where the type of pottery being considered is not found (Jope 1963).

A further problem concerns the variable quality of the samples of pottery. In analysing distributions for regression analysis it is necessary to count the percentage of a particular ware in the total assemblage of pottery found in a museum as coming from one site. These percentages must be considered highly unreliable if the sample is bad. For example, many collections of pottery as they now exist in museums, are only a selection of the finer or more interesting sherds found at the site. Even in modern excavations not all the coarse wares are always kept, and frequently not all the body sherds. Similarly, field walkers often only pick up 'interesting' sherds, while some fabrics are less visible than others on the ground. As a result of this selective quality of the samples, it is especially common to find in an assemblage a high proportion of finer wares. Usually there is little interest paid to the remaining coarse pottery and there appears to have been less general systematic retention of one type of Romano-British coarse ware in preference to another. For this reason, it might be considered desirable to count percentages excluding the finer wares. However, in addition to selection by the archaeologists, any group of pottery from a pit or living floor is not a random or representative sample of the pottery that was used on the site – its composition will vary with functional differences across the site. This introduces a further variability into the studied samples.

The unreliable nature of the samples also relates to their size. The number of sherds available may vary from 10 to over 500. Small samples give some idea of whether types are present or absent, but they seriously distort percentages. For example, one sherd in a collection of 10 is 10 % of the assemblage. In practice, it was found in the study of Romano-British pottery that samples of over 30 sherds resulted in fairly consistent spatial trends, and the assemblages could be divided on this basis. Clearly, further reliability could be obtained by increasing the minimum sample size, but this may quickly reduce the number of samples which can be taken into account, and decrease the likelihood of being able to pick up detailed distributional patterns.

Another major problem in analysing samples of this sort is that of dating. Many collections have a very wide date range. It is in any case extremely difficult to be accurate about the date of small collections of coarse Romano-British pottery since most types have a long time-span, and since associated fine wares which are more easily dateable often seem to have been retained long after their manufacturing date. At best, even for Roman Britain, it is usually possible only to provide broad date brackets of the type 'first/early second centuries A.D.' 'second/mid-third centuries' or 'late third/fourth centuries'. Clearly, the time-span of the assemblage relative to the time-span of the kiln production will seriously affect the percentages. As far as possible, therefore, sites should be distinguished according to date range, although this may be even more difficult in a prehistoric context. The effect of different time-spans of different functional groups of pottery on the relative percentages of pottery in assemblages has been discussed by David (1972). Long-lived types tend to be relatively less well represented.

A further difficulty in using percentage counts may result from the size of the sherds. Clearly by breaking every sherd of a particular ware into two or more smaller sherds its percentage in the assemblage can be increased. Where there is no evidence that this has happened, i.e. that at certain sites sherds of particular wares are all smaller (or larger) than other sherds, it may be thought reasonable to use counts instead of weights (Evans 1973). Statistical work on the evaluation of methods of measuring relative proportions of different wares or categories is in progress (Orton 1975).

One result of all the above variation in the quality of the samples is that apparently contemporary assemblages from different parts of the same site often yield rather different percentages. For example, the percentages of Malvern pottery at Dymock were found to vary from 1 % to 6 % in different deposits. Also, percentages of Savernake pottery from Windmill Hill in different museums vary from 45 % to 51 %. Where this occurs, the maximum possible sample size may be used so as to get a general picture of the amount of pottery of a particular type getting to the site.

Having mentioned some of the difficulties involved we can examine a number of archaeological artifact distributions for which sufficient data exist to see whether interesting spatial trends emerge from a regression analysis. It must be borne in mind that any patterning in the data could be affected by, or be the result of, the variable quality of the data themselves. The aim of the following study is to see whether archaeological distributions can indicate contact or, to use a general term, interaction with a production, marketing or service centre. In particular, variations in the b (gradient) and α values of the fitted regression lines are to be examined to find out whether they are systematic and of interest. This was thought to be of possible interest because variation in these values has been the subject of much study by geographers (e.g. Taylor, P. J. 1971), and has been shown to relate to differences in the type of interaction underlying the pattern. Archaeological distributional information exists in a number of different forms and a first step is to examine whether these differences have a great effect on the results of the regression analysis.

Three types of information are considered. The first type of interaction data is the percentage of a type of object from a known source in the total assemblage of such objects on each site. A second type of information is the density of sites with objects from a common source in concentric bands around that source. This type of data is, however, easily disturbed by spatial differences in fieldwork. For example, the distribution of neolithic axes in Yorkshire is strongly concentrated in an eastern zone, but Keen and Radley (1971, 29) point out that this concentration is closely related to fieldwork. It is essential, therefore, when considering density information, to obtain some form of negative evidence to allow fieldwork variation to be noticed. Where density data have been used in this study such a check has been made. For example, the distribution of neolithic axe-hammers of picrite (Shotton, Chitty and Seaby 1951) can be compared with the even spread in the same area of axe-hammers not made of this rock (*ibid.*, fig.6). The fall-off in the amount of picrite axe-hammers with distance away from the source cannot therefore be interpreted as the result of differential fieldwork. To allow comparison between data sets in which the total number of sites varies considerably, the density has been adjusted by dividing the number of sites in each band by the total number of sites. A third type of information is the number of sites with an object from a known source expressed as a percentage of all the contemporary sites in that band.

To examine the effect of these different types of information on the regression analysis, the three types of data have been collected for the same two examples of Romano-British pottery distributions. In the case of Savernake ware (fig.5.7 and Hodder 1974*b*), the best-fit regression curves for both the percentage of pottery at each site, and the density of sites are similar in form and in gradient. On the other hand, the data for the percentage of sites (the third type of data), give completely different results, especially in that they show a straight-line relationship (equation 5.1). Similar results have been obtained for a type of Romano-British pottery from the west Sussex region (Hodder 1974*c*). Therefore the third type of information – that is the percentage of sites with objects from a known source – appears in these cases at least to be insensitive and has not been included in this study.

The following data sets have been examined. Peacock (1969*a*) has made a petrological study of neolithic Hembury 'f' ware made in the Lizards Head area in Cornwall. He plotted the distribution of the ware and gave its percentage in the total pottery assemblage of each site. Other neolithic distributions for which good data exist are those of the

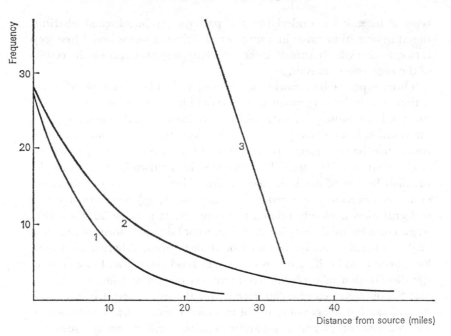

Fig.5.7. The decrease in the frequency of Savernake ware with distance from its main source. 1, Density of sites in bands around the centre; 2, the percentage of pottery at each site; 3, the percentage of sites in bands around the centre. Source: Hodder 1974*a*.

neolithic axes. The distribution of picrite axe-hammers in the west Midlands, and derived from the Cwm-Mawr source, has already been mentioned. Axes of Group I and Group VI have a much wider distribution, the former coming from a source near Penzance in Cornwall, and the latter from the Great Langdale axe factories. Detailed work on the distribution of these types has been completed in two areas in England: the southwest (Evens *et al.* 1962) and Yorkshire (Keen and Radley 1971). To obtain the necessary quantitative data from these distributions, a regular grid was imposed in both regions and the number of Group I and Group VI axes determined at the apex of every four cells of the grid as a percentage of all the grouped and ungrouped axes falling in those cells (see fig.5.7*b*). In most areas the total number of axes is too small to give reliable percentages, but in several areas, including the Avebury and Stonehenge districts for example, the total number of axes in the cells is above 35, and these samples appear to give more reliable percentages. Data for Near Eastern obsidian have also been studied. The distribution and percentage of obsidian in the total chipped stone industry at a number of sites have been published (Renfrew, Dixon and Cann 1966 and 1968; Dixon, Cann and Renfrew

1968), and a preliminary regression analysis undertaken (Renfrew 1969). The two main sources for the obsidian studied by spectrographic examination are in Anatolia and Armenia. Unfortunately no data are available from sites within 370 km of the latter source, and since therefore a large part of this distance-decay relationship is missing, the Armenian obsidian data have not been used in this study.

Late Iron Age coin distributions have already been examined by a form of regression analysis (Hogg 1971) and some of the problems in using these data discussed. In the study, only the Dobunnic coins (Allen 1961 with the addition of more recent finds) have been used since in other areas (e.g. Cunobeline coins) more than one dispersal centre seems to have been involved or the identity of the centre is not clear (e.g. Durotriges). The data used are the densities of find spots in bands around Bagendon, since the overall map of inscribed coins shows no marked areas of differential survival.

A number of Romano-British pottery and tile distributions have also been included in this study. All the pottery distributions consist of percentage data although sometimes duplicated by site density data. Savernake pottery is a coarse pottery of the first and second centuries A.D. which was made in the Savernake kilns (Annable 1962) and marketed largely through the nearby town of Mildenhall in North Wiltshire (Hodder 1974*b*). In the southeast Hampshire and west Sussex area are found two types of grey ware of the second and third centuries which seem to have been made at the Rowlands Castle kilns (Hodder 1974*a*). The distribution of a type of pottery made in the Malverns in the second century A.D. has already been plotted by Peacock (1967). This distribution has been re-examined in order to count percentages and to add more recent find spots (Hodder 1974*d*). In the late third and fourth centuries A.D., finer wares were being produced in centres in the New Forest and at Oxford. The percentages of types from these kilns have been collected at a number of sites (Fulford 1973*c*; Fulford and Hodder 1974). Several types of stamped tiles have a localised distribution around Cirencester, and a distribution of some of these has been published (Hodder 1972). The density of find spots with all these types of tiles (Clifford 1955 with recent additional finds) has been calculated in bands around Cirencester.

Clearly, some of the above data sets may be considered insufficiently reliable for a detailed study. It is hoped however that, in spite of this, some general and informative trends might emerge. The approach followed here has been to find for each data set the distance transformation which gives the best-fit regression line. Thus, for both the single-log and double-log cases, α was varied from 0.1 to 2.5 in steps of 0.1 arbitrary units, and the regression equation calculated for each α value. This was achieved by a computer programme. With this programme the standard error of estimate is also calculated so that the best-fit value of α can be identified. Variation of this with different α values is shown in fig.5.8. P. J. Taylor (1971), using a similar method, found that variation of the standard error of estimate in the double-log case was much less than in the single-log case, and indeed with the archaeological data studied here, marked variation is only found with the single-log function in which interaction (the *Y* variable) is logarithmically transformed. The same procedure has also been applied to a

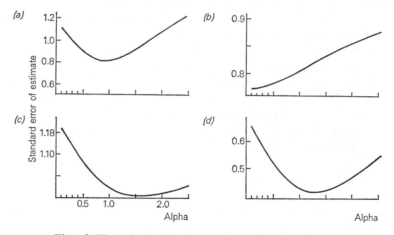

Fig.5.8. The relationship between α and the standard error of estimate. (*a*) Anatolian obsidian; (*b*) New Forest pottery; (*c*) neolithic pottery; (*d*) Dobunnic coins. Source: Hodder 1974*a*.

form of the regression function in which only distance (*X*) is transformed. This again results in little variation in the standard error of estimate. The *r* values for the relationship between the two variables are all high (above 0.8) and have not been subjected to a significance test because of the difficulties discussed above (p. 101). Examples of some of the relationships are shown in fig.5.9.

With the information supplied by the above analysis both the gradient (*b*) and the distance transformation (α) can be compared for all the data sets, bearing in mind the limitations imposed by the quality of the data. An initial question is whether the gradient slope varied in an interesting fashion. To allow comparison, gradients are considered for the single-log case with α = 1. Among the data sets for which site density information has been used, the Dobunnic coins (*b* = −0.06) from Bagendon have a less steep gradient than the Romano-British tiles around the equivalent later centre at Cirencester (*b* = −0.10). The value is also less than that for Savernake pottery (*b* = −0.13). This difference may be because the coins are a finer product than the more bulky tiles and coarse pottery (see below p. 141). The coins also come from a larger centre than at least the Savernake pottery (below

p. 141). Similarly, the neolithic pottery distribution has a steeper gradient ($b = -0.03$) than the neolithic axes (Group I, $b = -0.002$) coming from much the same area. This may be partly the result of the

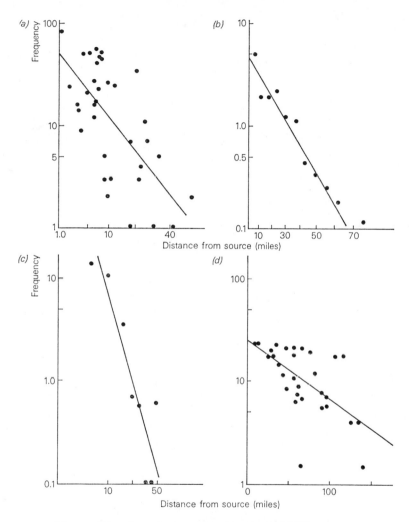

Fig.5.9. Some best-fit regression situations. (*a*) The percentage of Savernake pottery; (*b*) the density of Dobunnic coins; (*c*) the density of Roman tiles; (*d*) the percentage of Oxford pottery. Source: Hodder 1974*a*.

different nature of the commodity. The picrite axe-hammers have a steeper gradient ($b = -0.077$) than the more widespread Group I and Group VI ($b = -0.02$) axes and can be identified as one of a number of smaller, more local, axe production centres (for example Group XIV,

Shotton 1959). By plotting all the gradients in fig.5.10 a clear general
trend shows that the gradient slope is partly dependent on the relative

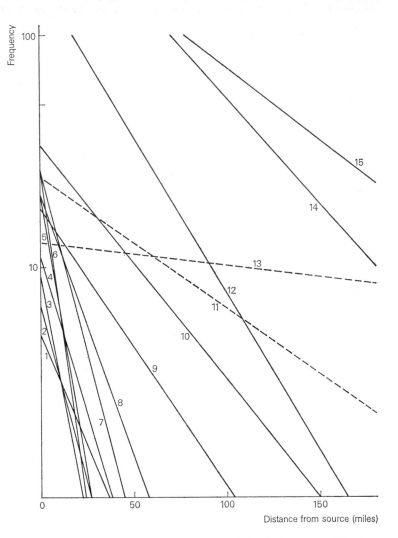

Fig.5.10. Regression gradients. Dashed lines indicate the fall-offs
in neolithic Group I axes (13) and Oxford fine ware (11). For
other number references see Hodder 1974a. Source: Hodder
1974a.

size of the output at the source. It is useful to identify this general trend
because it allows deviants to be noticed. For example, the neolithic
axes from Cornwall (Group I) have a very gentle gradient. Although
it seems to have been a small concern which did not flood the market

near the source, the products travelled a long way with the aid of sea movement. Sea trade is indicated by the coastal distribution of these axes in Yorkshire (see fig.5.78). The distribution of the finer Romano-British wares from the Oxfordshire centre also has a distinctly gentle gradient. This seems to have been a much more efficient industry than any of the other examples in this study. It had a wide network of marketing contacts through which the products could be profitably channelled (Fulford and Hodder, in press). Thus, for this series of data sets the gradient does often vary informatively and in a way which is comparable to recent examples.

The best-fit α values which have been obtained in this study may be suggested as falling into two groups. These groups may be compared with those identified in previous work on distance transformations in regression equations (p. 144). The first group has α values from less than 0.1 to 0.6 and includes comparatively small-scale local concerns producing the commoner and coarser products such as tiles and coarse pottery. For the distribution of such products distance seems to have had an important friction effect. Characteristic of this group is the distribution of Romano-British roofing tiles around Cirencester ($\alpha = 0.2$). This is clearly a common, bulky product supplied to a localised area which may be interpreted as the immediate service area around Cirencester (Hodder 1972, 903). A similar coarse, bulky product is early Romano-British Savernake ware (percentage data, $\alpha = 0.4$, site density data, $\alpha = 0.6$). A discussion of the distribution of this pottery (Hodder 1974b) has suggested that it was marketed mainly from one town (Mildenhall), perhaps involving fairly frequent and direct contact with this market centre. The Romano-British Malvernian pottery ($\alpha = 0.2$) is handmade and is a very coarse product within its own context. It seems to have been marketed by localised, and possibly fairly direct, contact with a few major towns (Hodder 1974d). The New Forest products (α less than 0.1) are certainly finer than those so far considered, but the kiln centre was much smaller than the comparable Oxford production centre (Fulford and Hodder 1974) and apart from one form, the products have a restricted local distribution around the kilns (Fulford 1973b). As far as the prehistoric material is concerned, the neolithic axe-hammers of picrite ($\alpha = 0.6$) have a very localised distribution around the source at Cwm-Mawr and in this area axes of this rock type are 'three times as abundant as any other rock type' (Shotton *et al.* 1951, 160). On the other hand, the distribution of axes of Group I (α less than 0.1) is far from localised. However, the size of the industry, as seen in the distribution of rough-outs and the relative amount near the source (fig.5.78), is much smaller than the Group VI industry. The comparison of gradients has already identified the Group I axes as having a distinctive distribution form based largely on extension by sea movement. Certainly their distribution cannot be considered as similar to a random walk process (section 5.3), a feature which is characteristic of the second group of α values.

The group of data sets with higher α values (0.9 to greater than 2.5) consists of very large scale concerns associated with fine products. There is less friction caused by distance and the overall pattern of contact appears in all cases to have been complex and indirect, and to be comparable to a random walk process. Characteristic of this group are the late Iron Age Dobunnic coins ($\alpha = 1.3$). This is clearly a valuable product and Hogg (1971) has shown by a different method that the diffusion of these coins from Bagendon approximates to a random walk movement. In the Roman period this group is represented by the distributions of pottery from Oxford ($\alpha = 1.0$) and southeast Hampshire ($\alpha = 1.1$). The fine-ware production at Oxford was on an extremely large scale and the products covered a wide area (Young 1973; Fulford and Hodder 1974). The marketing (Hodder 1974d) seems to have involved a number of complex mechanisms and certainly involved little direct contact with the production centre. The multiplicity of factors affecting the distribution may in aggregate have produced a pattern of contact similar to that represented by a random walk process. The Rowlands Castle centre in southwest Hampshire appears to have been producing good quality grey wares on a large scale (Cunliffe 1971a; Hodder 1974c). The distribution of the products indicates that a number of marketing mechanisms were being used involving little direct contact with the kiln centre (Hodder 1974c). Three neolithic data sets also have high α values. The distribution of obsidian from the Anatolian source ($\alpha = 0.9$) has been discussed by Renfrew. He interpreted the flattening of the regression curve near the source where high percentages are found as a form of within-group exchange. Only outside this 'supply zone' was the steeper gradient seen as 'down-the-line' movement (Renfrew 1969, 1972b). Since, however, this 'plateau effect' (Taylor, P. J. 1971) near the origin is a characteristic of regression relationships resulting from a random walk process (fig.5.3 and Pearson and Blakeman 1906), and has been discussed as a normal characteristic of interaction behaviour (Golledge 1967), the obsidian curve need not be divided into two. The whole pattern of contact may be seen as 'down-the-line' random walk movement. The neolithic pottery coming from west Cornwall ($\alpha = 1.6$) can certainly be considered as a fine ware. 'In technique they [the pots] are well above the general run of British neolithic ceramics' (Peacock 1969a, 147). The distribution covers a wide area and production on a large scale may be indicated by the high percentages near the source. The neolithic axes of Group VI from the Great Langdale factories (α greater than 2.5) are found over a very extensive area and completely flood the market in areas near the source, such as Yorkshire (fig.5.78). The large size of this production concern is reflected in the widespread distribution of axe rough-outs (Manby 1965).

It seems possible to detect, therefore, two groups of data sets as indicated by their regression α values. Further discussion of the interpretation of these different types of distance-decay relationships will be left until section 5.3.

Data provided by M. Fulford allow one pattern of fall-off to be examined over different time periods. A detailed study of the Romano-British pottery types from the New Forest kilns has enabled Fulford (unpublished) to identify three phases of production. An early (*c.* 270–320 A.D.) and middle (*c.* 320–350 A.D.) phase are followed by a decline of the industry in its latest period (after 350 A.D.). The overall pattern of fall-off has an α value of less than 0.1. The α value for the early and middle phases is 0.5 in both cases, with the gradient (*b*) being −0.533 and −0.719 respectively. In the period of decline the gradient is much less steep ($b = $ −0.101). This is because, although there is less production in the latest phase, the products managed to reach similar distances to those reached before, presumably because the marketing channels still existed (Fulford, personal communication). It is interesting that the α value shows little change in the latest phase ($\alpha = $ 0.3).

A further study of a distribution of Romano-British fine pottery illustrates the value of examining the pattern of residuals or deviations from the best-fit regression line. Late Roman fine wares (colour-coated, painted wares and mortaria) had two major production centres in central and southern England. These were located in the Oxford area and in the New Forest, although other minor centres also existed (Fulford 1973*a*). The percentages of the products of the Oxford centre, which can be identified by eye, have been counted at a number of major sites (Fulford 1973*c*) and these data have been made available to the authors. In spite of the variable nature of the samples concerned (p. 105), it is hoped that some marketing patterns might be recoverable from the data, although the dates of the pottery studied covered a long period (*c.* 250–400 A.D.).

A regression line of exponential form fitted to the Oxford products (fig.5.11) shows a generalised fall-off in percentages with distance from the production centre. There is, however, a considerable amount of variation from the best–fit linear curve. This could be accounted for by the unreliability of the samples, but it is thought worthwhile to see if there is any patterning in the variation from the curve. Spatial patterning can be investigated by calculating the deviation of each site percentage from the regression line, and plotting these residuals on a map (fig.5.12).

Two factors are apparent in the pattern of residuals:

(1) There is a marked distribution to the west and east of Oxford

of positive residuals (that is, more Oxford pottery is found in these areas than is expected according to the overall trend of decrease with

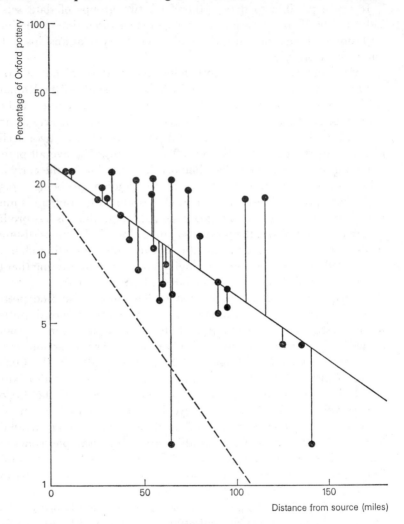

Fig.5.11. The decrease in Oxford pottery with distance from source. Dashed line indicates the decrease in New Forest pottery away from the New Forest kilns. Source: Fulford and Hodder 1974.

distance). Negative residuals are found to the north and south of this area.

(2) High negative residuals occur in a localised area around the New Forest.

These two factors can be considered separately.

(1) The area of high positive residuals may indicate further undiscovered centres producing wares indistinguishable from Oxford wares. There is, however, no evidence of this as yet, and a further explanation must be found. All the sites with high positive residuals are in areas to which some water transport of pottery could have been involved. Indeed the Oxford kilns are centrally situated for eastward movement down the Thames to London, Canterbury and Richborough, and

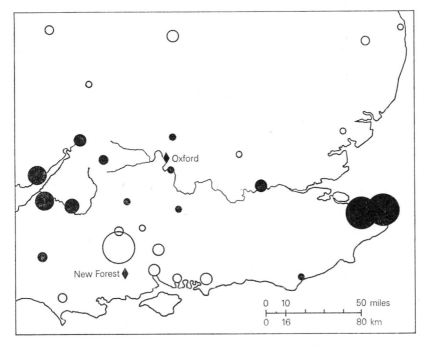

Fig.5.12. Regression residuals. ●, positive residuals; ○, negative residuals. The size of the circle indicates the magnitude of the residual. ◆, Oxford and New Forest kilns. Source: Fulford and Hodder 1974.

westward movement to sites flanking the Severn estuary. The same scatter of points as those graphed in fig.5.11 can be divided in to those sites to which water transport may have been involved, and those best reached by land (fig.5.13). The scatters of points can be interpreted as two curves. The 'by-land' curve is of similar gradient to the New Forest curve (fig.5.11), while the 'by-water' curve has a much less steep gradient suggesting greater and probably cheaper movement of pottery longer distances. This hypothesised cheaper transport of pottery in the Roman world has been discussed by Hartley (1973, 39), Fulford (1973*b*) and Jones (1964, vol. 2, 841–2; vol. 3, 283), and in ethnography by, for example, Foster (1966).

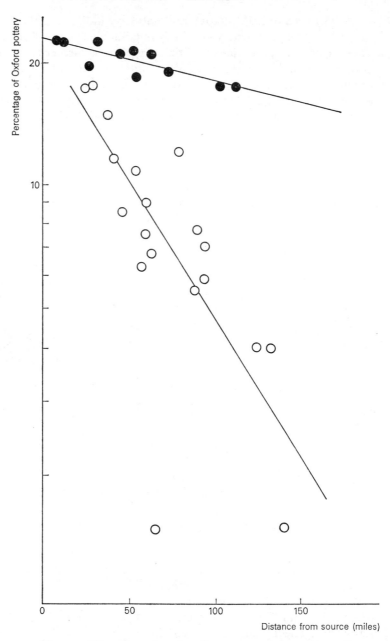

Fig.5.13. The effect of modes of transport on the amount of Oxford pottery found at sites. ●, Sites to which water transport could have been important; ○, sites best reached by land. Source: Fulford and Hodder 1974.

(2) The high negative residuals around the New Forest kilns may occur because in this area the New Forest products were able to compete successfully with the Oxford products. A closer examination of the distributions around the two centres and an assessment of their competitive relationship will be undertaken in section 5.6.

It will be shown (section 5.4) that a rather more satisfactory approach to these Romano-British fine-ware data is supplied by trend surface analysis.

The discussion of regression analysis and its use in archaeology has so far only considered data such as the percentages of pottery or the density of sites. Regression analysis can also be used to investigate how the similarity between artifacts decays over space. The similarity between two objects may be taken as the Y variable, and the distance between them as the X variable. One method is to take an artifact characteristic of one area and plot the fall-off in similarity with that artifact. This is unsatisfactory because the choice of the reference artifact is arbitrary and it is difficult to obtain an overall view of spatial patterning.

A more satisfactory approach which avoids this difficulty is to take a large number of artifacts and to examine the relationship between similarity and distance for each pair of objects. Regression analysis can be used to determine this relationship, with the similarity between objects i and j as the dependent variable, and the distance between objects i and j as the independent variable. A problem here is that if 100 objects are taken, and each object is compared with all other objects, this involves regressing 4950 distances against 4950 similarities. The Cambridge University IBM 370 computer which was used for an analysis of this sort was unable to take numbers larger than this so that the maximum possible sample of artifacts is 100. A Fortran IV programme has been adapted by the authors from the regression programme provided by Davis (1973). The programme assesses the Gower coefficient of similarity between all objects and computes the distances between objects from the co-ordinates.

The 100 objects which were chosen for a series of regression analyses are some middle Bronze Age palstaves in southern England studied by Rowlands (1970 and Rowlands and Hodder unpublished). The first 100 palstaves used in the analysis are from non-hoard contexts. The similarities between each pair of palstaves have been assessed in a variety of ways. The traits used to describe a palstave may be divided into primary traits, such as the presence or absence of a loop, or the presence of absence of 'shield' decoration on the blade face, and secondary traits which are subdivisions of the primary traits. These include the position of the loop, and the type of 'shield' decoration present. Another important distinction between traits would seem to be between those which are related to style and form and those related to function.

Although it is an extremely arbitrary procedure in practice, some attempt has been made to divide the palstave traits according to this distinction. The style and decoration features include the plan and cross-section of the blade, the height and shape of the flange, and the type of decoration on the blade face. The functional traits include the presence or absence of a loop, the type of stop-ridge, the length, the ratio of blade width to blade length, and the ratio of socket length to blade length.

The similarities between objects were assessed using different combinations of traits. These similarities were regressed against the

Table 5.1.   *Regression parameters*

	100 palstaves not in hoards		100 palstaves in hoards	
Secondary stylistic and	r	0.227	r	0.399
decorative traits	a	0.558	a	0.611
	b	−0.0006	b	−0.0010
Primary stylistic and	r	0.225	r	0.397
decorative traits	a	0.552	a	0.611
	b	−0.0006	b	−0.0010
Both stylistic (primary) and	r	0.238	r	0.357
functional traits	a	0.625	a	0.643
	b	−0.0004	b	−0.0005
Functional traits	r	0.081	r	0.041
	a	0.682	a	0.693
	b	−0.0001	b	−0.0000

distances between objects and the resulting regression parameters are shown in table 5.1. The aim was to see if, by defining the palstaves in different ways, different degrees of spatial patterning emerged.

Table 5.1 shows that the degree of correlation (r) between similarity and distance is in all cases fairly low. It is difficult to assess the significance of these r values when using data for which the necessary conditions which have to exist before using the tests (such as normality) cannot be assumed. An alternative approach which gives an approximate idea of the significance of these results is to randomise the array of 4950 similarities and to recompute the regression parameters and correlation coefficient. The results for five such randomisations, using all primary traits to assess the similarities are shown in table 5.2. This shows no r values above 0.1, while all the gradients of the regression lines are near zero – that is almost horizontal. Low values of r and b

(gradient) are only found for the original data for similarities computed with the functional trait list. Very few randomisations have been carried out, but since the data set is very large, it seems reasonable to suggest that the other higher values of r and b would be unlikely to have been obtained by chance. The results suggest that the functional traits as a whole do not show spatial patterning. Their variation must therefore largely relate to non-spatial factors. If we consider all the primary traits (a mixture of stylistic and functional information) then a slight fall-off in similarity with distance is seen. For the stylistic traits on the other hand there is a sharper gradient, indicating greater localisation

Table 5.2. *Regression parameters after randomisation*

Randomis- ations	r	a	b
1	0.029	0.085	−0.0001
2	0.022	0.061	−0.0001
3	0.010	0.075	−0.0000
4	0.006	0.072	−0.0000
5	0.040	0.091	−0.0001

of the types. It appears, then, that the traits most important for spatial variation in this sample are the stylistic ones relating to decoration and form. The major stylistic traits (primary) are sufficient to determine the degree of spatial variation since the secondary traits do not show any greater localisation.

Little has been said so far about the hoards which contain palstaves. The same approach as that outlined above has also been applied to palstaves which are all from hoards. The results (table 5.1) show the same overall pattern with the functionally defined palstaves having no spatial dependency, and the stylistic traits showing greater spatial variation than the mixture of stylistic and functional traits. Of interest, however, is that in the cases where the similarities do show a fall-off with distance the regression gradient is steeper for the palstaves in hoards than it is for those not in hoards. This suggests that palstaves in hoards are more similar to each other than other palstaves, so that the fall-off in similarity with distance from a palstave in a hoard is steeper than for palstaves not in hoards (fig.5.14). It is indeed the case that palstaves from one hoard are often extremely similar (Rowlands 1970), suggesting that they were finished objects deposited prior to dispersal.

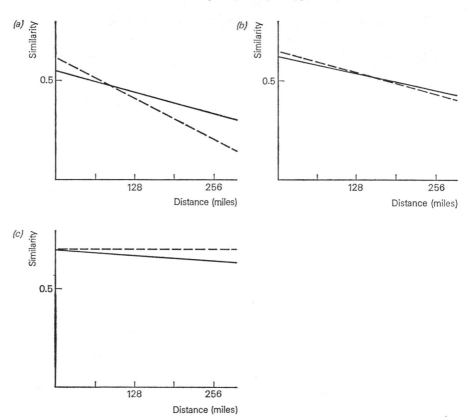

Fig.5.14. The regression lines fitted to the fall-off in similarity with distance. Parameters as in table 5.1. Solid line = palstaves not in hoards; dashed line = palstaves in hoards. (*a*) Secondary and primary stylistic and decorative traits; (*b*) stylistic and functional traits; (*c*) functional traits.

To some extent the difference in the gradient for hoard and non-hoard palstaves reflects the influence of dispersal factors, the spreading out of similar palstaves from the hoarded groups causing a decrease in the fall-off in similarity with distance.

It should be remarked that the model used for the regression analysis is a straight-line relationship between the two variables. This is because a model in which the similarities are transformed to their natural logarithms does not seem to provide a better fit to the data. If such a model is invoked for the first group of non-hoard palstaves using all the primary traits, the resulting value for r is 0.225, for a is 0.514, and for b is —0.0008.

The computer programme used to calculate the parameters of the regression equation also calculates the difference between each observed similarity and that expected according to the fitted model. It is thought

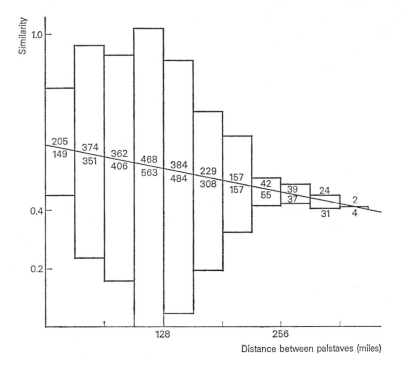

Fig.5.15. Best-fit regression line showing histograms summing the numbers of negative and positive residuals in equally spaced distance blocks.

that these residuals might release further information about spatial patterning. The first point to consider, however, is that the pattern of residuals may be due to the use of an inappropriate model – for example, a straight-line model as opposed to an exponential one. This possibility can be examined visually for the first group of palstaves using all primary traits. Rather than plotting all 4950 points on a graph, an indication of the residual pattern may be obtained by summing the number of positive and negative residuals in equally spaced distance blocks. These totals are shown as histograms either side of the best-fit regression line in fig.5.15. Since there is a slight tendency for there to be more positive residuals than negative at close distances, and less in the middle range, some form of exponential model might have provided a slightly better fit. But the generally comparable numbers of residuals at similar points on either side of the regression line suggest that the straight-line model is not wholly inappropriate.

Since the residual pattern is not to any great extent accounted for by the model used, it is possible to look at the spatial distribution of these residuals to see if they show any structure. This can be achieved by connecting with a straight line (continuous) on a map those palstaves

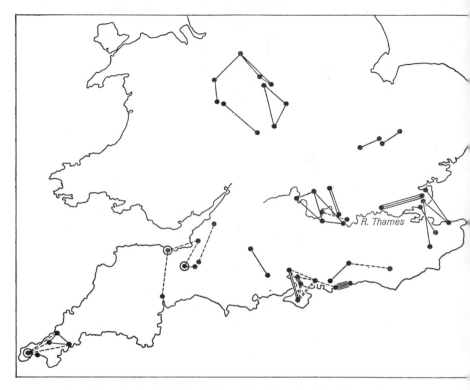

Fig.5.16. Spatial distribution of palstave residuals in southern England. Solid lines = positive residuals; dashed lines = negative residuals. Circles indicate palstaves likely to have been traded from one area into another.

which are more similar than we would expect according to the overall pattern of fall-off in similarity with distance (positive residuals), and by joining with a broken line those palstave pairs which are less similar than expected (negative residuals). Residuals above +0.30 and below −0.30 have been plotted in fig.5.16, and only palstaves up to 50 km (5 cm on the original map) apart are included since it is only the local patterning that is to be examined. Information from three groups of 100 palstaves is included on the map, their similarities having been computed using all the primary traits.

The pattern of positive residuals appears to identify the regional groupings already seen in a straightforward typological clustering of the artifacts (Rowlands 1970). In fact the regression method picks out some of these regions rather better than has been possible otherwise. The regional groupings have palstaves which, for a given distance are markedly more similar than expected. It is not easy to see why this should be so nor to see why the positive residual connections are not spread more haphazardly over the whole of southern England. One possibility is that the greater density of palstaves in the regional groupings means there is a greater chance of obtaining positive residual connections at the close distances being considered. This is not a satisfactory explanation because there are few such connections in the area of highest density (Cambridgeshire Fen area), and many where there is a lower density (for example, in the Midlands). It may, then, be the case that the areas of high positive residuals indicate the districts over which the products of one man or group of men were distributed so that it is this localised pattern of manufacture and distribution which makes up the regional styles and groupings. The groupings of positive residuals may also indicate areas where a strong tradition has been maintained by social bonds. Since the clusters of positive residual links often occur round major waterways, they may also reflect easier or greater contact and interaction along water routes.

The occurrence of high negative residuals appears to reflect two factors. The first of these is exemplified by the area immediately northeast of the Isle of Wight. Here negative residual links are found between two areas of high positive residuals. These two areas represent the two regions covered by a type of palstave found to the west of Southampton Water, and a type found to the east. The negative residuals in fact connect palstaves of two different traditions which remain markedly different even when spatially close. There is a sharp boundary between the two areas, which is sharper than expected according to the overall relationship between similarity and distance. Such a boundary could be due either to competition (in a broad sense) between two closely spaced production areas, or to a division relating to social factors.

The second factor pertaining to the negative residuals is that the method appears to be able to identify palstaves likely to have been traded from one area into another. For example, in Cornwall (see fig.5.16) palstaves in a regional group linked by positive residuals are all joined in addition by negative links to one nearby palstave. This palstave is much less similar to the others in its vicinity than expected from the overall pattern. In fact this palstave is very like the palstaves from the Thames valley. Similarly, in the Somerset area the two encircled palstaves are of a type characteristic of the Dorset/Isle of Wight/south Hampshire area, while the three palstaves to which they are connected by negative residual links are of more local types.

Thus regression analysis enables us to see how, by defining the artifacts in different ways, different spatial patterning occurs. The greatest degree of localisation is seen in decorative and formal traits as opposed to those designated as having some relation to function. The pattern of residuals or marked differences from the overall relationship of similarity to distance suggests a localised distribution of products, although some widespread trade or exchange is also evident.

Generally, it seems that regression analysis is a valuable method for describing trends in archaeological data and that the form of these trends and the differences between them may lead to insights about the data. Perhaps most promising is the analysis of residuals from the fitted regression lines. A major problem which remains for the archaeologist is whether he can confidently interpret the spatial trends in his data and at what level of detail. It may be that one form of regression relationship can be produced by a variety of different spatial processes. Some attempt at investigating this possibility will be made in the following section.

5.3 *The simulation of artifact dispersal*

The aim of the following series of simulations is to investigate whether different spatial processes produce different forms of fall-off curve. Can identification of different types of fall-off curve help in the interpretation of the process behind the pattern, and if so, within what limits?

The basis of the simulation will be a *random walk process*. That is, the distances and directions moved by points progressing from a source are chosen within specified limits, at random. Isaac (1972) has discussed the use of the random walk process to model change in space and time of palaeolithic tool types.

> If we accept that there may be wide tolerances for the morphology of tools with equivalent functions, and that 'tradition' itself may be subject to change through time and space, then it becomes apparent that *stochastic models* may provide an important alternative to phylogenetic or activity difference models. . . . A stochastic model allows for 'random walk' drift of 'craft norms' within the constraints of functional and technological limits [Isaac 1972, 178].

Clarke (1972, 20–3) has suggested the application of the random walk model to simulate the spread of early neolithic settlement across the European loess zones. Deetz (1967, 99) has compared certain types of diffusion of archaeological traits with Brownian Movement. Hogg (1971) has looked at the movement of Iron Age coins from their production centres in these random walk terms. It is to model the movement of objects from a source that the random walk process will be used here. This is a useful way of approaching the complexity of real-world patterns of trade and exchange. One can consider, for example, the complexity of the movement of axes by ceremonial gift exchange outlined by Clark (1965).

The general strategy followed here, therefore, is to use the computer (programs written by Hodder) to simulate random walks of points from a central source. Initially the rules for the 'walks' have been kept simple. The effect of making these gradually more complex can then be monitored. To aid comparison, the total number of points moving from each source has been kept to 100. The basic variables in all the simulations which determine the pattern of the random walk are the direction taken at each step, the length of that step, and the total number of steps allowed per walk. In addition we can select which of these variables or how many of them are to have values chosen randomly, within what limits, and according to what probability distribution.

The archaeological situation to have in mind is the movement of, for example, stone axes or obsidian which are capable of being handed-on more than once. The simulations do not consider, initially at least, the situation in which an object travels directly from source to destination without further or intermediate movement.

5.3.1 *Simulations of simple random walks*

In the first trials the direction taken at each step is chosen at random but the length of step and number of steps are fixed beforehand. The computer program used, which retains the same structure in all the later simulations, starts the process at an origin. From here, a point is allowed to move a stated distance in any direction with each of 360 degrees having an equal and independent chance of being chosen. From its new position the point is again allowed to move the same distance in a direction chosen at random. This single walk continues for the number of steps stated. The walk being finished we note how far from the origin the point has reached and return to the origin. The whole process is repeated with, for every walk the final position of the point noted. Some random walks of this sort are shown in figs.5.17 and 5.18. Some general characteristics of the walks in these figures should be noted. One is the gradual outward movement through 'time' and the other is the uneven pattern of spread. A random walk does not necessarily mean equal movement in all directions.

In the above examples the path taken by each point has been drawn out on the plotter by the computer. For the simulations to be described below, however, 100 points are allowed to walk and the total number reaching particular distances from the origin summed. These summations are made for 10 regularly spaced and concentric distance bands around the origin. Each band is 1 cm wide. The fall-off in the totals for each distance band are then drawn out on the plotter. The whole procedure is always repeated five times in order to gain some idea of the possible variation in fall-off curve. An example of the end result is shown in fig.5.19. However, to allow presentation of a large amount of information it has been necessary in the following diagrams to take the mean of the five fall-off curves and to show this as one curve. Single

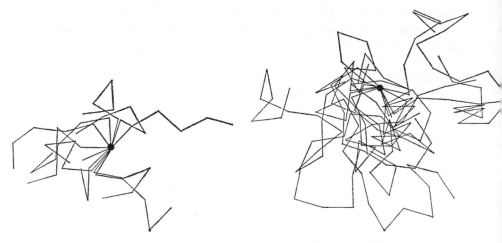

Figs.5.17 and 5.18. Two examples of random walks.

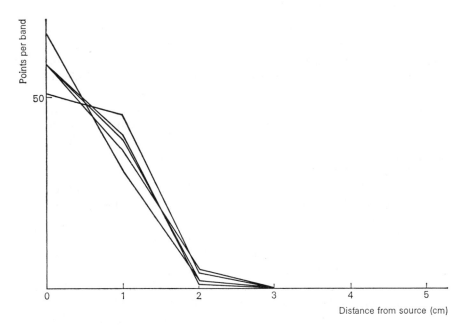

Fig.5.19. Variation in the simulated fall-off patterns.

fall-off curves therefore represent the average pattern that occurs for any random walk process.

Initially the length of each step has been put at 0.25 cm, and the number of steps moved for each walk set to 2. Of course, all the resulting end points are within the first 1 cm band. If we increase the number of steps to 6, some points reach the second band. In fact, by gradually increasing the number of steps allowed at each walk we can cause the

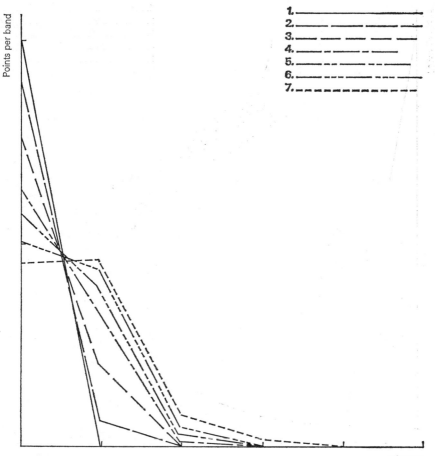

Fig.5.20. Step length fixed at 0.25 cm. Step numbers fixed.
1: 2 steps; 2: 6 steps; 3: 10 steps; 4: 14 steps; 5: 18 steps;
6: 22 steps; 7: 26 steps.

fall-off curves to change from being steep and concave (few steps) to being flattened or convex towards the origin (more than 14 steps). This change is shown in fig.5.20.

If the length of step is increased to 0.5 cm (fig.5.21), then a curve flattened near the source occurs with only 6 steps. As the number of steps is allowed to increase, the high point on the fall-off curve is found away from the source and gradually spreads wider and flatter.

The effect of increasing the length of step is shown in fig.5.22, for 6 steps. The end result is an ever flatter representation of the pattern already observed, with the high point on the fall-off curve gradually moving outwards.

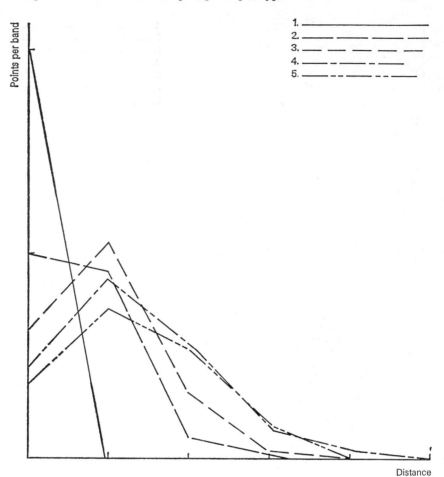

Fig.5.21. Step length fixed at 0.5 cm. Step numbers fixed.
1 : 2 steps; 2 : 6 steps; 3 : 10 steps; 4 : 14 steps; 5 : 18 steps.

As a summary of this rigid and rather unrealistic spatial process, it seems that we can produce sharply concave fall-off curves with walks of a few short steps, and curves flattened near the origin with many short steps. By increasing the length of the steps a situation occurs in which the point of highest frequency is not at the source. The latter is a pattern which is not common amongst prehistoric material.

An alternative procedure is to allow points to move only outwards from the source although, within this restriction, the direction is still chosen at random. This is an extreme case of the 'down-the-line' movement suggested by Renfrew (1969; 1972b) for the dispersal of Near Eastern obsidian. For the curves in fig.5.23, the step length was fixed at 0.25 cm, and the number of steps was fixed, increasing from

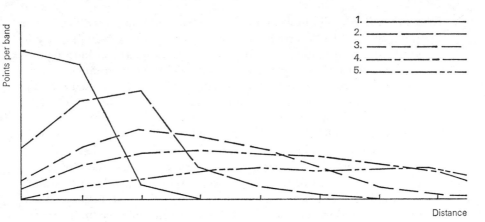

Fig.5.22. Step number fixed at 6. Step length fixed. 1: 0.5 cm step length; 2: 1.0 cm step length; 3: 1.5 cm step length; 4: 2.0 cm step length; 5: 3.0 cm step length.

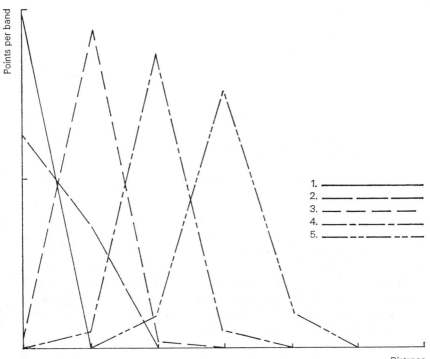

Fig.5.23. Outwards movement only. Step length fixed at 0.25 cm. Step number fixed. 1: 2 steps; 2: 6 steps; 3: 10 steps; 4: 18 steps; 5: 26 steps.

2 to 26. For small numbers of steps the pattern differs from the former (fig.5.20 in which the step length is also 0.25 cm) by being gentler in gradient. For example, compare the pattern at 6 steps in both figures. As the number of steps increases the high point on the frequency curve moves outwards and flattens. If the length of step is increased then the movement outwards is simply quicker and the zone of high frequencies is much flatter (not figured).

If we again allow moves in all directions, the process can be made slightly more realistic by choosing the values for the other variables (length of step and number of steps) at random. First the step length will be selected in this way. It is necessary to decide what probability distribution these lengths should have. One possibility is to choose them at random and with equal probability between arbitrary limits such as 0.0 and 2.0 cm. Perhaps more realistic, however, is that there should be more short lengths than long lengths of step, as is shown diagrammatically in fig.5.24. This can be done by choosing the lengths at

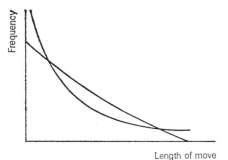

Fig.5.24. Two examples of possible frequency distributions for the lengths moved by points.

random from a negative exponential distribution with predetermined mean.

For the simulation of the random walk this mean has been set to 0.5 cm. The number of steps is fixed and increases from 2 to 18 in different trials. The resulting fall-off curves (fig.5.25) are similar to those in fig.5.21 in which the length of step is fixed at 0.5 cm. However, with the length of step chosen at random, the fall-off curves are much flatter. For example, with 2 steps the sharp fall-off seen in fig.5.21 is much more gradual. In both cases, as the number of steps increases, flatter fall-off curves occur.

Having seen the effect of letting the step length be chosen at random, we can investigate the effect of keeping the length fixed while allowing the number of steps moved at each walk to vary. To produce the fall-off curves in fig.5.26, the length of all steps has been fixed at 0.5 cm, but the number of steps per walk has been chosen at random between the limits

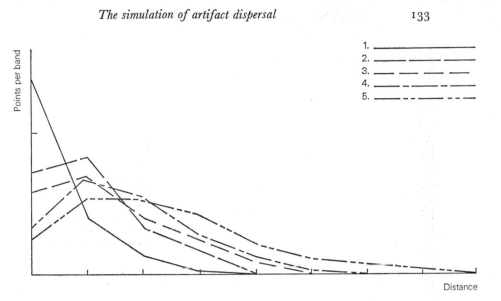

Fig.5.25. Step number fixed. Step length chosen from a
negative exponential distribution with mean of 0.5 cm.
1: 2 steps; 2: 6 steps; 3: 10 steps; 4: 14 steps; 5: 18 steps.

shown in the figure. Each number within these limits has an equal
chance of being picked. By comparing with fig.5.21 in which the step
length was also 0.5 cm but the number of steps was fixed, it is clear that
by allowing the latter to vary we avoid most of the high frequency
peaks away from the source (although a slight peak occurs when the
limits for the number of steps are broad (between 1 and 18)). By
increasing the step length to 1.0 cm (fig.5.27) we find much gentler
gradients and a peak occurring away from the source when only 10
steps is the maximum allowed.

We have investigated how one variable performs when its value is
chosen at random while others are predetermined. We can now consider the more complex situation in which all the variable values are
picked at random. It is reasonable to suppose that high-value objects
move longer distances and perhaps move more steps than heavy,
coarse, low-value objects (section 5.6), but for any one type of object a
range of step numbers and step lengths is to be expected, resulting in a
complex pattern. In fig.5.28 the first four curves have been produced by
walks in which the length of step is chosen at random from a negative
exponential distribution with a mean of 0.5 cm, and in which the number
of steps walked is picked at random between the limits shown. It
appears that, as the upper limit of this range is increased, the always
concave curves become flatter. There is a complete lack of the peaking
away from the centre which has often been found before, and the
curves have a gentler gradient than when one of the variables is fixed.
In this figure the procedures which produced the last two curves

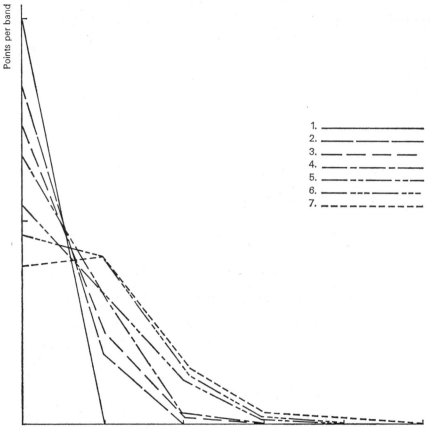

Fig.5.26. Step length fixed at 0.5 cm. Number of steps chosen between the following limits. 1: 1 and 2; 2: 1 and 4; 3: 1 and 6; 4: 1 and 8; 5: 1 and 10; 6: 1 and 14; 7: 1 and 18.

(5 and 6) used a step length distribution with a larger mean. This immediately produces a very flat fall-off curve even when the maximum number of steps allowed is few. These last fall-off curves show the sort of pattern occurring with Group I neolithic axes from a source in Cornwall. The axes from this source have a very gradual fall-off with distance because some of them travelled a long way to areas such as the Yorkshire coast, apparently by sea movement. The peak of highest frequency, however, remains near the source.

In fig.5.29, by comparing curve 1 with 3, and 2 with 4, it is possible to see the effect of choosing step length and number at random but only allowing movement outwards from the source. As might be expected, the curves are flatter since the points move out rather faster.

We can further investigate what results if a semi-permeable barrier

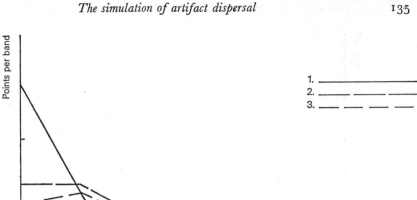

Fig.5.27. Step length fixed at 1.0 cm. Number of steps chosen
between the following limits: 1: 1 and 2; 2: 1 and 6; 3: 1 and 10.

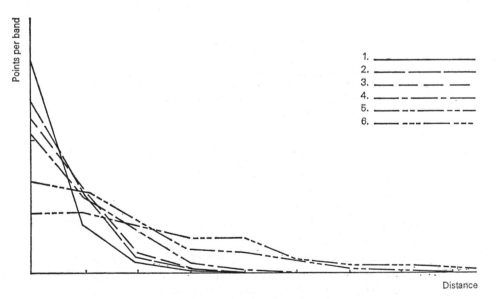

Fig.5.28. Curves 1 to 4. Step length chosen from a negative
exponential distribution with a mean of 0.5 cm. Numbers of
steps chosen between the following limits. 1: 1 and 2;
2: 1 and 4; 3: 1 and 6; 4: 1 and 8.

Curves 5 and 6. Step length chosen from a negative
exponential distribution with mean 1.5 cm. Number of steps
chosen between the following limits: 5: 1 and 2; 6: 1 and 4.

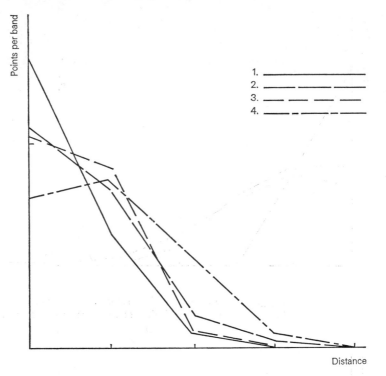

Fig.5.29. Curves 1 and 2. Step length chosen between 0 and 1 cm.
Number of steps chosen between the following limits.
1: 1 and 4; 2: 1 and 8.
Curves 3 and 4. As for 1 and 2, but only outward movement
allowed. 3: Step number between 1 and 4; 4: step number
between 1 and 8.

is put in the way of the points (cf. Yuill 1965). This has been achieved
by placing a circular barrier around the central source at 0.75 cm or
1.50 cm distance. When points are allotted a direction which takes
them across this barrier they are only given a 0.5 chance (one in two) of
being allowed to do so. If not allowed, then another direction is chosen
at random which, if this again means crossing the barrier, has the same
chance of success. If a point does succeed in crossing the barrier it is
allowed to proceed unhindered. In the simulations the length of move is
fixed at 0.5 cm, and the number of steps per walk is chosen at random
between the limits shown in fig.5.30.

This semi-permeable barrier is probably more realistic than a non-
permeable one since, if it is considered to represent a social division,
mechanisms usually exist for between-group exchange (Sahlins 1965).
It may be helpful to bear in mind the case of the late Iron Age inscribed
coins (Hogg 1971) which might have had less or different value outside

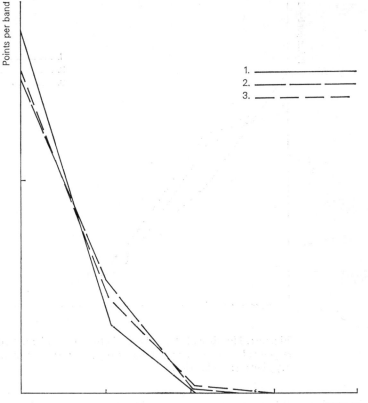

Fig.5.30. Number of steps chosen between 1 and 6. Step length fixed at 0.5 cm. 1: Barrier at 0.75 cm; 2: barrier at 1.5 cm; 3: no barrier.

a political unit, a difference which might be expected to be reflected in the spatial distribution of the coins.

The results of the simulations (figs.5.30 and 5.31) show that the presence of a barrier only makes a slight difference to the fall-off curves, especially when only a few steps are involved. If more steps are allowed, a marked difference is seen only if the barrier is near the source. In this case the curve changes shape from being flattened near the source to being entirely concave. This is disappointing, for in a situation in which, as with the Iron Age coins, the supposed boundary is towards the edge of the distribution, it is difficult to see how such a boundary could reliably be identified from the artifact distributions. This is the conclusion suggested by the simulations, although Hogg (1971) has claimed to have distinguished such boundaries for a few of the Iron Age coin distributions.

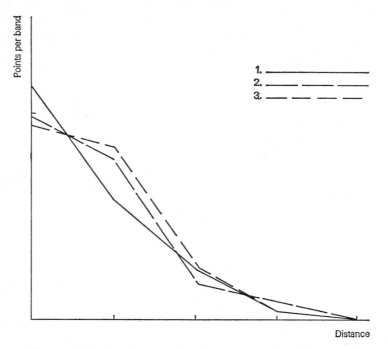

Fig.5.31. Number of steps chosen between 1 and 14. Length of step fixed at 0.5 cm. 1: Barrier at 0.75 cm; 2: barrier at 1.75 cm; 3: no barrier.

Is it possible to reach any conclusions as a result of simulating the simple random walk process? Can we make any comments which might be helpful in understanding archaeological material? In fig.5.32 are collected a number of curves of similar form, all fairly steeply concave. It is clear from the discussion so far, and from this diagram that the same *form* of fall-off curve can be produced by different spatial *processes*. This is to a certain extent disappointing for the archaeologist. However, all the curves in fig.5.32 have been produced by random walks of only a few steps, the maximum number of steps allowed (6) being when a boundary was present. In all cases the length of step is short (around 0.5 cm).

In fig.5.33 are collected curves flattened near the source. Again it appears that different processes can produce very similar patterning. However, the number of steps moved is in all cases comparatively large (the maximum allowed being from 6 to 22), while all step lengths are again comparatively short (around 0.5 cm). It seems that visually different curves can be produced by increasing the number of steps taken per walk, but keeping the length of step fairly short. It is interesting that, in fig.5.33, the sole case in which the maximum number of steps allowed is small (4), is when only outward movement is allowed.

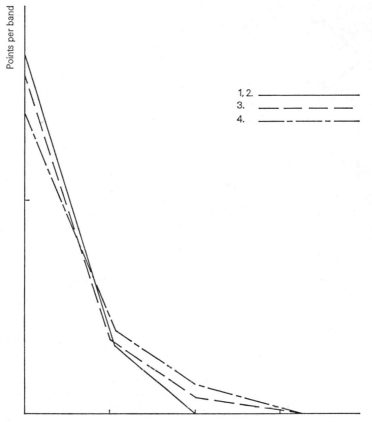

Fig.5.32. 1: Step length fixed at 0.5 cm. Step number chosen between 1 and 4. 2: Step length fixed at 0.5 cm. Step number chosen between 1 and 6. Barrier at 0.75 cm. 3: Step length chosen from a negative exponential distribution with mean of 0.5 cm. Step number chosen between 1 and 2. 4: Step length chosen from a negative exponential distribution with a mean of 0.5 cm. Number of steps fixed at 2.

This, then, may be useful for empirical cases in which the type of fall-off curve flattened near the source is found, although there is reason to believe (from the type of artifact) that the number of steps moved by artifacts may have been small.

In fig.5.34 are shown two curves of a much flatter type, which have in common that the length of move used is comparatively large (generally above 1 cm), although the number of moves is fairly small. This very gradual fall-off is the sort which, as has been mentioned, may occur with the Cornish neolithic Group I axes, for which some long steps may have been possible by sea movement.

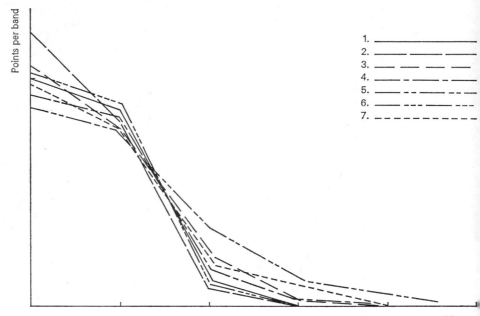

Fig.5.33. 1: Number of steps chosen between 1 and 14. Step length fixed at 0.5 cm. 2: Number of steps fixed at 18. Length fixed at 0.25 cm. 3: Number of steps chosen between 1 and 8. Step length chosen between 0 and 1 cm. 4: Number of steps fixed at 22. Step length fixed at 0.5 cm. 5: Number of steps fixed at 6. Step length chosen from a negative exponential distribution with mean of 0.5 cm. 6: Number of steps chosen between 1 and 14. Step length fixed at 0.5 cm. Barrier at 1.5 cm. 7: Number of steps chosen between 1 and 4. Step length chosen between 0 and 1 cm. Only outward movement allowed.

A further type of curve which has occurred is one in which the point of highest frequency is not at the source. This is not a common type amongst archaeological data, but it seems to be produced in the simulations by very long steps or by large numbers of them. It also occurs when the direction of movement is outwards only.

Some mention has already been made of the relationship between the simulated patterns and those observed in the archaeological material. How can we compare the two? One possible method is to compare the distance exponents of the fitted regression curves, since these α values (section 5.2) summarise the shape of the curves. Values of α for the curves shown in fig.5.35, which represent a range of different forms and different processes, are given in table 5.3. To allow comparison with the archaeological data in section 5.3, the gradients for the exponential

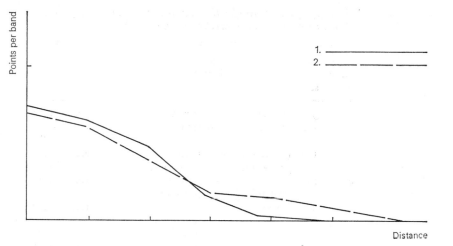

Fig.5.34. 1: Number of steps chosen between 1 and 6. Step length fixed at 1.0 cm. 2: Number of steps chosen between 1 and 2. Step length chosen from a negative exponential distribution with mean of 1.5 cm.

form ($\alpha = 1$) are also shown. The model used to find the best-fit α value and the gradient (b) is that of equation 5.2.

Some general comments may be made from table 5.3.

(1) The gradient is less sensitive than the value of alpha to changes in spatial process, although, in general, steeper gradients (greater b values) are found, as might be expected, with fewer steps. In the large number of distance-decay studies of modern spatial interaction conducted by social scientists, systematic variations of the gradient of the regression line have been noticed. It tends to be lower (less steep) in urban than in rural areas (Chisholm and O'Sullivan 1973; Hägerstrand 1957, 116). The angle of the gradient is also a function of the size of the centre with which interaction is occurring. The smaller the centre, the steeper is the gradient (Claeson 1968; Olsson 1967). This is the principle underlying the gravity models to be discussed below (section 5.6). The purpose of the trip or the type of commodity involved also influences the gradient so that, for example, bulky goods like coal and building materials have higher values (steeper gradients) than more highly valued goods (Carroll and Bevis 1957; Huff 1964; Olsson 1967). A number of studies have found that the gradient value decreases with time (Hägerstrand 1957; Taaffe 1962; Olsson 1965), suggesting a relationship with the level of technical, social and economic development in society (Olsson 1967). Similar trends have been found in the archaeological data (section 5.2). However, the differences in gradient are often only slight, and, as suggested by the random walk simulations, the α value is perhaps more sensitive to variations in spatial processes.

Table 5.3.   *The results of fitting regression curves to fall-off patterns obtained from 12 different simulated spatial processes*

Curve no.	No. of steps		Step length (cm)		Comments	α	b
I	5	(fixed)	0.5	(fixed)		2.5	−0.098
2	1–6	(equal probability)	1.0	(fixed)		2.4	−0.047
3	1–3	(equal probability)	0–1	(equal probability)		2.2	−0.130
4	1–2	(equal probability)	0–1	(equal probability)		1.3	−0.152
5	2	(fixed)	0.5	mean (exponential distribution)		1.1	−0.076
6	1–14	(equal probability)	0.5	(fixed)		2.1	−0.077
7	1–10	(equal probability)	0.5	(fixed)		1.9	−0.077
8	1–6	(equal probability)	0.5	(fixed)		1.8	−0.112
9	1–14	(equal probability)	0.5	(fixed)	Barrier at 1.5	2.3	−0.072
10	1–6	(equal probability)	0.5	(fixed)	Barrier at 1.5	1.7	−0.107
11	1–14	(equal probability)	0.5	(fixed)	Barrier at 0.75	2.1	−0.072
12	1–6	(equal probability)	0.5	(fixed)	Barrier at 0.75	1.4	−0.114

(2) From table 5.3 and fig.5.35 it is the less concave and more convex curves which have the higher α values. Such curves are produced by a comparatively large number of short steps. For the archaeological data it was noted (p. 114) that higher 'value' goods had fall-off curves with higher α exponents. It is the higher 'value' which can be supposed to be related to the greater mobility suggested by the simulations. Objects of higher value may be handed on with greater frequency and be in demand over a wider area. Thus Near Eastern obsidian has been discussed (Renfrew 1969) as being handed across a wide area by neighbourhood 'down-the-line' contact. A high frequency of moves is also appropriate for the Iron Age Dobunnic coins and the fine neolithic Group VI axes, both of which have high α values (section 5.2). The result of the regression analysis for the second simulated curve in table 5.3 shows that higher α values occur if we increase the step length of the random walk but leave the range of step numbers taken per walk fairly low. The higher values that were obtained for the finer Romano-British pottery and fine neolithic pottery (p. 114) might be related

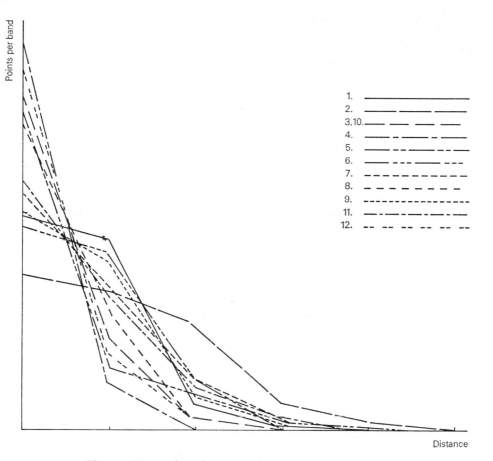

Fig.5.35. For explanation see table 5.3.

to this greater distance moved per step and to the small number of steps. The pots were of high 'value' but fragile. But attempts at interpretation of this sort are dangerous and speculative.

In modern contexts attempts have been made to compare patterns of interaction with the idea of a random walk (Cox and Miller 1965) away from a centre.

> It is logical, for example, to find out whether the patterns of contact are a product of normal diffusion, as if people randomly walked in various directions to different distances, and each walk was unrelated to any other. Here the mean information field would best be fit by a normal spatial distribution. In fact such a pattern of contact is extremely rare. Rather, there is greater contact at very close and at rather great distances. Limitations of time, as the length of day and the strong tendency to repeat the easier contacts already made, strongly reinforce the short distances.

At the same time widespread modern communication systems help lengthen the interaction distances of individuals (Morrill and Pitts 1967, 411).

Pearson and Blakeman (1906) showed that a number of organisms progressing from a point source by random walk obtain a close approximation to a 'normal' distribution ($\alpha = 2$ in the single-log case – see section 5.1) after seven or more steps (*ibid.*, 24). This is just the same distribution form as the diffusion of gas according to kinetic theory. Brownlee (1911), however, found that the exponential model ($\alpha = 1$ in the single-log case) gave the best representation of both epidemic distribution in space and time and random migration. Bateman (1962) reviewed a number of studies of the movement of bees and flies and found the exponential model to be the most appropriate but with a movement of α towards 2 with time. Similar results have been obtained for insect and wind pollination away from a particular pollen source. Tendencies towards a process which can be represented by random walk movement have also been discovered in human behaviour. Morrill and Pitts (1967) found that the exponential function gave the best fit for a series of marriage and migration data. 'There is a feeling that moves are more accidental than purposeful' (*ibid.*, 412), and more permanent and costly than in the journey-to-work case. P. J. Taylor (1971) gave greater detail to this tendency in the same data by examining the α values in both the single-log and the double-log cases. Kulldorf (1955) also found that higher α values gave the best fits to the migration data. Clearly, individual moves can in no sense be considered random, but in certain cases it may be possible to simulate the aggregate of moves by a random process.

In both archaeological and modern interaction data, then, high α values relate to more costly moves. Comparing the archaeological data with the simulated patterns, it is of interest that, with one exception, α values do not reach above 1.6 for the archaeological data, while higher values are common for the simulated patterns. This might suggest that most of the archaeological data examined have been produced by processes involving few steps in comparison to the 6, 10, 14 or more allowed in the simulations. The exception amongst the archaeological data is the higher α value obtained for the neolithic Group VI axes. Their movement may have involved complex gift exchange with much handing on of the objects. However, for this sample, particular caution is necessary because large areas of the distribution were still missing (fig.5.78) at the time of the analysis.

(3) Table 5.3 and fig.5.35 also show that the lowest α values describe those curves with most concavity. By comparing curve 3 with 10 and curve 7 with 11 it is clear that the presence of a few points at long distances from the source (producing a tail to the curve) can lower the α value for concave curves even when these have very similar

gradients near the source. Thus lower α values relate to greater numbers near the source with some points moving longer distances. In general it seems that the spatial process involves shorter walks of short step length. The lowest α value occurs with a curve (5) produced by walks of very few steps, the length of most steps being short although some are much longer (since they are chosen from a negative exponential distribution). In modern contexts lower α values have been found in cases where there is greater contact both at very close and at rather great distances. This type of contact is best exemplified by journey-to-work data (for example Helvig 1964) in which the α value in the single-log form of the distance-decay function has been found to vary around zero. For example, Gleave (1970) found such values to give the best fit to the data in a study of the journey-to-work pattern in Newcastle, while the double-log case applied to the same data sets produced α values mainly between 1 and 1.5. Morrill and Pitts (1967) found that regression formulae involving similar α values best described purposeful, non-permanent and non-costly moves.

It is interesting, therefore, that the archaeological data (section 5.2) provided low α values with spatial processes which might be supposed to have involved a few short steps because of the difficulty of movement (for example with Romano-British roofing tiles and coarse pottery, and the large, coarse, neolithic picrite axe-hammers). Notable, however, is that none of the simulated curves have α values as low as those of the archaeological data (below 0.6). Thus the degree of concavity found amongst the archaeological data is greater than has been produced by random processes. It seems reasonable to suggest that the spatial process behind the archaeological data involved extremely close and frequent contact with a centre, perhaps with only one-step moves being most common. This is acceptable for the objects in question which had high localised demand or low value and/or transport difficulties (Romano-British tiles and coarse pottery and neolithic axe-hammers). Great concavity is also produced by a long tail when a few items reach long distances. Indeed the archaeological distributions studied usually do show a few examples of the item reaching long distances. In an early prehistoric context most of, for example, the picrite axe-hammers may have been obtained directly from the source while a few were passed over greater distances by secondary trade and exchange. The neolithic Group I axes have a low α value because of a long tail to their distribution rather than because of especially intense interaction near the source.

Although some interpretations of fall-off curves have been discussed above, one of the main results of the simulation experiment is to show that different spatial processes can produce very similar fall-off curves. This advises great caution in any attempt at interpretation. Thus the imposition of a boundary or barrier can be seen to cause some changes in the α value of the fall-off curve. But the differences between these curves are slight and it would be dangerous to suggest a boundary for prehistoric material on this sort of evidence. Clearly, the use of simulation has not allowed us to give precise interpretations of archaeological data. What it has done perhaps is to allow consideration of the sorts of possible procedures which might result in the observed archaeological patterns.

Consideration so far has been of a situation which has greatest similarities in a prehistoric context to some form of reciprocal exchange (Sahlins 1965). Most exchange of this sort takes place by neighbourhood or local contacts. An idea of the sort of ceremonial gift exchange which could lead to a large number of steps being taken by highly valued objects is provided by Clark (1965). He discusses the pattern of the axe trade in Australia, Melanesia and New Zealand, where most axe movement was by reciprocal gift exchange, and often between rival groups. Marriage ties and relationships were maintained by the giving of gifts of goods. The objects involved could, therefore, move hundreds of miles without the people themselves moving very much at all. However, in certain cases (for example in New Zealand) special long-distance trips were made to obtain axes of precious rock.

5.3.2 *Simulations of more complex random walks*

Rather different types of exchange are those which are often collected under the general heading of redistributive exchange. In the following discussion the term will be used in a very broad sense to mean a system in which the goods flow via a central place to and from a surrounding region. In a non-market economy this implies social obligations and dependence on the centre, while in a market economy it is represented by the hierarchy of central places. Renfrew (1973*b*, 117) has mentioned the importance of being able to distinguish reciprocal from redistributive exchange in prehistoric archaeological data.

> We must hope to trace, in successive prehistoric societies, the development of exchange systems which gradually made possible an increasing degree of interdependence and specialisation. This we can indeed do in the Aegean, although commercial trade did not develop until the second millenium B.C. and markets a thousand years later. In central and northern Europe, too, we shall have to examine the evidence afresh in order to learn to what extent the developing metal industry of the bronze age depended on a system of redistribution.

The following is an attempt to employ simulation techniques similar to those used above in order to investigate whether, and under what circumstances, we can identify fall-off curves produced by a general redistributive process.

Figures 5.36 and 5.37 introduce the approach followed. In fig.5.36 a number of points proceed by random walks from the main centre.

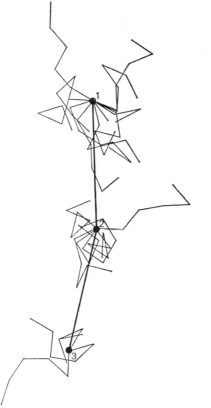

Fig.5.36. A number of points proceeding by random walks from one main centre (1) and through two others (2 and 3).

Points or goods may also move to a second centre from which lesser numbers of points may proceed. A third centre receives less points which in turn move outwards from it. The amount of points walking from each centre depends on distance from the main (original) source. The existence of strong connecting links between centres is characteristic of redistributive processes. The location of the centres is determined by a random walk from the origin which follows the same rules as the walks of the points, except that the centres are not allowed to locate too near each other. The random walk of centres is simply a convenient method for locating the centres. In certain cases, however, it may be given a chronological significance, the outward expansion of minor redistributive centres often being the way that large states expand (Friedman and Rowlands 1974). Figure 5.37 shows basically the same procedure although repeated three times, and with a relatively large number of points proceeding from the main centre.

We can now outline in greater detail the simulation procedure used to produce the fall-off curves. From each centre points are allowed

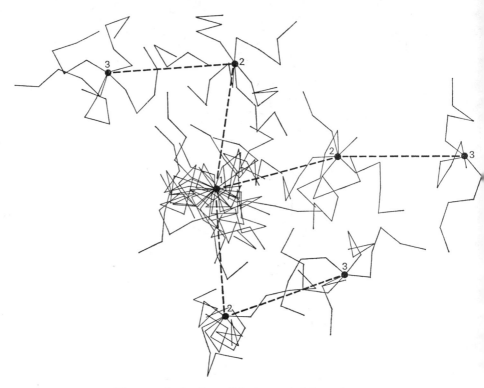

Fig.5.37. As for fig.5.36 but repeated three times.

to walk any number of steps between 1 and 3 or 4, the number being chosen at random and with equal probability. The length of step taken is between 0.0 and 1.0 cm, any figure within that range having an equal chance of being picked. The total number of points moving from the first centre is set to 100. The number from the other centres is calculated using a negative exponential distribution. The distance (D) between the centre in question and the main centre is computed. The number (X) of points moving from the centre in question is therefore

$$\log X = \log 100 - 0.05\,D. \tag{5.4}$$

The number 0.05 is the gradient of the fall-off curve and we shall examine the effect of varying this value in the simulations. Two centres walk from the main centre, and these in turn each produce one further centre. The distance moved by the centres at each step is a further variable. If a centre locates within a predetermined distance of another centre an alternative position is found. As in the simple random walk procedure, the number of end-points in 1 cm bands around the main centre is calculated and plotted out as a frequency curve. The whole process is repeated 25 times to obtain an idea of the possible variation in fall-off pattern.

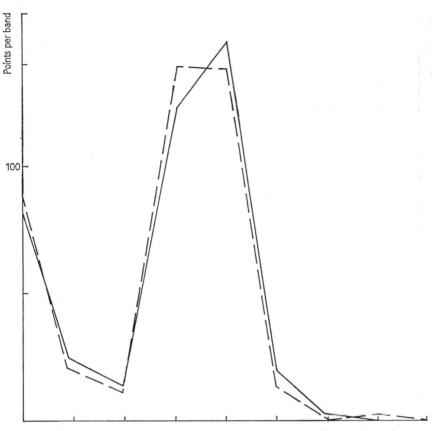

Fig.5.38. A simplified fall-off pattern resulting from redistribution. Lines of different symbols indicate the results of different simulations.

There are a large number of variables involved in the redistributive procedure, but the first trial has been simplified by allowing 100 points to move from all centres. The upper limit for the number of steps taken per walk is 3. The distance moved by centres is fairly large at 4.0 cm. This is also the minimum distance allowed between centres. Examples of the fall-off patterns which result around the main centre are shown in fig.5.38. As might be expected an unmistakable double peaking occurs.

In a second series of simulations the number of points walking from second and third centres is obtained by using equation 5.4 with the gradient set at —0.1. The upper limit of steps for each walk is again 3. The distance walked by centres is 2.0 cm and the minimum distance between centres is also 2.0 cm. A greater variety of fall-off curves is obtained for this and other redistributive processes than was found for

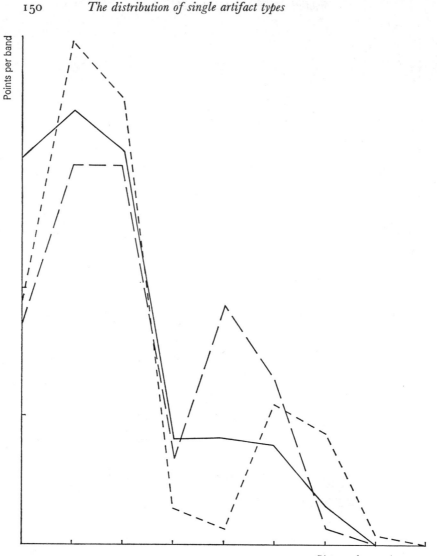

Fig.5.39. A variety of fall-off curves obtained by using an equation of the form of equation 5.4. Different lines as in fig.5.38.

the simple random walk. Some idea of the range of variation resulting in this case is given in fig.5.39. The curves are all characterised by 'plateaus' and secondary peaks. If the maximum number of steps allowed for each individual walk is increased to 4 while keeping the other variables unchanged, similar fall-off patterns occur (fig.5.40) although these are sometimes smoother. The smoother curves are of comparable form to those produced by the simple random walk.

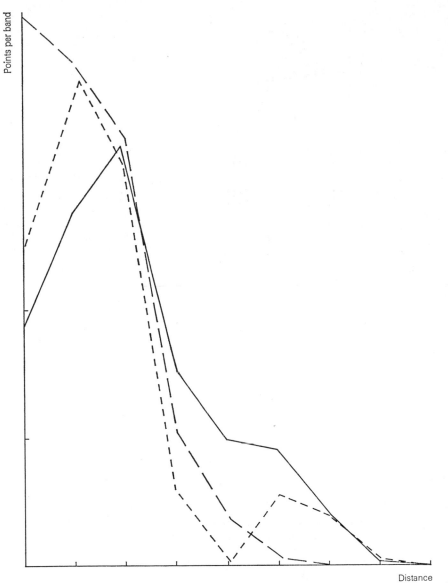

Fig.5.40. The results of a random walk procedure similar to fig.5.39, but with the number of steps increased. Different lines as in fig. 5.38.

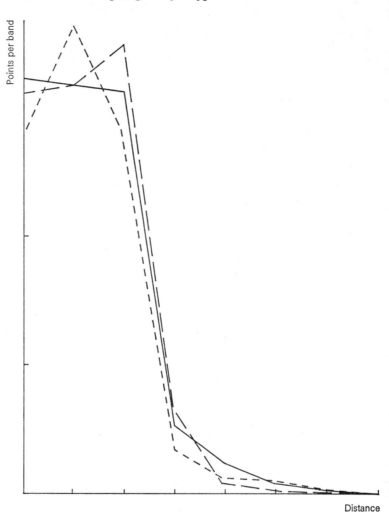

Fig.5.41. As for fig.5.39 but using an increased gradient in equation 5.4. Different lines as in fig.5.38.

The fall-off patterns produced in fig.5.41 are the result of the same process as above with the upper limit of steps for each walk again set to 3. A change has been made for equation 5.4 by increasing the gradient to −0.5. This implies a much steeper fall-off so that second and third centres produce much fewer points relative to the main centre. Although some peaks and plateaus result, the overall pattern is often smooth so that it is not easy to distinguish a 'redistributive' form.

In a further trial the gradient in equation 5.4 has been set to −0.1, but the distance moved by the centres has been decreased to 1 cm and this is also the minimum distance allowed between centres. As a result (fig.5.42) it is still less easy to identify a redistributive process from the form of the fall-off curves, and smooth curves are often found. The centres are too close together for their distribution areas to appear as separate, and points from each mingle. It seems that by further increasing the number of centres and varying the number of points they produce it would be possible to generate fall-off patterns even more similar to those resulting from the simple random walk process examined earlier.

It is apparent that redistributive processes can often produce fall-off curves which are visually distinctive. Plateaus and secondary peaks occur as opposed to the smoother fall-off presented by the simple random walk. However, in certain cases, the redistributive fall-off pattern is not easy to distinguish, especially when the number of points walking from minor centres is relatively small, or when centres are so close together that points from each intermix considerably. With real-world data it is possible that the further complexity involved would make it still more difficult to identify redistributive processes. For example, in the simulations the number of minor centres has been kept unrealistically small. Also the distances between centres have been determined with some regularity. In a real-world situation they might be located with more of a random pattern and this would produce further blurring of any peaks and plateaus in fall-off curves. Blurring and smoothing would also occur if a number of minor centres were allowed to locate in the interstices between larger centres.

As example of this more complex real-world situation where something is known about the redistributive system is the pattern of Romano-British fine-ware products occurring at sites in southwest England (fig.2.4). Much of this pottery was channelled through marketing centres but the overall pattern is very complicated and it is only at the periphery of the distribution that it is perhaps possible to see this marketing redistribution effect. Around Dorchester (Dorset) and Ilchester there seem to be some concentrations of high percentages of fine pottery. The fall-off of this pottery away from these two walled towns is contoured in fig.2.4. Even in this instance, however, the evidence is too meagre to be able to be confident that the pattern is the result of redistribution.

The spatial patterns for which sufficient data exist and which produce distinctive redistribution fall-off curves are likely to be identifiable from their spatial distributions as reflecting some form of redistributive process. It is not evident that examining regression curves will help in this identification, or provide much insight. Indeed these more complex processes are perhaps best examined by fitting three-dimensional surfaces and examining their residual patterning. This is the approach to be discussed in the next section.

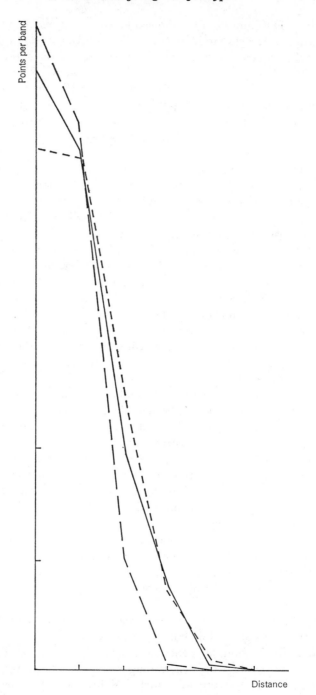

Fig.5.42. The results of another redistributive process. For
explanation of the process, see text. Different lines as in fig.5.38.

5.4 *Trend surface analysis*

Trend surface analysis is the name used widely in, for example, meteorology, geology and geography for methods of smoothing the values of some mapped variable. A generalised surface is derived from, or fitted to, the mapped data and two components or trends extracted – that of a regional nature, and local fluctuations.

'Trend analysis . . . is potentially one of the most exciting and powerful techniques for probing archaeological data, although at the time of writing no archaeologist has yet used this technique' (Clarke 1968, 428). Although some application has now been made (Bradley 1970), the method has still not been widely used by archaeologists. This is perhaps surprising since in many ways it offers a useful approach towards the handling of the often complex archaeological material. For example, an archaeological distribution or diffusion map is often the result of many interlocking factors and is thus not easy to study and interpret. The value of a mapped variable is affected by a multiplicity of processes and conditions (for example, the pattern of diffusion, the existence of major redistributive centres, environmental conditions, and the pattern of fieldwork) and by the simultaneous interaction and variation of these factors. It is difficult to disentangle the broad regional trends from the local variations and to interpret these different levels. Similarly, the distribution of finds within an archaeological site often presents a complex pattern in which it is difficult to differentiate significant trends from local anomalies. In an excavation of a Beaker settlement at Belle Tout, the localised patterning resulting from a trend surface analysis of finds density was able in certain cases to go far towards confirming expected but exiguous structures (*ibid.*, 318). 'This method is also useful in trying to isolate "activity complexes" . . . For example, by preparing a trend map of the distribution of flint waste it is possible to put on a proper basis the intuitive recognition of certain parts of the area as knapping areas. In the same way areas of disturbed hearths may be recovered with some confidence' (*ibid.*).

Thus, the value of trend surface analysis is in distinguishing regional and local trends, and in providing a certain degree of objectivity in this procedure. It further allows generalisations to be made from complex patterns, and makes interpolation and prediction possible.

5.4.1 *The methods*

In the following summary of the methods of trend surface analysis extensive use has been made of the summaries by Davis (1973) and Chorley and Haggett (1965). The formation of trend surfaces may be compared to the simple drawing of contours. However, when contouring, each data point at which a variable has been measured contributes information only for the immediately adjacent area. Lines are simply drawn between a data point and its immediate neighbours. For the methods described as trend surface analysis, however, each point contributes information over a wider area. In the first method to be discussed, trends are obtained by averaging the values at a number of points to produce one more general value. One way of doing this (*ibid.*, 199) is the 'parallel-profile' method, in which equally spaced parallel profiles are constructed, smoothed out by eye, and used to construct a three-dimensional map, two dimensions being the spatial co-ordinates of the map and the third being the value of the variable measured. A grid of 'intersecting profiles', adjusted at their intersections, can also be used to obtain a regular grid of values from which a contoured map may be constructed. A further approach is to place a circle of chosen radius at a regular series of points and to calculate the average value of the variable concerned within the circle. The resulting average values at the grid points provide the basis for a generalised contoured map. Alternatively, a series of square cells or quadrats may be placed over the area and the value within each cell calculated. The larger the size of cell used, the broader the regional trend obtained. Positive and negative residuals from the regional trend can also be mapped.

Some examples of this grid generalisation method can now be presented. As an initial example, and to test the sensitivity of the method, an analysis has been made of a rather scanty distribution of Romano-British pottery which is skewed around the known production centre in Hampshire (fig.5.43). For a description of the type see Hodder (1974c). In general terms it seems that objects made in, or distributed from, one centre often maintain a concentration around that centre. For example, the widespread distribution of Romano-British pewter objects has a concentration around the manufacturing centres such as Lansdown (Wedlake 1958). When the centre is unknown, can we predict its location by finding the high point or highest frequency on the smoothed trend surface? We can investigate this by comparing the high points (modal centres – Warntz and Neft 1960) on the trend surface of the Romano-British pottery with the location of the known kiln.

In fig.5.43 the number of sites in each quadrat of size x in a continuous grid has been counted. The numbers in every adjacent four of these have been summed at y to provide a more generalised figure for the number of sites. Areas with the highest values at y, that is the high points on the smoothed density surface, are shaded in figs.5.43–5.45. The eastern cluster appears to have the highest density of sites with the pottery type although the kiln centre is in the western group. In fig.5.44 the y values have been obtained by summing the x values which occur in the large quadrat around each y point. A much smoother density surface is therefore produced. In this case the area of highest

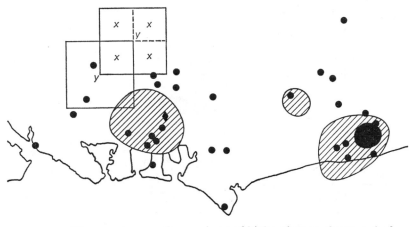

Figs.5.43 to 5.45. Comparisons of high points on the smoothed density surface of Romano-British Rowlands Castle pottery with the location of the known kilns (◆). Areas of highest densities of sites with Rowlands Castle pottery are shaded or blackened according to increasing density of sites.

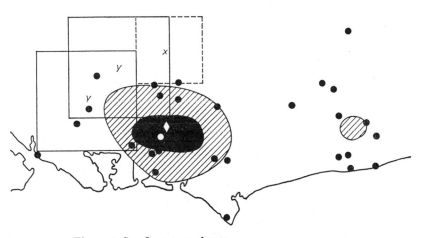

Fig.5.44. See fig.5.43 and text.

density does incorporate the kiln centre. If the quadrat size is still further increased (fig.5.45), the quadrats are large enough to include both the western and eastern clusters so that the point of highest density shifts towards the area between them.

From this example it is clear that the quadrat size has a great effect on the location of the highest point on the smoothed density surface. If the quadrats are too small then the point of smoothing the densities is lost. A number of similarly dense, small areas are produced. If the quadrats are too large, on the other hand, and include more than one

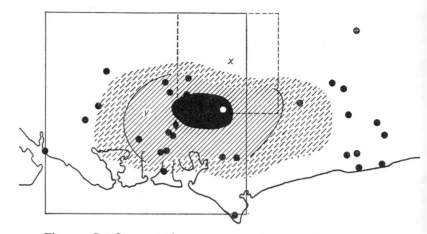

Fig.5.45. See fig.5.43 and text.

important cluster, then the modal centre can be located between clusters in an 'empty' zone. This should clearly be avoided. How much smaller than this the quadrats should be must be chosen subjectively when the centres of manufacture or distribution are unknown. In his study of neolithic stone axe distributions in Britain, Cummins (1974) suggested several instances in which the distributions were not centred over factory sites. In certain cases this may have resulted from the size and placing of the grid squares, rather than from prehistoric exchange mechanisms. Some attempt should have been made by Cummins to determine the variation in results occurring with the use of different lattices.

In fig.5.46 grid generalisation methods have been applied to the total distribution of sites or find spots with late Iron Age inscribed coins. It was hoped to be able to identify some regional trends by moving above the wealth of complicated local variation in the distribution. Some further indications of wealth at this period are also shown – the distribution of imported amphorae (Peacock 1971), that of rich Welwyn-type burials (Stead 1967), and the main oppida. In certain cases the areas of highest density of coins do seem to relate to other distributions, but it is also clear that peripheral densities of coins (made up of coins from more than one area) occur. These peripheral high density areas may be due to patterns of fieldwork, or they may prove to have some further significance. But the precise patterning of the density groupings, as is always the case with this class of methods, will vary as different lattices are used.

Another example of the use of grid methods to produce trend surfaces is provided by Bradley (1970) in his study of the distribution of finds within a Beaker settlement. First, an overall trend map of the density of finds across the site was constructed, and this is reproduced

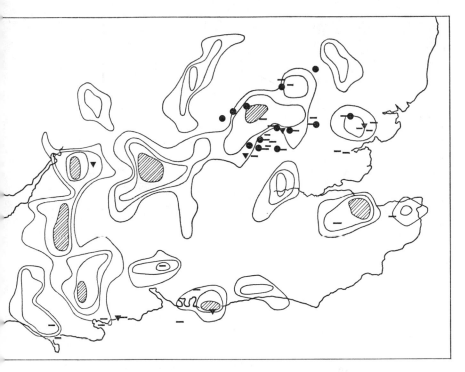

Fig.5.46. Trend surface fitted, by grid generalisation methods, to the distribution of find spots with late Iron Age inscribed coins in southern England. ▼, Main oppida; ●, Welwyn-type burials; horizontal bars = imported amphorae. Areas of highest density of find spots with coins are shaded.

in fig.5.47. Patterns of positive and negative residuals from this trend could then be studied in relation to possible post-hole structures. For example, in fig.5.48 the area within a series of post holes has positive residuals while negative residuals occur around the periphery.

There are some considerable problems associated with this first group of methods. These mainly stem from the lack of objectivity involved. For example, in constructing the map in fig.5.46 some subjectivity was encountered in the drawing of the contours. More serious is that the results of such methods rely heavily on the size of grid selected. We have been trying to separate regional from local trends, but what is meant by 'regional' and 'local' is largely subjective.

The second type of trend surface analysis may be considered more objective because it does not use quadrat averages and because it uses an operational definition of trend and deviation. The method is a form of regression analysis (cf. section 5.2) in which instead of fitting a two-dimensional line to a scatter of points on a graph the three-dimensional surface is found which best fits the variable plotted on a map. In this

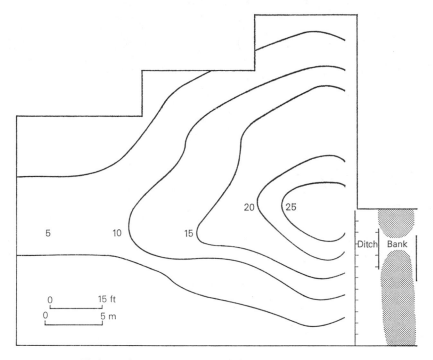

Fig.5.47. Trend surface fitted to the number of Beaker finds to the square metre throughout area II at Belle Tout. Contours are at intervals of five finds per square metre. Source: Bradley 1970.

case a trend may be defined as a 'linear function of the geographic co-ordinates of a set of observations so constructed that the squared deviations from the trend are minimised' (Davis 1973, 324).

Figure 5.49 shows the relationship between two-dimensional curves that can be fitted by regression analysis, as discussed in section 5.1, and three-dimensional surfaces. For the moment we will consider linear trends only (equivalent to a straight line in two dimensions). The function describing the three-dimensional linear surface has the form $Z = a + bU + cV$ in which U and V are geographical co-ordinates, and Z is the value of the variable on the trend surface. Lower-case letters indicate coefficients (see section 5.1). As with regression analysis these coefficients are obtained by minimising the squared deviations from the trend. The trend can therefore be regarded as a function having the smallest variance about it. However, an archaeological trend may not be a linear plane but may be extremely complex, although we rarely have any idea about what the form of the trend should be.

> Physicists can state that the path of a falling projectile should be a parabola, because they know something of the controlling forces,

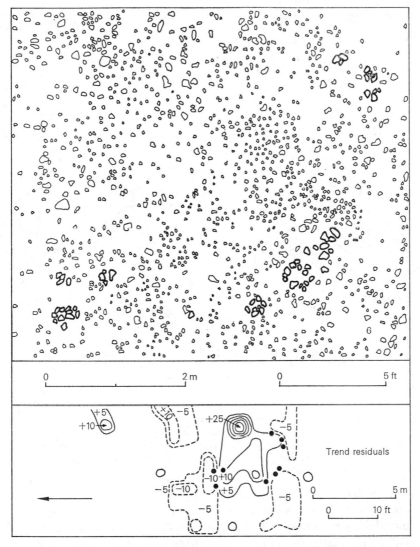

Fig.5.48. *Top:* Structure 6 as excavated at Belle Tout. Pitched flints belonging to the suggested outline of the structure below are given in bold relief.
Bottom: The structure in relation to residuals from overall trend of the density of Beaker material. Post holes are represented in solid black. Positive residuals are defined by solid contours at intervals of five items to the square metre and negative residuals are shown at similar intervals by broken lines.
Source: Bradley 1970.

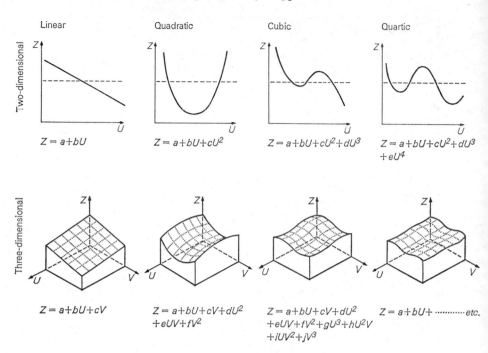

Fig.5.49. The relationship of four orders of two-dimensional polynomial curves to their three-dimensional couterparts. Source: Chorley and Haggett 1965.

i.e., the acceleration of gravity and the conservation of momentum. Geologists can seldom speak with any authority about what form a geologic surface or distribution 'should' take. Instead, they do the next best thing, and approximate the unknown function with one of arbitrary nature [*ibid.*, 330].

The archaeologist and geographer must follow the same path. A polynomial generalisation of the linear trend surface is usually used, introducing powers and cross-products of the geographic co-ordinates. Polynomials are extremely flexible, and at high orders, can conform to very complex surfaces. They can be fitted with the use of computers.

It should be stressed that polynomials can only be used in an archaeological context as a matter of convenience. They are comparatively easy to work with on the computer, but their use does not mean that prehistoric spatial processes conform to polynomial functions. These processes are of unknown or perhaps unknowable nature, and the polynomial expansion can only be an approximation.

Localised patterning is obtained from the residual difference between the observed value of Z and that predicted by the fitted function. These positive and negative residuals may show some spatial patterning not accounted for by the general trend, or they may relate to differences in the type of site. For example, for the distribution of some exchanged item, we might find that larger centres have larger residuals than other centres because of their redistributive function. On the other hand, the residuals may be unsystematic and appear to vary from the main regional trend by chance. In this case there is only one scale of trend and the randomly distributed, unexplained component can be termed 'noise' (Chorley and Haggett 1965, 207). Such variation may result from a number of different sources such as errors of identification and measurement, differences in the detail and care of excavation or field survey (although the last factor may cause trends at certain scales), and real variation in the data due to a great complexity of factors which can best be seen as random. A method for discerning whether regression residuals show any spatial pattern will be discussed in the following section.

The problem remains of how well a trend surface fits the data. This is an important consideration but tests of goodness-of-fit such as analysis of variance are not appropriate for an archaeological context since the assumptions necessary for the use of these tests cannot justifiably be made for most archaeological data. The correlation coefficient may provide a scale of increasingly good 'fit', but what values are to be considered as acceptable? Perhaps the most fruitful approach will prove to be by randomisation. By producing randomly generated data sets having the same range of values as the actual data we can obtain some idea of the likelihood of obtaining the observed correlation by chance. This method has been followed to a limited extent for the two-dimensional surfaces fitted to some middle Bronze Age palstave data (p. 121) and also to some data to be discussed below, but the whole matter will repay future investigation.

It is important to mention some of the problems associated with the use of trend surface analysis but which have not been discussed above. Most important is that there should be sufficient data points for the analysis. The number and spacing of these points have a direct influence on the scale of local patterning that can be detected. At an absolute minimum, the number of data points must exceed the number of coefficients in the polynomial equation (15 in a fourth degree (quartic) expansion) or the results of the regression are invalid (Davis 1973, 349).

A difficulty to be encountered below occurs when the data points do not extend to the edges of the map area (see figs. 5.55 and 5.56 for example). In this case the surface trends are extrapolated outwards to the edges of the map and may take on extreme values. It may, in certain cases, be possible to avoid these edge effects by including data points outside the boundary of the map area being studied.

The effects of the spatial arrangement of data points on the trend surface analysis have been investigated by Doveton and Parsley (1970). First a second-degree (quadratic) trend surface was constructed with

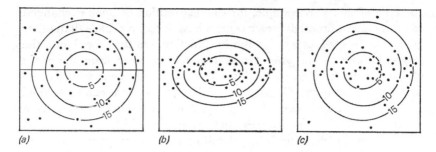

(a)   *(b)*   *(c)*

Fig.5.50. Influence of data-point distribution on trend
surfaces. (*a*) Original test surface with randomly placed data
points; (*b*) distorted trend produced by sampling original test
surface along a narrow band; (*c*) nearly correct trend produced
by adding a few outlying points to the narrow band of
observations. Numbers in the diagrams indicate values on the
fitted trend surfaces. Source: Davis 1973.

randomly spaced data points (fig.5.50*a*). Tests were then run to examine
the effect of having different arrangements of data points. For example,
if the data points are along a central band (*b*) the form of the fitted
surface is rather different from the original pattern. It is only necessary
to have a few points outside the band for the fitted surface to correspond
more closely to the first (*c*). Similarly, in fig.5.51 a test surface has been
constructed and clustered data points taken to see if this surface can be
reproduced from them. The data points and the fitted surfaces produced by using them are shown in fig.5.51*b* and *c*. In both cases the
fitted surface is closely similar to the test pattern. Although these
experiments suggest that the effects of clustered data points may not
always be serious, they were carried out for idealised models without
local random 'noise', and more severe distortions are to be expected in
the presence of local variation. The effects of clusters of data points are
further discussed by Gray (1972).

5.4.2 *Application to archaeological data*

The value of applying the regression type of trend surface analysis to
archaeological data can be examined by using the comparatively
reliable and well-studied set of data which was taken for some two-
dimensional regression analysis (p. 115). These data are the percentages of Romano-British fine pottery from the Oxford kilns found at
sites in England. Twenty-nine data points are available, the information for each being the two grid co-ordinates of the site and the percentage of pottery found there. The trend surface program used and
run on the Cambridge University IBM 370 is that supplied by Davis
(1973, 332–5). This program fits a polynomial trend of specified

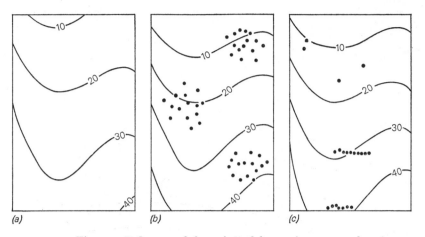

Fig.5.51. Influence of clustering of data points on trend surfaces.
(*a*) Original third-degree test surface; (*b*) trend surface obtained
from data points placed in clusters on the test surface;
(*c*) trend surface obtained from data points located along
traverses across parts of test surface. Source: Davis 1973.

degree, calculates the predicted and residual values of Z for each data
point and the correlation coefficient, and plots out a contoured map of
the fitted surface. The maps to be shown in the following diagrams are
derived directly from the computer print-out.

In studying the distribution of the Oxford products, it seemed
useful to examine the structure of the pattern and to see the effect of
fitting trend surfaces of different orders. In fig.5.52 a surface of second
degree (quadratic) has been fitted to the data. This clearly picks out the
main east–west trend that was noticed in an earlier study and related
to the main river system. It also brings out the fact that this central
east–west axis is more strongly weighted westwards. There is no
indication of the effect of the contemporary New Forest industry on the
pattern, however. The correlation coefficient for the 'fit' of the surface
is 0.84 and was considered sufficiently high so as not to warrant further
examination. The second degree surface, then, identifies the main
regional trend. Much the same is true for the third-degree (cubic)
trend surface (fig.5.53). This provides little more detail although the
high percentages to the east are brought into the picture. With the
fourth-degree (quartic) trend, however, the results are more complex
and the effect of the few more northerly sites is to produce some rather
extreme patterns. These sites seem to have exerted a greater influence
than is perhaps desirable. On the other hand, the fourth-degree surface
is sufficiently sensitive to pick up the lower values of Oxford pottery in
the area around the competing centre in the New Forest. It is of
interest that the main concentration of finds from this latter centre is to

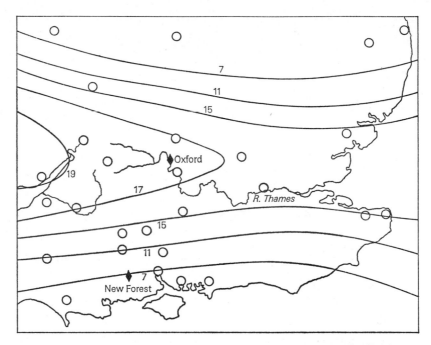

Fig.5.52. Second-degree trend surface fitted to the distribution of Romano-British Oxford products. Sites shown as circles. New Forest and Oxford kilns (◆) indicated. Numbers in the diagram indicate predicted values for the percentages of Oxford pottery according to the fitted trend surface.

the west of the kilns and it is to the west also that the low values on the trend surface occur. This surface provides a good fit to the data, and the residuals show no spatial patterning. Neither can their magnitude be correlated with the type of site involved. They may be seen then as the result of random 'noise' to which differences in excavation techniques must contribute a large part.

A close look at figs.5.52 to 5.54 brings out some of the problems associated with the use of polynomial surfaces. For example, all three show a 'peak' in the distribution in the Severn/South Wales area, 5.53 (third-degree surface) shows a secondary peak in the east Kent/English Channel area, while 5.54 (fourth-degree surface) shows a 'plateau' stretching away into East Anglia. In no case is the Oxford kiln area at the peak of the fitted surface, which must cast doubt on the ability of the method to predict an unknown centre. While these anomalies can be partly explained by 'edge effects' (see p. 163), they also reflect the unsuitability of polynomial surfaces for dealing with distributions which have relatively few data points scattered irregularly over a wide area. Such surfaces are better at approximating to an unknown surface over a relatively small area. Just as in the two-dimensional case

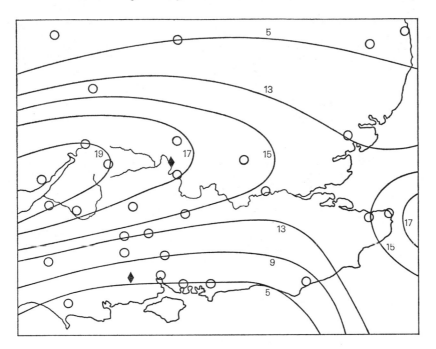

Fig.5.53. Third-degree trend surface fitted to the distribution of Romano-British Oxford products. Symbols as for fig.5.52.

(section 5.1), some transformation of the data might be useful. A different way of looking at the distributions would be to use polar co-ordinates (with the kilns taken as the origin), and express the trend surface in the form

$$Z = f(d, \theta) \tag{5.5}$$

where d represents the distance from the kiln to a site, and θ the direction. The relationship between Z and d would reflect the fall-off rate and any observed relationship between Z and θ would indicate directional differentiation. This approach could not be used if the position of the kiln was unknown. The 'plateau' of fig.5.54 seems to be due to the lack of sites in this area – even one value here could alter the picture dramatically.

A second example uses prehistoric material from the early Bronze Age. The aim is to examine whether, from a complex pattern, the degree of localisation of manufacture and dispersal, and the structure of local and regional trends can be obtained. The data consist of measurements taken on 67 spearheads of the Bagterp type in Scandinavia and North Germany studied by Jacob-Friesen (1967). This type of spearhead is socketed and is often highly decorated towards the base of the socket. Other decoration which sometimes occurs consists of a row of

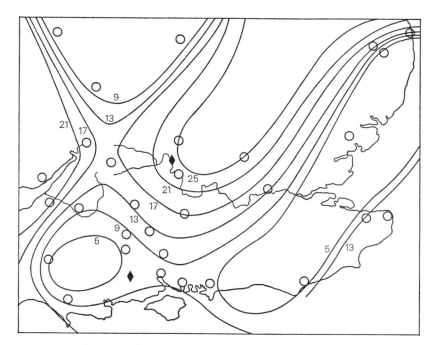

Fig.5.54. Fourth-degree trend surface fitted to the distribution of Romano-British Oxford products. Symbols as for fig.5.52.

points bordering the shaft along the blade face. Measurements taken on 67 of these spearheads were used to construct a length/breadth index which is defined as (*ibid.*, 90) (greatest breadth × 100)/greatest length. This index was shown by Jacob-Friesen to vary considerably about a mean but there was no attempt made to examine the spatial structure of the variation. Were the spearheads made in one centre and traded over the area, or did the type diffuse as an idea, with much local manufacturing, and what was the scale of this local production? Although there are other ways of tackling this problem (section 5.5), one approach is to use trend surface analysis.

The fourth-degree surface which best fits the data is shown in fig.5.55. Since the scatter of data points does not reach the edge of the map, some marked 'edge-effects' occur (p. 163). Some local areas are suggested, some of which indicate coastal trends. Since the correlation coefficient is only 0.49 caution should be exercised in interpreting the pattern, although, as will be shown, the patterning can be substantiated by the distribution of other traits on the spearheads. The residuals from the fourth-degree surface are shown in fig.5.56. These suggest some spatial patterning not picked up by the regional trend. The sample is perhaps too small over too large an area to be able to identify confidently highly localised patterning. Indeed this does not seem possible

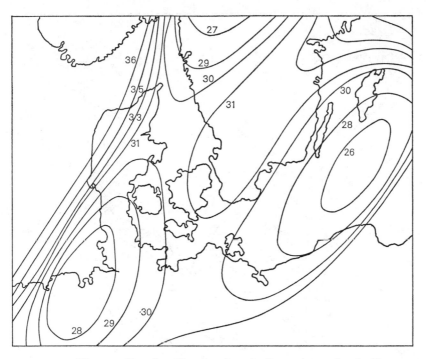

Fig.5.55. Trend surface fitted to the Bagterp spearheads. For data points see fig.5.56.

for part of the area. Some areas of high and low residuals do seem to occur, however, and some of these are extremely small. Coastal trends, especially of negative residuals, are detectable.

Some degree of localisation can be seen in other aspects of the spearheads. For example, no decorated examples are found in north Germany (*ibid.*, map 1), while the Danish and northern Bagterp spearheads nearly always occur in graves. In north Germany they occur in hoards. The decoration on the spearheads is quite varied (*ibid.*, 92) and a study of this allowed Jacob-Friesen to suggest some spatial patterning. For example, the decoration is richer in Sweden, Norway, the large Danish Islands and north Jutland, than it is in middle and south Jutland (*ibid.*, 93). It is thus of interest that this latter area is picked up in both figs.5.55 and 5.56. In certain cases pairings of extremely similar decorated spearheads could be made which were separated on the ground by distances on the scale of the smaller groupings suggested in fig.5.56. The spatial variation in decoration was discussed by Jacob-Friesen in terms of workshop areas. His findings would certainly seem to be corroborated by the quantitative and rather more objective approach followed here.

Another example of the use of trend surface analysis on archaeological

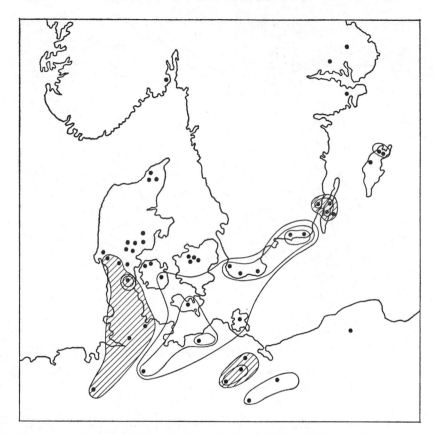

Fig.5.56. Residuals from the trend surface in fig.5.55. Areas
of positive residuals shaded. Areas of negative residuals
contoured.

data attempts to throw some light on the study of the late La Tène in
an area including Trier along and to the south of the Moselle. Mahr
(1967) has plotted the distribution of a number of pottery types in this
area at this time. One such distribution is that of the percentage thrown
on a fast wheel amongst the wheel-thrown and hand-made pottery at a
site (fig.5.57). Percentages were counted at 27 sites. Mahr noted that
sites farther south from the Moselle had higher percentages of this
pottery, and this distribution was used to support an argument concerning the origin of the technique of using a fast wheel. Hawkes had
suggested that the Marne area obtained the fast wheel first from the
Rhineland together with cremation and certain other ceramic types,
while Marien has suggested, for the Belgian use of the fast wheel, a
transfer from the east and southeast, probably from the Rhineland.
Mahr, on the other hand, suggested that the sporadic appearance of the
slower but older wheel in the area between the Marne, Thuringia and

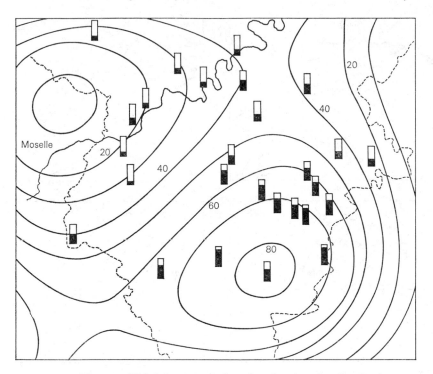

Fig.5.57. Third-degree trend surface fitted to the distribution of La Tène wheel-made pottery. The percentage of this pottery at each site is indicated by the filled part of the vertical bars.

Middle Danube could not have any causal relationship with the development of the fast wheel in the Trier area, and could not suggest an eastern influence (*ibid.*, 63). He looked in preference to the west and south for the necessary influences both for this and other elements of the late La Tène culture in his area. From the evidence of his maps 'the conclusion is clear, that the "progressivity" of the bearers of our culture lagged behind in the remoter, mountainous areas south of the Mosel, and especially in the Hochwald' (*ibid.*, 57).

Mahr was concerned with spatial trends which seemed to have a chronological significance and which could be used to support theories about the origin of new influences in his study area. No attempt was made, however, to examine these regional trends on a systematic basis. Trend surface analysis supplies such a basis, and it has been applied to the map discussed above (fig.5.57). The correlation coefficient for the fit of the third-degree surface is 0.89. The trend surface fitted to the percentage of wheel-thrown pottery confirms the regional trend described by Mahr, the more northerly areas having lower values. The data cannot, however, as suggested by Mahr, really support the hypothesis of an origin to the southwest.

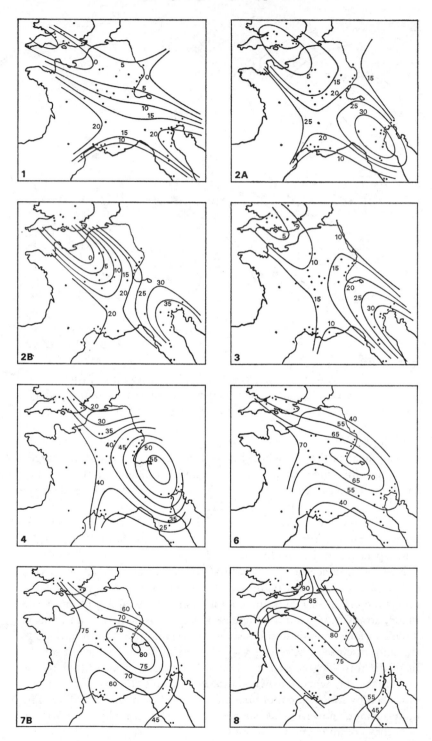

Trend surface analysis has also been applied to data for the distribution of coins in the western Roman Empire. The percentage of coin types at sites has been assessed for the twelve phases from 27 B.C. to 259 A.D. outlined by Reece (1973). A study of the spatial variation of these percentages (Hodder and Reece, unpublished) concentrated on the percentages of sestertii amongst the total sestertii and lower-value middle-range bronze coins (dupondii, asses and folles). The aim of the study was to see if any interesting regularities could be noted in the spatial variation of these percentages through time. It was also hoped that some sites would have high residuals from the fitted trend surfaces at all periods, and that this would throw light on the nature of money flows in the Roman world.

Figures 5.58 to 5.65 show the third-degree trend surfaces fitted to the percentages of sestertii at different time periods. The lowest correlation coefficient obtained for these data was compared with randomised data (Hodder and Reece, unpublished and see p. 163). Moving from map to map it is clear that the high points on the trend surfaces (that is the areas with highest percentages) gradually shift across Europe from north Italy to England. In phase 1 the high point is in north Italy with a spread westwards. In phases 2*a*, 2*b* and 3 this high percentage area expands a little towards the Rhine. In 2*b* there is a fairly sharp fall-off in percentages away from north Italy, but by 3 this has spread to produce a smoother fall-off. In phase 4 the high point is no longer in Italy and by 6 it has moved to the upper Rhine area. By phase 7*b* there is a sharper fall-off between the upper Rhine and north Italy. In phase 8 there is less spatial variation, with all areas having high percentages of sestertii relative to middle-bronze coins, but the high point on the trend surface has moved to England.

High levels of sestertii relative to lower value coins may perhaps be taken as indications of inflation, with coins of greater value becoming more used. If this is the case the movement across Europe indicated by the maps may reflect the spread of inflation from Italy to England. It is of interest that the route followed is along the Danube–Rhine military frontier rather than across central France. The greatest inflows of money in the Empire were those that went to pay the army. Thus it is at the frontier zones that any attempt to control money flows or compensate for changes in local money values would have had the greatest impact.

The same point is of interest in regard to the regression residuals. A number of sites have positive residuals on all the trend surfaces. At all

---

Figs.5.58 to 5.65. Third-degree trend surfaces fitted to the percentages of sestertii at sites in the western Roman Empire at different time periods. The phases are indicated in bold type on each figure.

periods, then, they have higher percentages of sestertii than is expected from the overall trend. These residuals do not show much spatial patterning, but they do often seem to relate to one class of site – those with strong military connections. It is to such sites that larger numbers of sestertii travelled.

The application of trend surface analysis to the Roman coin data has allowed a spatial process of spread to be identified and has helped to suggest reasons for the form that the diffusion took.

Trend surface analysis, in spite of the difficulties associated with its use, can sometimes provide a systematic and relatively objective or at least well-defined way of finding pattern in the often complex archaeological data. In particular it allows regional trends to be distinguished from more local ones. This may often have immediate significance for the interpretation of the data.

5.5 *Spatial autocorrelation*

There are a large number of situations in which the archaeologist wishes to know if the distribution of some variable has a spatial structure. In the diffusion of an artifact or a style, in the dispersal of objects through redistributive centres and in the density of artifacts across a site, he may wish to know whether the values of the variable are distributed haphazardly, at random, or whether the value of the variable at one point is related to values at nearby points. For example, in fig.5.66 is shown the distribution of the length/breadth index for the Bagterp spearheads discussed in the previous section (5.4). This is clearly a complex pattern and the shape of the spearheads may have no spatial structure. The correlation coefficient for the trend surface that was fitted was not high, and it is not immediately apparent to the eye that much spatial structure exists. Are the values of this index placed randomly or do they show some pattern which could then be interpreted? Similarly, light would be thrown on the controversy (Binford 1972; Bordes 1973) over the interpretation of the Mousterian industries in southwest France if it could be shown that the percentage of a tool type at one site was closely related to the percentage of that tool at nearby sites. Other tool types might show no spatial structure or a structure of a different sort. 'If the presence of some quality in a county of a country makes its presence in neighbouring counties more or less likely, we say that the phenomenon exhibits *spatial autocorrelation* . . . It is also possible to test for spatial autocorrelation among variate values collected at points' (Cliff and Ord 1973, 1). If the archaeologist can detect spatial autocorrelation amongst his data, which are often highly distorted by survival factors so that clear patterning is not easy to distinguish, then he has something to explain and interpret. Rather than be led into interpretations of chance patterning it is important that the existence of

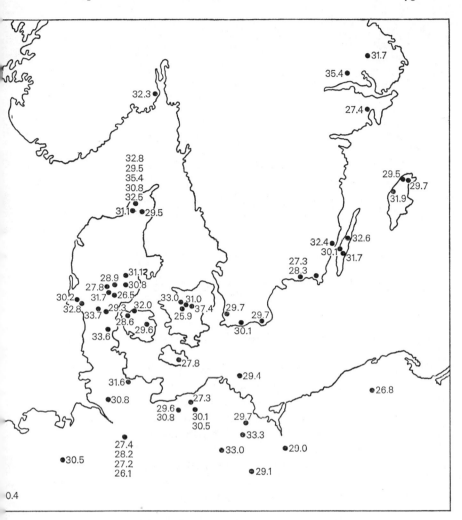

Fig.5.66. The distribution of the length/breadth index for the Bagterp spearheads.

structure should be exhibited. For such problems spatial autocorrelation methods are appropriate.

5.5.1 *The methods*

Davis (1973, 232–46) discusses autocorrelation in time series, itself an interesting field for the archaeologist. The present account is confined to spatial autocorrelation and is derived from the study by Cliff and Ord (1973). The measures of spatial autocorrelation are the same whether a variable value has been obtained for 'counties' or some other

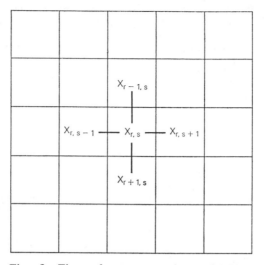

Fig.5.67. First-order autoregressive model for a regular lattice. Heavy solid lines indicate joins.

unit, or for data points, and no distinction will be made in the following discussion.

The value of variable X in county i is called x_i. If, for every pair of counties (or points) i and j in the study area, x_i and x_j are uncorrelated, then there is said to be no spatial autocorrelation. Conversely, spatial autocorrelation exists if the values are not all pairwise uncorrelated. Let us consider a regular lattice with R rows and S columns (fig.5.67). A simple autoregressive model for such a lattice, considering only interactions between cells with a common edge, would be

$$x_{r,s} = ax_{r-1,s} + bx_{r+1,s} + cx_{r,s-1} + dx_{r,s+1} + e_{r,s},   (5.6)$$

where a, b, c and d are parameters and $e_{r,s}$ is random disturbance.

The tests for spatial autocorrelation which are now described can be discussed according to the kind of data (nominal, ordinal or interval scaled) for which they may be used. An example of nominal data is a binary classification in which, if a county has some quality present it is colour-coded black (B), and if it has not, the county is colour-coded white (W). If two counties or cells have a boundary in common then they are said to be *joined*. A join between two B counties is called BB, between two W counties WW, and a BW join links a black and white county. To determine whether the presence or absence of the variable in neighbouring counties is spatially autocorrelated or not, we count the numbers of BB, BW and WW joins which occur in the study area, and compare these numbers with the expected numbers of BB, BW and WW joins we would expect under the null hypothesis of no spatial autocorrelation among the counties. Intuitively a 'lot' of BB joins implies some clustering of the B counties in the area.

It is also necessary to know whether a particular county or point is adjacent to another. For the moment we will put a weighting, $w_{ij} = 1$ if the i and j counties are joined, and $w_{ij} = 0$ otherwise. Other forms of 'weight' will be discussed below. Let $x_i = 1$ if the ith county is B, and $x_i = 0$ if the ith county is W. The observed number of BB joins in the study area is then defined as

$$BB = \tfrac{1}{2}\Sigma_{(2)}w_{ij}x_ix_j \tag{5.7}$$

and the observed number of BW joins is given by

$$BW = \tfrac{1}{2}\Sigma_{(2)}w_{ij}(x_i - x_j)^2 \tag{5.8}$$

where

$$\Sigma_{(2)} = \sum_{\substack{i=1 \\ i \neq j}}^{n} \sum_{j=1}^{n} \tag{5.9}$$

The observed number of WW joins is given by

$$WW = W - (BB + BW) \tag{5.10}$$

where

$$W = \Sigma_{(2)}w_{ij} \tag{5.11}$$

Cliff and Ord (1973, 153) have shown that, for binary data of the type discussed above, BW performed better than BB. Commonly, however, we wish to code the counties in more than one of two ways. Each possible value may then be assigned one of k colours. We can then proceed to count the number of joins between counties of (1) the same colour (2) two different colours, and (3) all counties of different colours. Each of these cases is studied as for the case when $k = 2$.

> The usual method employed to determine whether BB, BW and WW depart significantly from random expectation is to use the fact that these join count statistics are asymptotically normally distributed, and to assume that these results hold approximately for moderate sized lattices. The first two moments of the coefficients are then used to specify the location and scale parameters of the normal distribution [*ibid.*, 5].

The evaluation of these parameters for two colour and k colour cases is given by Cliff and Ord (*ibid.*).

Dacey (1973) has applied these methods to archaeological data. He was able to discern the degree of patterning in the distributions of end-scrapers, carinated scrapers and burins at the Sole Divshon site. As he points out, the results of this type of analysis are dependent on the size of cell used.

For ordinal data, in which the rank of a value in a county is known, or for interval data, in which the value of X in each of n counties is known, there are two further coefficients which assess the degree of spatial autocorrelation between the x_i in joined counties. The first of these, I, is due to Moran (1950).

$$I = \frac{n\Sigma_{(2)}w_{ij}z_iz_j}{W\sum\limits_{i=1}^{n} z_i^2} \qquad (5.12)$$

where $z_i = x_i - \bar{x}$. The second coefficient, c, was suggested by Geary (1954).

$$c = \left(\frac{n-1}{2W}\right)\frac{\Sigma_{(2)}w_{ij}(x_i - x_j)^2}{\Sigma z_i^2} \qquad (5.13)$$

If $c = 1$ there is no spatial autocorrelation present, while values of c less than 1 indicate positive spatial autocorrelation and those greater than 1 indicate negative spatial autocorrelation. For interval data, I has been found to perform better than c, although this conclusion has only been validated for normal data (Cliff and Ord 1973, 153).

The significance of the departure of these statistics from the null hypothesis of no spatial autocorrelation can be evaluated under either of two assumptions:

1. Normality. Here we assume that the x_i are the results of n independent drawings from a normal population (or populations),

2. Randomisation. Whatever the underlying distribution of the population, we consider the observed value of I or c relative to the set of all possible values which I and c could take on if the x_i were repeatedly randomly permuted around the counties or sites. There are $n!$ such values. This second approach is clearly of greater value to the archaeologist. It is discussed in greater detail by Cliff and Ord (1973, 29).

Something more should be said on the choice of weights (w_{ij}) for the above equations. The types of weight chosen have a considerable effect on the results of the analysis and must therefore be in accordance with some prior considerations or hypotheses about the data. For example, if differenthypotheses are proposed about the degree of contact between neighbouring areas, different weights might be used to investigate these hypotheses. For data collected at points or sites we can consider some of the variety of weighting possible.

(1) $w_{ij} = 1$ if i and j are first nearest neighbours, $w_{ij} = 0$ otherwise.

(2) $w_{ij} = 1$ if i and j are first or second nearest neighbours, $w_{ij} = 0$ otherwise.

(3) $w_{ij} = d_{ij}^{-a}$ where d_{ij} is the distance between i and its nearest neighbour j, and $w_{ij} = 0$ otherwise. a is an exponent which may be set to 1 or 2 for example.

(4) $w_{ij} = d_{ij}^{-a}$ if j is the first or second nearest neighbour of i, and $w_{ij} = 0$ otherwise.

In a county system, let the proportion of the perimeter of county i which is in contact with j be $\beta_{i(j)}$, and exclude from the perimeter of i those parts which coincide with the boundary of the study area. We might then wish to use a weight which takes into account this measure of join as well as the distance between the centre of the two counties (or rooms on a site, for example). Thus w_{ij} might be set to

$$w_{ij} = d_{ij}^{-a}(\beta_{i(j)})^b \tag{5.14}$$

Different values may be chosen for the exponents a and b, or particular values may be preferred according to the specific hypothesis being tested. Since the choice of weights, w_{ij}, is often difficult it may be advisable to compute the autocorrelation measures using a number of different weights.

In the preceding section it was noted that a researcher may wish to examine maps of residuals from trend surfaces in order to see if they show any spatial patterning. The use of spatial autocorrelation measures to discern this patterning has been fully discussed by Cliff and Ord (1973).

5.5.2 *Application to archaeological data*

The first data used to examine the potential for spatial autocorrelation analysis of archaeological material are the measurements of early Bronze Age Bagterp spearheads discussed in the preceding section (5.4). Initially w_{ij} is set to 1 if the spearheads i and j are less than 1 cm apart on the map, this being approximately 66 km on the ground, $w_{ij} = 0$ otherwise. A programme written by Cliff and Ord was made available and this was adapted to calculate the value of w_{ij} between each pair of spearheads from their spatial co-ordinates. The results are that the expected value of I under the null hypothesis of no spatial autocorrelation is -0.015 and the observed value is 0.448. The expected value of c is, as always, 1.000, and the observed value is 0.549. Positive spatial autocorrelation is therefore detected and for both statistics this result is significant at $p = 0.01$ under the assumption of randomisation. This suggests that the value of the length/breadth index measured on one spearhead is related to the values on spatially close spearheads and that the values are not randomly intermingled in the map.

The spatial autocorrelation measures can also be used to construct spatial correlograms in which the way that the autocorrelation function between values of the variable decays over space can be examined. Thus the I statistic, for example, can be computed so that the degree of autocorrelation is assessed for increasing distances between spearheads:

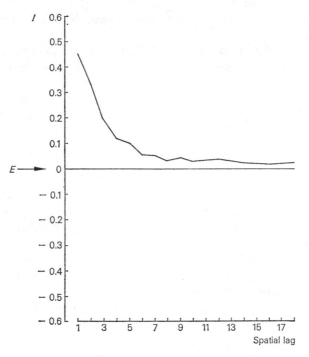

Fig.5.68. Bagterp spearheads. Correlogram for I.
E = expected value under null hypothesis.

w_{ij} is set to 1 for distances within a specified band, and 0 otherwise. The first band is 0–5 mm on fig.5.66 (0–33 km), the second 5–10 mm and so on. These distances are termed spatial lags. In this way we can see how the degree of spatial autocorrelation between spearhead shapes varies over space. The value of I for a number of spatial lags is shown in fig.5.68. It decreases rapidly until at distances greater than about 140 km no spatial autocorrelation can be detected. This very much suggests the scale of localised patterning indicated by the map of trend surface residuals in fig.5.56. The fact that the decrease in spatial autocorrelation occurs immediately at lag 2 in fig.5.68 suggests that the spearheads may have been manufactured (and perhaps dispersed) in very small areas, although broader regional similarities in shape also occur. The construction of spatial correlograms may provide much useful information for the archaeologist since alternative patterns to those in fig. 5.68 may be found. Other fall-off patterns which have been obtained by Cliff, Haggett and Ord (1974) show, for example, lags with negative autocorrelation and secondary peaks of positive autocorrelation. Such a pattern might result from a redistributive system of artifact dispersal in which areas around each centre have high percentages of the item and intermediate areas low percentages. For example, the distribution of Romano-British fine pottery could be

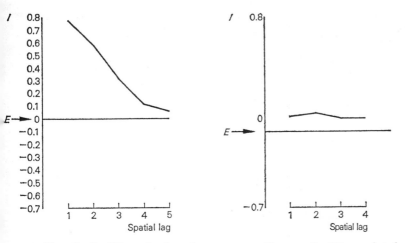

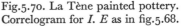

Fig.5.69. La Tène wheel-made pottery. Correlogram for *I*. E as in fig.5.68.

Fig.5.70. La Tène painted pottery. Correlogram for *I. E* as in fig.5.68.

examined in this way to try and identify clustering of high percentages around market centres.

Spatial correlograms have also been constructed for the distribution of late La Tène pottery in the Trier area which has already been discussed. The spatial lags used are at 2.54 cm intervals on the map. For the wheel-made pottery both *I* and *c* are significantly different from expected ($p = 0.01$) at lag 1, but fig.5.69 shows that this difference decays at increasing spatial lags. There is no evidence of redistribution in that no secondary peaks of high spatial autocorrelation and no zones of negative spatial autocorrelation are visible.

A similar analysis has been carried out of the painted pottery which occurs in the latest La Tène phase in the same Trier area (Mahr 1967, 57 and 78) (fig.5.70). This type is compared by Mahr with an older style of linear polish decoration. The relative percentages of the painted pottery amongst the painted and polish decorated pottery on sites of more than three occurrences of sherds could be obtained in 11 cases. The correlogram derived from these percentages shows no evidence of significant deviation from the null hypothesis of no spatial autocorrelation ($p = 0.05$). This indicates that in this small sample there is little evidence that the percentage values are spatially autocorrelated. It would therefore be difficult, for example, to justify the fitting of trend surfaces to these data. It may be advisable, always to carry out tests for spatial autocorrrelation prior to such trend surface analysis.

Tests for spatial autocorrelation have also been applied to the Roman coin data (Hodder and Reece unpublished; Reece 1973) discussed in section 5.4.2. The results for the percentages of sestertii amongst sestertii and middle-range bronze coins at the 56 sites are shown in

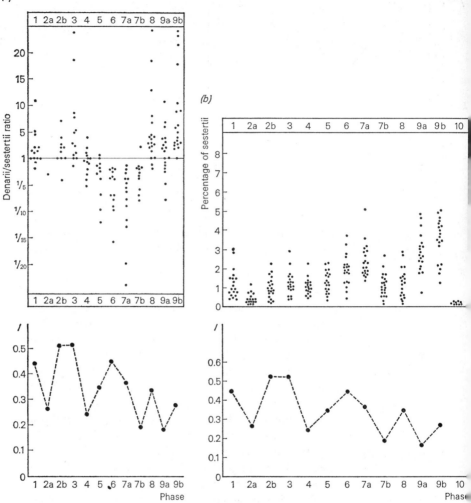

Fig.5.71. The bottom two graphs show changes in spatial autocorrelation (*I*) for the Roman coin distributions in phases 1 to 9*b*. These changes can be compared with:
(*a*) changes in the ratio between denarii (silver coins) and sestertii (bronze coins) in North France. Ratios with more denarii than a one to one ratio are above the central line.
(*b*) The upper graph shows the percentages of sestertii at Roman sites in north Italy. For the upper graphs in (*a*) and (*b*) see Reece 1973. Source: Hodder and Reece (unpublished).

fig.5.71 for each of the 12 periods. The variation in the spatial auto-correlation coefficients relates quite closely to variation in the composition of the money supply. This can be seen by comparing the graphs in fig.5.71. In fact the high levels of spatial autocorrelation occur whenever new trends develop – for example, when more coins of a particular type are flowing into the system. High levels of spatial autocorrelation can be interpreted as periods of contagion in which new trends are spreading through the Roman Empire – so that there is some spatial trend in the percentages of coin types at nearby sites. In intermediary periods, in which new developments are not spreading at such a rate, the values at nearby sites are less closely related.

The high levels of spatial autocorrelation in phases 2*b* and 3 (see section 5.4.2) relate to a period of high inflation with many denarii (silver coins) relative to bronze sestertii. This is brought to an end in phase 4 by Trajan's policy, which was possibly to withhold denarii. This temporary stoppage of money flow upsets the growing trend successfully.

The high level in phase 6 results from a gradually increasing deflation with many sestertii relative to denarii. The high point in phase 6 suggests that this was the period of greatest change even though the period of greatest inflation is in many places in phase 7*a*. Spatial autocorrelation decreases in 7*a* and 7*b* as inflation slowly increases.

The coinage debasement by Severus in phase 8 may have resulted in the inflow of many denarii into the system. Because there is this money flowing into the Empire, a peak of spatial autocorrelation occurs at this time.

It does seem that, in this case, measures of spatial autocorrelation are extremely sensitive to changes in the structure of spatial variation of an item. A rather different approach which does include an allowance for spatial autocorrelation effects, is to build a model incorporating both space and time dimensions. For example, let $p_i^k(t)$ denote the percentage of coin type k at location i at time t. A general model might be written as

$$p^k(t) = b_0 1 + b_1 p^k(t-1) + b_2 M p^k(t-1) + e(t) \quad (5.15)$$

where b_0, b_1, b_2 are parameters to be estimated by ordinary Least Squares, and M is a weights matrix with weights of the form outlined on p. 178. Residuals from the fitted model may indicate sites or areas which are earliest to adopt new trends and may provide further information about spatial processes since a time factor is included.

5.6 *Some factors affecting artifact distributions*

5.6.1 *Some important factors*

Up to this point in the discussion the spatial variation in an artifact type has been correlated only with distance and survival and recovery factors. This is a convenient oversimplification and some of the other factors affecting artifact distributions must now be considered. For example, a relatively greater amount of movement and interaction

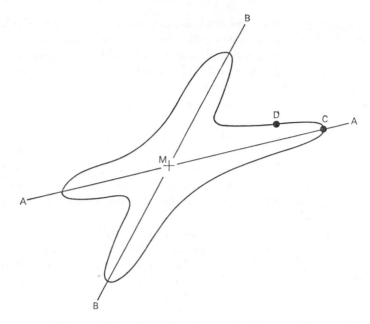

Fig.5.72. The effect of roads on a service area. Source: Alonso 1964.

might be expected along rivers or roads than over difficult terrain, and this may be visible in the archaeological distributions. For Roman Britain, the presence of a link by water to the Oxford kilns has already been shown to correspond to a relative increase in the amount of pottery obtained from there (p. 117). Similarly, marketing models often assume a circular trading area around the market centre. However, if we realise that roads exist only in some directions, then it is clear that transport costs will increase away from the marketing centre in an irregular fashion. In fig.5.72 is shown a hypothetical situation in which the curved line around the centre (M) joins points of equal transport costs. A–A and B–B are main roads, although a similar situation will occur with waterways. 'Although point D is nearer than C to M, it is as expensive to reach, since part of the travel must be over routes inferior to A–A' (Alonso 1964, 98). Figure 5.73 shows an example of this effect for a type of Romano-British coarse pottery (Hodder 1974*c*).

Another important factor affecting artifact distributions is the type or value of the artifact involved. This is similar to the concept of the range of a good (Abler *et al.* 1971) used by geographers in studies of interaction. The quantity of a good sold per person will decrease with distance from the centre as transport costs rise.

The range of a good can be defined as having a lower and upper limit (Berry and Garrison 1958*b*). The lower limit, or threshold, is the

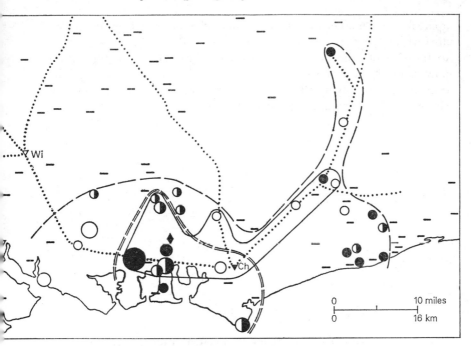

Fig.5.73. The distribution of jars with sharply everted rims
made in the Rowlands Castle kilns in the second and third
centuries A.D. These sometimes have batch marks incised on the
shoulder. The size of the circle at each site indicates the
percentage of the pottery type among the total coarse pottery.
◑, Assemblages of more than 30 sherds and including sherds
not from the second and third centuries; ●, assemblages of
more than 30 coarse-ware sherds and of second and third
century dates; ○, assemblages of less than 30 coarse-ware
sherds; ▽, walled towns, Winchester (Wi) and Chichester (Ch)
indicated; ◆, Rowlands Castle kilns. Dotted lines = roads;
double dashed lines = area of main concentration of finds;
single dashed line = total area of distribution; solid contour
line = area covered by jars with batch marks; horizontal
bars = contemporaneous sites without the pottery type.

minimum amount of purchasing power necessary for a place to supply
a central good. It is necessary to have a minimum amount of people or
demand for a good in a given area for a centre to provide that good. The
upper, or outer, limit may be seen as the point beyond which the price
of a good is too high to be sold because of transport costs, or because of
an alternative competing centre (Berry and Garrison 1958a).

The range of a good varies with local purchasing power, and the type
or value of the good. A centre providing goods which are costly, or
for which there is little demand, needs a wider area to obtain sufficient
purchasing power than does a centre providing commoner goods.
Certain goods are, therefore, only provided by centres located farther

apart from each other than smaller, more closely spaced centres. In an area with *n* types of good, we can rank the goods from 1 to *n* according to the size of area around a centre, or the amount of purchasing power, needed for the good to be supplied from that centre. The central place supplying all *n* goods will require the largest market area (in terms of the amount of purchasing power).

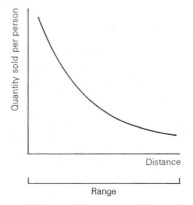

Fig.5.74. The range of a good as often used by geographers in studies of interaction. Source: Abler *et al.* 1971.

In Roman Britain there was a low and dispersed demand for the expensive service of installing a mosaic. As a result, the centres providing this service were widely spaced, and served a wide area (Hodder 1972). Roofing tiles, on the other hand, were in high demand. These were supplied by local, closely spaced centres to small areas. The ranges of the two goods differed considerably. The fine ware products of the late Romano-British Oxford, Nene valley and New Forest kilns cover much wider areas than the coarse-ware products made at a large number of local kilns (Hodder 1974*d*).

It seems that this same general model may be of importance in the analysis of prehistoric distributions. Objects of high value and/or low local demand might be expected to cover a wider area than objects which were of lesser value or which were used frequently. The 'value' of the artifact has been shown to be important as a factor causing variation in the curvature of a wide range of fall-off curves (section 5.2). In addition, the very coarse picrite hammer-axes of neolithic Britain have a much more localised distribution than the very fine axes of much harder rock from the Great Langdale source. Similarly, the neolithic Hembury 'f' ware made in Cornwall has a distribution comparable to the neolithic axes made in an adjacent area. The main difference, however, is that the bulky, fragile pottery is found much less widely than the axes.

Rowlands' (1970) study of middle Bronze Age metalwork in England showed that the spearheads and rapiers in this period have a distribution markedly different from the ornaments and palstaves. Localised groupings of types are not found, and the typological differences which can be identified do not relate to spatial differences. Each typological variation is found widely across southern England.

Sahlins (1972) has discussed the concept of relative value in primitive society and shown that, although it may appear similar to concepts in a more advanced supply and demand economy, the actual situation is much more complex. Nevertheless it would appear that range and value are important concepts for our understanding of archaeological distributions. 'The idea that, in both monetary and non-monetary economies, different commodities will move with unequal ease depending on their desirability, implies that long distance trade will tend to be limited to luxury durables that will retain a consistently high value' (Rowlands 1973, 595). 'Thus in many non-monetary economies, subsistence goods and particularly food-stuffs, that are widely available and do not travel well, tend to have a lower exchange value and a much narrower circuit of exchange (both in distance travelled and in their trade with other commodities) than durable, prestige or luxury items' (*ibid.*, 594). However, 'although goods can have an intrinsic value that may be expressed in a set of mutually accepted exchange rates with other goods in a network, desirability is not necessarily an absolute quality but can change in relation to factors like distance, mode of transport, freedom of exchange and accessibility to other exchange networks as alternative sources of goods' (*ibid.*).

In some cases such as the distribution of neolithic axes (Clark 1965) artifacts from one source have spread outwards without apparent regard to the location of other similar and contemporary centres. In other cases the location of competing centres does appear to affect patterns of movement. This possibility has been discussed by Bradley (1971) who provides a number of examples. In addition, the idea that interaction is more likely with the nearest centre than with any other similar centre, has recently been made explicit in a number of archaeological examples by the drawing of Thiessen polygons around hillforts (Cunliffe 1971*a*), Romano-British walled towns (Hodder 1972), neolithic long barrows (Renfrew 1973*a*), Mayan ceremonial centres (Hammond 1972) and Maltese temples (Renfrew 1973*b*). These Thiessen polygons simply enclose areas nearer to the site in question than to any other similar contemporary site.

5.6.2 *Gravity models*

Although it may be the case that interaction is more likely with the nearest centre than with any other similar centre this is only true if the two centres are of the same importance. One indication of importance is size. Larger centres tend to attract interaction from larger areas than smaller centres, so that the interaction (I) between centres i and j can be expressed as

$$I_{ij} = a\frac{P_i P_j}{D_{ij}{}^b}$$

(5.16)

in which P is the population or size of a centre, D_{ij} is the distance between them, and a and b are constants. The historical derivation of this model from Newtonian gravitational theory has been discussed by Carrothers (1956), although it can also be arrived at by an entropy maximising procedure (Wilson 1971). The b exponent is usually taken as 2 (Olsson 1965; Reilly 1931), although a value of 1 has also been used (Zipf 1949) and further studies have shown it to vary from less than 1 to 3.5 (Chisholm and O'Sullivan 1973; Olsson 1965). A value of 2 does however seem to be most appropriate in rural areas (Berry 1967, 41). Cliff, Martin and Ord (1974) have shown the effect of spatial autocorrelation on the evaluation of the friction of distance parameter (b) in gravity models.

Reilly has re-formulated the equation so that the boundary or breaking-point between the service areas of two adjacent towns of different size can be calculated. Thus, for two centres i and j, the distance from the breaking-point (x) to centre j (D_{xj}) is

$$D_{xj} = \frac{D_{ij}}{1 + \sqrt{\dfrac{P_i}{P_j}}}.$$

(5.17)

The terms can be explained by the following diagram.

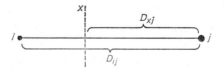

Thus the straight line distance between i and j is divided according to the population sizes of the two centres (P_i and P_j). By repeating the procedure for all towns adjacent to i, i's area of maximum influence can be estimated, although interaction, to a lesser and decreasing degree, will also occur outside this area.

There seems little point in applying this procedure generally to archaeological settlements such as hillforts when the relevance of the model cannot or has not been tested (Hogg 1971; Stanford 1972). There are cases, however, when such testing is possible. The distribution of early Romano-British Savernake ware has already been dis-

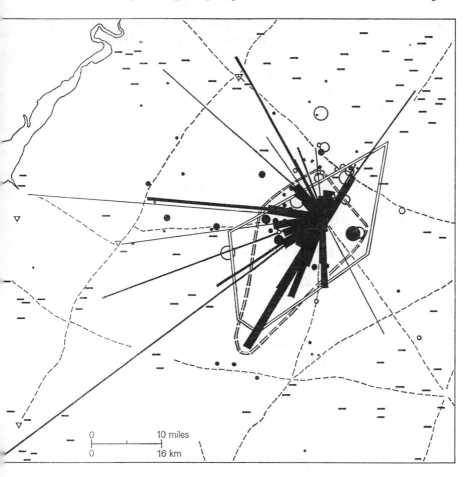

Fig.5.75. The distribution of early Romano-British Savernake
pottery. Radiating bars connect sites to the main marketing
centre at Mildenhall. Their width and the size of the circles
indicate the percentages of pottery found at sites.
Radiating bars = Sites with more than 30 coarse-ware sherds
and only first and second centuries A.D. pottery.
●, Sites with more than 30 sherds and more than first and
second centuries' pottery; ○, sites with less than 30 coarse-ware
sherds; ▽, walled towns.
Double dashed lines enclose the area covered by Savernake
ware lids; continuous double line = the market area of
Mildenhall predicted by the gravity model; dashed
lines = roads; horizontal bars = contemporaneous sites without
Savernake pottery. Source: Hodder 1974a.

cussed and its spatial distribution is shown in fig.5.75. The Savernake kilns, two miles south of the important centre of Mildenhall, produced a number of forms most of which are found over the whole area of distribution. The lids, however, cover a more restricted area which seems to correspond to the area around Mildenhall where high percentages of Savernake pottery are found. The Reilly breaking-point formula can be used to examine the hypothesis that this immediate marketing area corresponds to the market or service area of Mildenhall. The area of maximum influence predicted by the model according to the size and location of the neighbouring walled towns is shown in fig.5.75. It does seem to correspond quite closely to the area with high percentages of Savernake pottery and the area covered by the lids.

The same model has also been found to be of value in discussing the distribution of Romano-British types of pottery in southeast Hampshire and west Sussex (fig.5.76). The distribution of the products seems to be rather lop-sided in relation to the kilns. The hypothesis to be examined is that the observed pattern is in large part related to Chichester's market or service area. Chichester is an important walled town of cantonal capital status. Equation 5.17 has been used to predict the market area around the town of Chichester according to the size and location of neighbouring walled towns. Clearly this assumes that Winchester, for example, was marketing products at the same time and in competition with Chichester, and that the size (acreage) of the centres reflects their varying attractiveness.

In the late third and fourth centuries A.D., competition from neighbouring large kiln centres, such as the New Forest and Alice Holt, may have affected the distributions of these pottery types from southeast Hampshire (which are mainly of second and third century date). However, the hypothesis of competition from neighbouring towns, as examined by Reilly's model, does seem to explain rather well aspects of the distribution such as the marked westerly fall-off in finds and the general eastward bias. It may well be, therefore, that an important part of the distribution of products from the Rowlands Castle area in southeast Hampshire relied on the marketing mechanisms centred on Chichester. These mechanisms may have involved sale in the market at Chichester, or in addition, sale in the surrounding minor markets connected to the main market at Chichester by traders or pedlars moving according to some cycle of market days, in what is termed a periodic ring (Berry 1967, 94).

The gravity models may also be used to examine the relationship between the distributions of fine late Romano-British pottery from the Oxford kilns (p. 115) and of similar pottery from the New Forest centre (Fulford and Hodder 1974). It has already been shown that the New Forest kilns appear to affect the distribution of the Oxford pottery (p. 119). The graph in fig.5.77 shows the percentages of Oxford and New

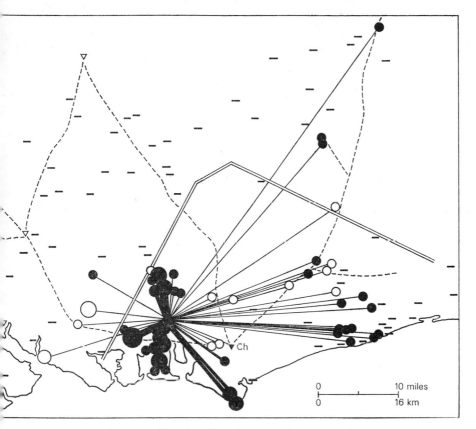

Fig.5.76. The distribution of two jar types made in the
Rowlands Castle kilns in the second and third centuries A.D.
The size of circle indicates the percentage of the jar types
amongst the total coarse pottery at each site. The sites are
connected by bars to Rowlands Castle.
▽, ▼, Walled towns. Chichester (Ch) is indicated.
Straight double lines = Chichester's market area as predicted
by the gravity model; horizontal bars = contemporaneous
assemblages without this pottery type. Source: Hodder 1974*d*.

Forest products on sites where they are both found (data supplied by
M. Fulford). Since all the sites are not on a straight line between Oxford
and the New Forest, the distance from each site is expressed as a ratio
of the total distance to both centres. The two patterns of fall-off show a
symmetrical relationship with distance which is to be expected in this
case because at each site the total percentage of fine wares from the two
centres is very constant.

   More interesting is that the point where the two curves cross, that is
where the percentages from each centre are equal, is not at the mid-
point between them, but in real terms is 62.8 km from the Oxford kilns

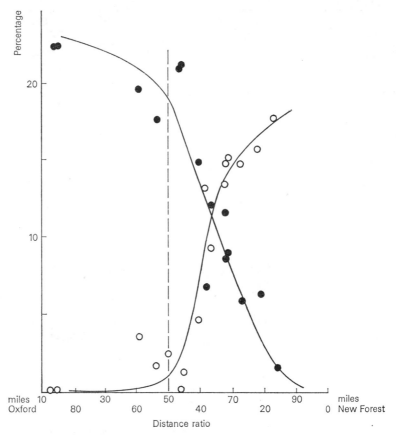

Fig.5.77. The percentages of Oxford (●) and New Forest (○) pottery on sites where they are both found. Dashed line = the mid-point between the two kiln centres. Source: Fulford and Hodder 1974.

and 34 km from the New Forest centre. The New Forest products are therefore predominant in a smaller area than the Oxford products. Its more restricted distribution can be seen by comparing its regression curve in fig.5.11. This difference in distribution can be adequately explained in terms of the difference in size of the two centres using Reilly's breaking-point formula. The size of the two centres can be roughly determined as the area containing the known kilns producing fine wares (Swan 1973, fig.1; Young 1973, fig.1). It is probable that further kilns will be found, but it seems unlikely that the total area covered will be significantly altered. According to Reilly's model, the distance from the Oxford kilns to the trade area boundary or 'breaking-point' should be

$$D_{x_{0x}} = \frac{96.6}{1 + \sqrt{(19.9/51.2)}} \text{ km} = 61.2 \text{ km} \qquad (5.18)$$

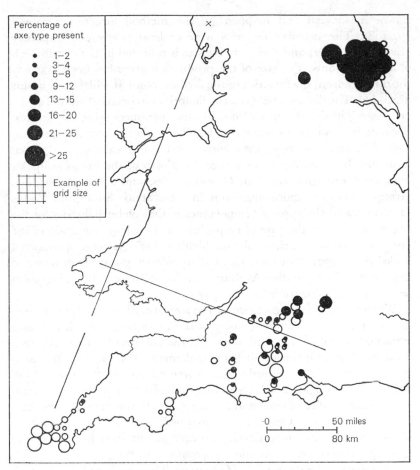

Fig.5.78. The distribution of Group I (○) and Group VI (●) neolithic axes from their respective sources in the southwest and northwest of England. The size of circle shows the percentage of axe type present in those grid cells for which sufficient data exist. The dashed line joins the two sources, and the continuous straight line indicates the boundary or breaking point between the areas supplied by the two sources as predicted by the gravity model. Source: Hodder 1974a.

This result is very close to the actual location of the breaking-point at 62.8 km from the Oxford kilns. This close correspondence encourages the suggestion that the relative importance of the two production concerns is reflected in the area size estimated for the centres, and that the observed uneven pattern of distribution of the products in the area between the centres is the result of competition.

The breaking-point model can also be applied to prehistoric data, for example the distribution of Group I and Group VI neolithic axes shown in fig.5.78 and mapped by the method already examined (p. 108). The two axe factories were at least partly contemporary (Evens *et al.* 1962) and their relative size is reflected in the distribution of axe rough-outs. The size of the production areas has been taken as the distance from the factories to the farthest point at which rough-outs are found. The distance between the factories has been calculated as the crude straight-line distance although other measures using the shortest distance by land gave similar results. The predicted breaking-point as shown in fig.5.78 appears to correspond quite well to the actual boundary between the two trade areas. North of the line, Group VI axes are more common than Group I axes, and south of the line, Group I axes are more numerous in most areas. Stone and Wallis (1951) stressed the apparent importance of the Avebury district for the axe trade. It was 'the capital emporium of the whole axe trade of the country. No other district or site has yielded so wide a range of imported rocks' (*ibid.*, 132). However, this variety of rock groups may occur at least partly because the Avebury district is on the breaking-point between two major trade areas.

When some reliable measure of the size of settlement clusters, such as the area covered or the density of sites, can be obtained, it is also possible to use equation 5.16 to predict the pattern of contact between clusters. The number of sites in settlement clusters, and the area covered, depend to a considerable degree on the relative intensity of fieldwork. In well-studied areas this difficulty can perhaps be minimised. The density of male and female graves in the early Bronze Age, period 2, in north Germany, as mapped by Bergmann (1970), is shown in fig.5.79. These density groupings, obtained from a square grid placed over the distribution, correspond to Bergmann's typological divisions of the material (*ibid.*, map 2). The number of sites in each group can be used as an approximate measure of the relative importance or size (P) of that group. The amount of interaction (I) between each pair of groups (i and j) is inversely proportional to the distance between their centres (D_{ij}) and directly proportional to their size, as in equation 5.16 (b set to 2). The pattern of contact predicted in this way (fig.5.79) does relate to much of the apparent 'distortion' and unevenness of the artifact distributions in the area (p. 215). Atkinson (1972) has also shown that gravity models might be used to indicate areas where there is a higher potential for contact. He suggests that in such areas there may be more cultural change. However, he also points out that if all the sites used for the analysis are not contemporaneous or if further fieldwork produces more sites, the results of the analysis can be seriously affected.

The gravity models would seem, then, to be generalisations which can be extended back into early historic and prehistoric contexts, and which seem adequately to account for some of the patterning in artifact

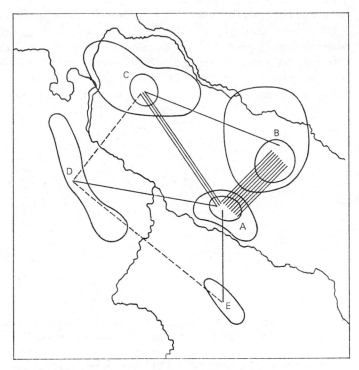

Fig.5.79. The predicted pattern of interaction between north German early Bronze Age site clusters. The density clusters are labelled and are referred to in fig.6.6.

distributions. An interesting further application is provided by Tobler and Wineburg (1971) and Clarke (1972, 50) has pointed to the potential of the model for within-site patterns.

5.6.3 *Social variability*

A further factor which might be thought to play a part in determining archaeological patterns is that of cultural or social bonds. It might be supposed that there is relatively greater contact within social units than across their boundaries, and this prediction has been made by Clarke (1968) in a review of some ethnographic material. Soja (1971) further suggests that territorial behaviour produces discontinuities and 'plateaus' in normally expected patterns of spatial interaction (fig.5.80). 'Territoriality is associated with a concentration of activities and communication within localised areas, inserting boundaries as it were into normal distance-decay relationships' (*ibid.*, 34). Even if Soja is correct in his assumption, it seems that archaeological material seldom reflects such patterning. It has been shown that the relative distance an artifact moves can often be related to its type or value. Ethnographic evidence confirms that there are many mechanisms for between-group exchange so that, given a broad archaeological view, objects and, therefore, perhaps styles and fashions (see for example Driver and Massey 1957) may move unhindered across social divisions. For this reason, archaeological artifact distributions can be satisfactorily or adequately discussed in terms of simple spatial mechanisms such as

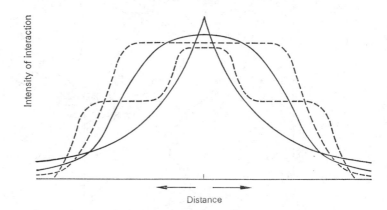

Fig.5.80. The effect of territorial behaviour on normally expected patterns of spatial interaction. Source: Soja 1971.

those outlined in sections 5.6.1 and 5.6.2. Sahlins (1972) has shown that spatial models and concepts derived from supply and demand economies are inadequate for understanding the underlying principles of primitive exchange. It may be the case that, as more evidence becomes available, simple distance-based models will have to be revised by the archaeologist.

Much present evidence, however, suggests that patterning in archaeological distributions is the result of normal distance-decay principles. For example, Soja (1971) has put forward the view that at the boundary between the areas around adjacent centres there might be a recognisable difference between territorial (fig.5.81*b*) and non-territorial (fig.5.81*a*) behaviour. This can be examined for archaeological data by plotting the distributions of late Iron Age Dobunnic coins around Bagendon and Cunobelin coins around Verulamium. These distributions have long been assumed (Allen 1944; Radford 1954; Rivet 1964) to be clear archaeological examples of tribal or cultural groupings. However, if we take a broad transect from Bagendon to Verulamium and assess the density of coins in sections along this transect, the pattern of fall-off from the two centres clearly does not suggest 'territorial' behaviour. In both cases (fig.5.82) there is a gradual decrease in density, with the Dobunnic coin distance-decay relationship being a good example of a type of random walk curve (section 5.3). Hogg (1971) has found a similar pattern of gradual

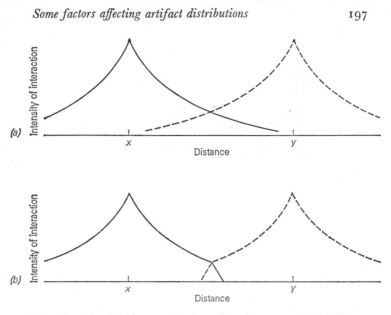

Fig.5.81. The significance of a boundary in non-territorial (*a*) and territorial (*b*) behaviour. Source: Soja 1971.

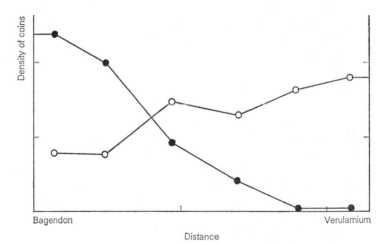

Fig.5.82. The fall-off in the density of Dobunnic coins (●) with distance from Bagendon, and Cunobelin coins (○) from Verulamium.

fall-off in discussing the relationship between the Dobunnic and Durotrigian areas. It is possible, however, that any sharp boundaries which did exist in the distributions have been disturbed due to the lack of detailed archaeological information. Changing boundaries at different dates may have produced a blurred aggregate pattern. This is a problem which can only await further study and more detailed chronologies.

6
The association between distributions

In the previous chapters, interest has centred on the pattern exhibited by the distribution of settlements or of a single artifact type. The factors controlling and determining pattern, however, are likely to affect many distributions in an area rather than just one, and much may be learned by investigating the way in which distributions are associated with one another. If two co-occurring distributions are affected by the same environmental factors, or if they have some effect, either of attraction or repulsion, on each other, their patterns will not be independent; the distributions will be associated, either positively or negatively. Association or the lack of it among pairs and groups of distributions is therefore of obvious archaeological interest. Some examples of the possible sorts of relationships between two point distributions are given in fig.6.1.

One context in which there has been increasing interest in spatial association is the distribution of tool types and other artifacts within a site (Dacey 1973; Whallon 1974). Co-occurrence in this situation might indicate 'tool kits' for example. Another area in which there is interest in association patterns is in the examination of archaeological cultures. Childe (1951, 40) defined the archaeological culture 'as an assemblage of associated traits that recur repeatedly'. Hodson (1962, 153) has used a similar definition. 'A classification into archaeological groups or "cultures" must start from an objective material basis, and in fact must simply recognise groups of types that are regularly associated together'. Clarke (1968) retains a similar emphasis on the recurring association of artifacts. 'An archaeological culture is a polythetic set of specific and comprehensive artifact-types which consistently recur together in assemblages within a limited geographical area' (*ibid.*, 285). Areas which have a degree of overlap of artifact distributions, termed here association groups, seem, therefore, to be the essence of archaeological cultures. In the sense in which it is used by Hodson (1964), only two or three generalised artifact types need to overlap in distribution

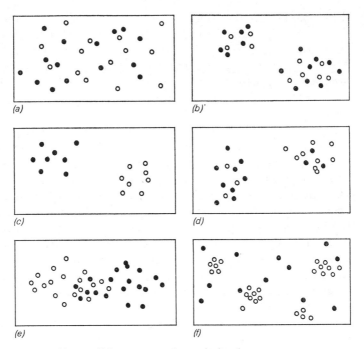

Fig.6.1. Six possible patterns of association between two
distributions. Source: Pielou 1961.

for a culture to be claimed. It has been noticed that the 'boundaries of
the several fields of culture do not necessarily coincide' (Childe 1951,
47). Different artifacts have different distributions, while Childe also
noted from anthropological and historical examples that there is often
a discrepancy between material culture and language or political
allegiance. In terms of distributions of artifacts, Clarke (1968) has,
therefore, preferred a polythetic definition. 'The available evidence
suggests that the individual distributions of the specific artifact-types
from one culture extend in irregular lobes in various differing directions,
many types also occurring as components in other cultural assemblages
in neighbouring areas, and vice versa' (*ibid.*, 248). These are all very
broad definitions, and there seems to be little clear idea of the structure
of archaeological cultures. Indeed, for some time there has been
considerable disillusion with the term. 'Are there really things called
cultures?' (Hawkes 1973, 177). It is not at all clear, in any case, what
archaeological cultures represent. 'Perhaps we might call its members
a people, but we should have no right to assume that this people as a
whole spoke a single language or acted as a political unit, still less that
all its members were related physiologically or belonged to one
zoological race' (Childe 1951, 49). There seems to have been little
development in the archaeological concept of culture since Childe's

definition, and for the moment the concept is too vague to be of value in interpreting archaeological material. There is clearly a need for the structure of archaeological cultures to be examined and defined. Hawkes (1973, 177), referring to the use of the term by English archaeologists, suggests that 'its popularity in English, owed largely to Gordon Childe, deserves a stricter analysis than it commonly seems to get'.

For both within-site and between-site association patterns it would be desirable if some degree of clarity and objectivity could be obtained in the analysis of often complex relationships. For example, in cases such as fig.6.1*d* it may be difficult to decide on the type and degree of association that occurs. This need for a more rigorous approach, especially when large amounts of data are being examined, has been felt in social anthropology where measures of association have been used to analyse the distribution of cultural traits (Driver 1961). Kluckhohn (1939) records that the approach in anthropology claims three things: first, an expression of distributional relationships more precisely and definitely than is possible verbally; second, the discovery of problems and clues not revealed by the usual ethnographic analysis; third, the reduction of the personal element in the treatment of data. It would clearly be desirable if these qualities could be introduced into archaeological analysis.

As an example of the value of a more rigorous approach, consider the following. Take a bounded surface and place a number of circular areas (for example circular discs) on to it, such that the centres of the circular areas are placed at random. Every point on the surface has an equal and independent chance of becoming the central point of an imposed circular disc. It is clear that in this pattern, there will be a number of areas of overlap which occur by chance. We have seen that a characteristic of archaeological distributions is that they often cover restricted but continuous areas. Even if the centres of these distributions are unrelated, because of their continuous nature, there will be much overlap and recurring association. In the case in which a number of distributions are located on a surface at random, there will be association groups (areas where a number of distributions overlap) which occur by chance. It will, in fact, generally be true that spatially close sites have similar assemblages. 'Random' association groups will be considered as 'cultures' if the accepted archaeological definition is used. The tests for spatial association to be discussed in this chapter allow us to determine whether two distributions are intermingled in such a way that they are comparable to two random distributions.

6.1 *Tests and measures of spatial association*

The methods available for the analysis of spatial association depend on the type of data being examined. The data may be in the form of measurements of two variables at a number of sites, or the presence and absence of two variables at sites or in quadrats of a grid. In the first instance, it is possible to use the correlation coefficient (r) to determine the degree of covariation between the two variables. This approach has been used in plant ecology (Greig-Smith 1964, 103) and extensively in geography (for example, Stewart and Warntz 1958; Warntz 1965). It has also begun to be used in archaeology (Green 1973; Longacre 1968; Redman and Watson 1970; Whallon 1973). The difficulties involved in using this method have been touched upon already (p. 101), and prevent the use of this coefficient as a rigorous test. In certain cases it may be applied to give a general measure of association. The effects of spatial autocorrelation on this type of analysis have been investigated by Martin (1974).

When presence/absence data are being studied a number of tests of spatial association are available. These have been developed primarily by plant ecologists and can be used in cases where the unit of observation is a site or where items of the two distributions never occur at the same location but whose nearness to each other is to be examined. The latter situation is important because much archaeological information does not occur in closed sites but is composed of single or 'chance' finds. Neolithic axes, Bronze Age palstaves and Iron Age coins are examples of this large category of data. The tests to be described allow the association between distributions of this type to be assessed.

The first group of tests and measures uses quadrat methods. Consider an area in which point distributions of two types (A and B) occur. The area can be partitioned into quadrats and the presence or absence of each type in each quadrat noted. From this information a contingency table of the following form may be built up.

Table 6.1. *A table in which the number of quadrats containing both type A and type B points is expressed as a, the number of quadrats which contain type B points but no type A points is given by b, and so on*

		Type A		
		Present	Absent	
Type B	Present	a	b	$e = a + b$
	Absent	c	d	$f = c + d$
		$g = a + c$	$h = b + d$	$n = e + f = g + h$

To test whether A and B are significantly associated we can compare the observed number in each cell of the contingency table with the number we would expect in that cell if the occurrence of each type was independent of the other. If the occurrence of type B is independent of that of type A, then, of the quadrats containing A (i.e. g), a proportion e/n would be expected to contain type B, i.e. the expected number of quadrats containing both types is eg/n. To test the significance of the difference between the observed and expected values in the cells we can use a χ^2 test. The most convenient form of the test for use with the contingency table (Croxton 1953, 273), is

$$\chi^2 = \frac{(ad - bc)^2 n}{efgh} \tag{6.1}$$

For archaeological applications see Hill (1968) and Williams (1968). Pielou (1969, 163) advises the use of the continuity correction

$$\chi^2 = \frac{[(ad - bc) - n/2]^2 n}{efgh}. \tag{6.2}$$

This is the test used by Dacey (1973) in his examination of the association of tool types on an archaeological site. For low observed frequencies (less than 5), Pielou (1969, 162) provides an appropriate exact test. The approach can be extended to consider the distributions of three or four types (Greig-Smith 1964, 97), but becomes impractical for more than this.

It is important to realise the statistical approach that is being followed here. When confronted with a 2 × 2 table of the above sort, Pielou (1969, 160) shows that there are two entirely different questions that can be asked. First, among the n units examined do types A and B occur independently of each other? Second, in the population as a whole are the two types independent of each other? The archaeologist can only ask the first question because his sample is not taken randomly from a population. We know that g of the n units contain type A and that e of them contain type B. The table's marginal totals are therefore fixed. The question thus becomes for the archaeologist: for these given marginal totals what are the probabilities of the various possible sets of cell frequencies (or partitions of n)? Is the particular set of cell frequencies that has been observed consistent with the hypothesis of independence? This approach is further discussed by Pielou (1969, 160–3) who also considers the use of the above tests to answer such questions.

As well as testing whether the null hypothesis of independence between the two distributions should be accepted or rejected, some measure of the degree of association can be obtained. One such measure (*ibid.*, 165) is

$$Q = \frac{ad - bc}{ad + bc} \tag{6.3}$$

For lower case letters see table 6.1. $Q = 1$ when either $b = 0$ or $c = 0$. This is the Q_2 measure used in anthropology (Gifford and Kroeber 1937; Kluckhohn 1939). Another measure is the V coefficient which has already been used in this study (p. 21)

$$V = \frac{ad - bc}{+(efgh)^{1/2}} \qquad (6.4)$$

This is the same as the r coefficient used by Milke (1935; Kluckhohn 1939) and the ϕ coefficient discussed by Driver (1961). Q and V vary from $+1$, when positive association is as great as possible, to -1 when negative association (that is segregation) is as great as possible. They equal 0 when there is no evidence of association – that is when the observed and expected frequencies are equal.

An important difference between Q and V is given by Pielou. Suppose type B occurs in more of the units than does type A. 'The positive association would be as great as possible if A was never found in the absence of B, though there would perforce be some units in which B was found without A. This degree of association can be called *complete*' (*ibid.*, 165). However, we might choose to assert that the association was 'as great as possible' only when neither type ever occurred without the other. 'This is called *absolute* association. In terms of the cell frequencies in the 2 × 2 table complete positive association requires that either b or c (not necessarily both) be zero. For absolute association we must have both $b = 0$ and $c = 0$' (*ibid.*). Consider the following tables.

Tables 6.2 and 6.3. *Frequencies of quadrats containing different combinations of A- and B-type points*

6.2		Type A			6.3		Type A		
		+	−	Total			+	−	Total
Type	+	80	80	160	Type	+	80	0	80
B	−	0	15	15	B	−	0	15	15
	Total	80	95	175		Total	80	15	95

+ presence, − absence.

The tables are very different. In table 6.2, although all the 80 units containing A also contain B, there are in addition 80 units with only B in them. In the table 6.3, on the other hand, neither type occurs without the other. For both tables $Q = 1$, whereas $V = 1$ only for table 6.3. For the table 6.2 $V = 0.281$ (Pielou 1969, 166). For most archaeological situations V would therefore seem preferable to Q. A characteristic of V which may be considered undesirable in certain cases in mentioned by Driver (1961). This is that a zero frequency for a

will only yield a perfect negative correlation (-1) when it is matched by a zero frequency in d (for definition of a and d see table 6.1).

A number of other measures which have been used by anthropologists have been discussed by Kluckhohn (1939) and Chaney and Ruiz Revilla (1969). The spatial autocorrelation measures may also be used to assess the degree of mixing between different 'coloured' cells (section 5.5).

A serious problem associated with tests based on quadrat counts is that the size of the quadrat has a great effect on the results of the analysis. With certain patterns negative association becomes positive and then association is not detectable as the quadrat size is increased (Greig-Smith 1964, 110). It is also the case that the V coefficient is greatly affected by the amount of area in which neither type occurs but which is included in the analysis. Thus Dice (1945) and Bray (1956) have suggested coefficients which disregard the d value in the contingency table (table 6.1). Bray's coefficient is $2a/(2a + b + c)$. Driver (1961) has suggested a measure to achieve the same end.

$$r_n = G = \frac{a}{\sqrt{(a + b)(a + c)}} \tag{6.5}$$

For definition of letters a, b, c see table 6.1. However, one cannot judge whether the value of the coefficient departs significantly from expectation, on the null hypothesis of independence of the distributions, without taking d into account (Pielou 1969, 176).

In view of these difficulties, tests based on distance measurements may often be more applicable. We have two distributions of types A and B. We can note the type of each point in the combined distribution, and also note the type of the point nearest to it. The following contingency table can then be constructed (table 6.4).

Table 6.4.   *A table in which the number of times that a type A point has another type A point as its nearest neighbour is given by a, and so on. For a definition of e, f, g, h, n, see table 6.1*

		Base point		
		Type A	Type B	
Nearest neighbour	Type A	a	b	e
	Type B	c	d	f
		g	h	n

The table can be extended to include second and third nearest neighbours. If only first nearest neighbours are used the method is sensitive

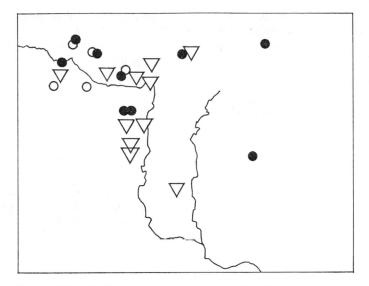

Fig.6.2. The distributions of types 76 (○), 67 (●) and 69 (▽). Source: Hänsel 1968.

to small scale patterning. The χ^2 test can be used to test for a difference between AA, BB and AB, BA relationships.

Pielou (1961) has suggested a coefficient of segregation (*S*).

$$S = 1 - \frac{\text{Observed number of AB and BA relationships}}{\text{Expected number of AB and BA relationships}}$$

$$= 1 - \frac{(c + b)N}{eh + fg} \tag{6.6}$$

S varies from $+1$ when the distributions are completely segregated, i.e. occur in different areas, to -1 when A and B are associated in isolated pairs made up of one A and one B. *S* equals 0 when the two types are randomly intermingled.

To examine the performance of this measure some distributions of the middle Bronze Age which are to be discussed below can be considered. We wish to examine the relationship between the three pin types in fig.6.2. If the association between types 76 and 67 is considered, the results in table 6.5 are obtained.

There is thus no evidence for significant difference between the distributions. In fact the negative value of *S* relates to the frequent occurrence of 76 and 67 type pins in isolated pairs.

However, if the relationship between the 76 and 69 types, which does give a visual impression of segregation, is considered, no significant difference between the two distributions is found.

Table 6.5. *A contingency table (see table 6.4) for the spatial association between types 76 and 67 in fig.6.2*

		Base point 76	67	Total
Nearest neighbour	76	1	5	6
	67	4	4	8
	Total	5	9	14

$S = -0.34$
$\chi^2 = $ (with Yates' correction for small numbers (Croxton 1953, 275–6)) 0.52 (not significant).

Table 6.6. *A contingency table for the spatial association between types 76 and 69 in fig.6.2*

		Base point 76	69	Total
Nearest neighbour	76	3	3	6
	69	2	8	10
	Total	5	11	16

$S = 0.31$
$\chi^2 = 0.48$ (not significant, corrected).

Similarly, the apparent segregation between the distributions of pin type 76 and of the pendant type 128 (fig.6.3) is not significant, although the S coefficient does indicate a tendency towards segregation.

Table 6.7. *A contingency table for the spatial association between types 128 and 76 in fig.6.3*

		Base point 128	76	Total
Nearest neighbour	128	9	2	11
	76	2	3	5
	Total	11	5	16

$S = 0.42$
$\chi^2 = 1.2$ (not significant, corrected).

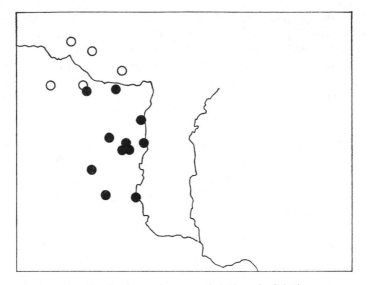

Fig.6.3. The distributions of types 128 (●) and 76 (○).
Source: Hänsel 1968.

Because of the small size of the sample and the sensitivity of the test to detailed patterning, significant segregation is difficult to obtain in these cases. The difficulty could be overcome by including second and third nearest neighbours. A rather different approach to examining spatial association is suggested by Whallon (1974) and is based on nearest-neighbour distances. It suffers from involving unjustifiable assumptions about the frequency distribution of nearest-neighbour distances in a clustered pattern, and from an inability to test the significance of the degree of association.

For spatial distributions, a number of statistics can be calculated which correspond to the mean, median etc. of univariate distributions. For a single distribution these statistics are purely descriptive and of no great practical use, but when more than one distribution is under consideration they can be used as a basis for comparison. The most commonly used of such statistics are outlined below.

Measures of location

(*a*) Arithmetic mean centre. It corresponds to the arithmetic mean of a univariate distribution, and is defined as the point at which the sum of the squares of the distances to all points of the distribution is a minimum. It can be most easily obtained by imposing x and y axes (e.g. north–south and east–west axes) on the distribution and calculating the means of the x and y values. The point $(\bar{x}, \bar{y})$ is the arithmetic mean centre.

(*b*) Median centre. It corresponds to the median of a univariate distribution, and is defined as the point at which the sum of the distances to all points of the distribution is a minimum. For this reason it is sometimes called the 'point of minimum average travel'. It *cannot* be calculated by finding the median *x* and *y* distances when a pair of axes is imposed, as the point so defined will depend on the orientation of the chosen axes.

(*c*) Modal centre. It corresponds to the mode of a univariate distribution, and is defined as the highest point of a smoothed or trend surface fitted to the density of points in the distribution (see section 5.4.1). This definition is unfortunately not unique, and different answers can be obtained by different methods of fitting the surface to the density.

(*d*) Harmonic mean centre. It corresponds to the harmonic mean (a little-used statistic) of a univariate distribution, and is defined as the point at which the sum of the inverses of the distances to all points of the distribution is a maximum. This in fact corresponds to the location of the 'peak of potential' in the gravity models (Warntz and Neft 1960, 50).

Measures of dispersion

(*a*) Standard distance deviation. It corresponds to the standard deviation of a univariate distribution, and is defined as the square root of the average of the squares of the distances from the arithmetic mean centre to the points of the distribution. It is a useful measure of the dispersion or spread of a reasonably symmetrical distribution, but is often of little use in other circumstances.

(*b*) Mean distance deviation. It corresponds to the mean deviation of a univariate distribution and is defined as the average distance from the median centre to all points of the distribution.

(*c*) Harmonic mean distance deviation. It is defined as the inverse of the average inverse distances from the harmonic mean centre to all points of the distribution, and is important in measuring the dispersion about the 'hub' of the distribution, its harmonic mean centre.

These measures are all discussed in greater detail by Neft (1966).

When two or more spatial distributions are to be compared, tests analogous to the common univariate tests can be used. For example, the Normal probability surface (analogous to the Normal distribution) can be used to test the difference between two arithmetic mean centres if the sample numbers are sufficiently large, and an analogue to the Students 't' test can be used if the sample is small (Neft 1966, 139).

An additional test

When assumptions cannot be made about the form of the distribution – often the case in archaeology – a non-paramatic test may be used. A useful additional and relatively simple test to apply is the *Runs test*. In the one-dimensional case, i.e. that of points on a line, we suppose that there are two samples of m and n points, which are denoted by A and B respectively. The As and Bs can be thought of as a sequence, e.g. AABABBB, ... and a block of consecutive As or Bs is called a 'run'. In this example there are four runs, namely AA, B, A, and BBB. Under the null hypothesis that the two samples come from the same population, the As and Bs will be well mixed, while if the null hypothesis does not hold, the number of runs will be smaller. The test procedure is to reject the null hypothesis if d, the number of runs, is less than a certain value d_0. The required value of d_0 is calculated by choosing a significance level α (e.g. $5\% = 0.05$) and finding the integer d such that (as nearly as possible) $\sum\limits_{d=2}^{d_0} h(d) = \alpha$ where $h(d)$ is the probability of there being exactly d runs. The formulae for $h(d)$ are

(i) d even:
$$h(d) = \frac{2\binom{m-1}{k-1}\binom{n-1}{k-1}}{\binom{m+n}{m}}, \quad k = \frac{d}{2},$$

(ii) d odd:
$$h(d) = \frac{\binom{m-1}{k}\binom{n-1}{k-1} + \binom{m-1}{k-1}\binom{n-1}{k}}{\binom{m+n}{m}},$$

$$k = \frac{d-1}{2}.$$

Unless m and n are both very small, these calculations can become very tedious unless a computer is available. Tables of $\sum h(d)$ are available (e.g. Swed and Eisenhart 1943), or if m and n are both greater than ten one can use the result that d is approximately Normally distributed with mean

$$\frac{2mn}{m+n} + 1$$

and variance

$$\frac{2mn\,(2mn - m - n)}{(m+n)^2(m+n-1)}$$

Putting $m + n = N$, $m = N\alpha$, $n = N\beta$, the distribution of d has approximate mean and variance $2N\alpha\beta$ and $4N\alpha^2\beta^2$ respectively.

These results can be generalised to the two-dimensional situation in one of two ways.

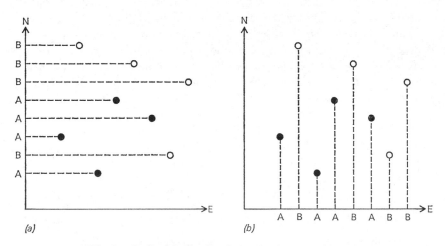

Fig.6.4. Referring distributions of points to (*a*) north–south axis and (*b*) east–west axis for Runs test. Number of runs = 4 in (*a*) and 6 in (*b*).

1. A transect (e.g. a north–south or east–west axis) can be drawn, and perpendiculars dropped from each point on to the transect (fig.6.4). This provides a sequence of As and Bs which can be tested by the above method.

2. The circular test. A central point or 'origin' is chosen (the arithmetic mean centre seems to be suitable) and a circle drawn about it. Perpendiculars are dropped from each point on to the circle (fig.6.5), providing a sequence of As and Bs, but this time on a circle instead of a straight line. The number of runs, *d*, can now only be even, and

$$h(d) = \frac{(n + m) \dbinom{m - 1}{k - 1} \dbinom{n - 1}{k - 1}}{k \dbinom{n + m}{n}}$$

For large *m* and *n*, we can use the result that *d* is approximately Normally distributed with mean

$$\frac{2mn}{m + n} \left(\frac{m + n - 2}{m + n - 1}\right) + 1$$

and variance

$$\left(\frac{2mn}{(m + n)(m + n - 1)}\right)^2 (m + n - 2)$$

which can as before be approximately represented by $2N\alpha\beta$ and $4N\alpha^2\beta^2$.

This test is particularly useful in that it is sensitive to differences in shape of distribution as well as to differences in location. Other tests,

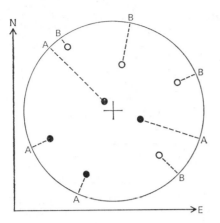

Fig.6.5. Referring distributions of points to circle for Runs test.
+, Arithmetic mean centre. Number of runs = 4.

which are sensitive to shifts in location, include the Median test (Mood 1954), the Wilcoxon–Mann–Whitney test (Wilcoxon 1945; Mann and Whitney 1947), and the Randomisation test (Lehmann and Stein 1949), which is the most efficient but also the heaviest computationally. It may well prove necessary to devise simple *ad hoc* tests to meet the demands of particular problems.

A completely new approach to the study of spatial relationships has recently been put forward by Atkin (1972; 1973*a*, *b*). The emphasis is on structural rather than distance relationships, and the methods used are based on an abstract geometry of the situation under study. They would seem to be particularly useful in the study of changes in patterns over time. Of the three reports so far published (*ibid.*), I is a general introduction to the subject, II concentrates on the mathematical theory and III contains a case-study based on an area in Southend-on-Sea. This new approach, as yet unexploited in archaeology, could have considerable potential, perhaps for urban archaeologists in particular.

6.2 *Some archaeological applications*

Figures 6.7 to 6.12 show the distributions of some north German early Bronze Age metal types studied by Bergmann (1970). For his second period in the area studied, Bergmann plotted 112 very specific types which occur more than three times. The objects appear in a range of contexts (indicated on the maps by different symbols) such as graves and hoards and as single finds. He found that the types were restricted to certain sub-regions which can be identified with the density groupings shown in fig.5.79. The groupings have been given a 'tribal' definition by Bergmann (1968, 236; 1970, 57).

A grid of the size shown in fig.6.8 has been constructed so that it

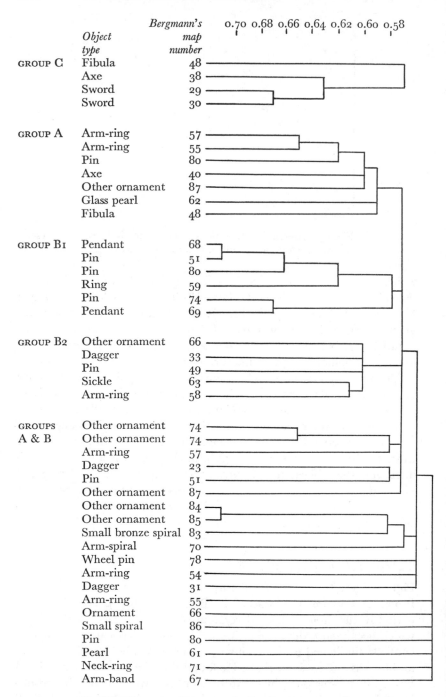

Fig.6.6. Clustering Bergmann's distributions according to the *V* coefficient.

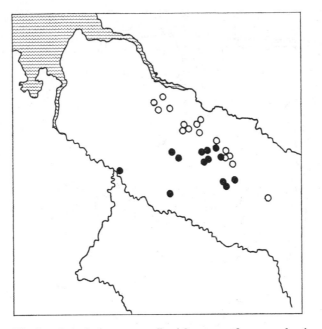

Fig.6.7. Association groups B1 (● – types 69, 74 and 59) and
B2 (○ – types 58, 63 and 49) in north Germany.

could be imposed on each distribution map, and the occurrence of
each type in the lattice noted. A computer programme was then used
to compute the V coefficient between every pair of distributions. It was
then possible to carry out a single-link cluster analysis based on the V
coefficients of association. Hodson (1969*a*) has discussed the inade-
quacies of this clustering method. One of these problems is apparent in
this example. As the level of similarity is lowered, large numbers of
distributions are added to the main group, producing a 'chaining
effect' (Hodson 1969*b*, 305). Figure 6.6, therefore, only shows those
distributions which are grouped at a high level of similarity. The
clusters indicated in fig.6.6 relate to the density groups in fig.5.79 and
to the spatial groupings suggested by Bergmann. Some closer definition,
however, is given, for the association groupings, B1 and B2, identify a
division within Bergmann's group (B) (fig.6.7). It is interesting that
these localised groupings are distributions of small ornaments such as
pins, pendants, finger- and arm-rings. Distributions of a similar range
of jewellery identify the B group as a whole, and the A group. An
example of the distinction between the A and B groups is shown in
fig.6.8. Moving up a hierarchy of groupings, we find that further types,
such as the dagger in fig.6.9, cover both the A and B groups. The C
group is identified very distinctly in the cluster analysis (fig.6.6) and its
distribution is shown by the sword types in fig.6.10 and 6.11. Other

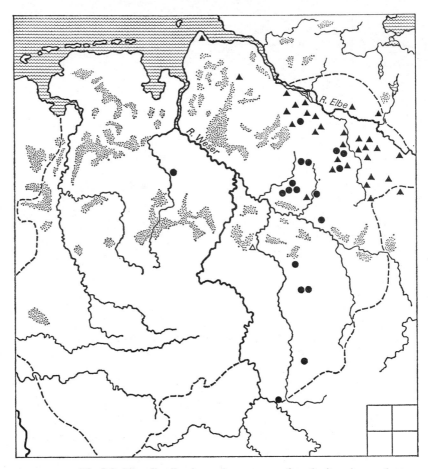

Fig.6.8. The distributions of two types of neck rings in north
Germany. The quadrats show the size of grid used in
measuring the association between distributions. Source:
Bergmann 1970, map 67.

types have a concentration in the same C area but are spread much
wider, for example the axe type shown in fig.6.12. It is of interest that in
the central area of this axe distribution, finds occur in hoards and
graves, while outside the core area they occur as single finds. This is a
recurring pattern. The C association group is distinctive in that it does
not contain a wide range of ornament types. Only a fibula type is
centred in this group, and this is a rare type of ornament at this
period. This difference may support Bergmann's hypothesis of a
cultural distinction between the groups.

There seems, then, to be a hierarchy of association groups, with small
localised groupings incorporated into larger clusters, until finally the
A, B (1 and 2) and C groups are covered by the distributions of more

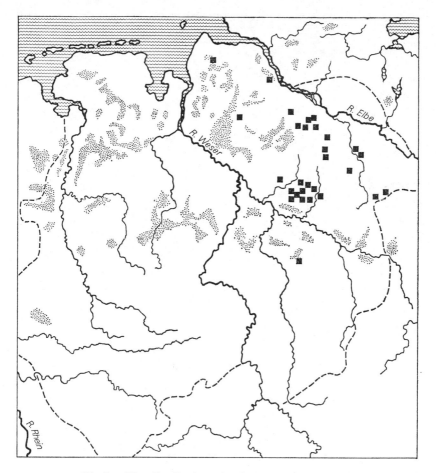

Fig.6.9. The distribution of a dagger type in north Germany.
Source: Bergmann 1970, map 31.

widespread types. It is of interest that the pattern of group formation is
as predicted by the gravity models (fig.5.79). The strong link predicted
between the A and B density groups is evident in a large number of
distributions covering this area. Similarly, the strongest predicted ties
from C are to the southeast, and this is indicated by a number of
distributions such as in figs.6.9 and 6.12 which run along this axis. This
method of analysis was unable to identify association groups at D and E.

There is also some indication that different classes of artifact define
different levels of association. Nearly all the localised types clustered
in fig.6.6 are ornaments. In fig.6.12 an axe type has a much wider
distribution although being centred on one of the smaller groupings.
Indeed the pattern of axe distribution is different from that of other
artifact types. This is clarified in the matrix (fig.6.13). In this matrix an

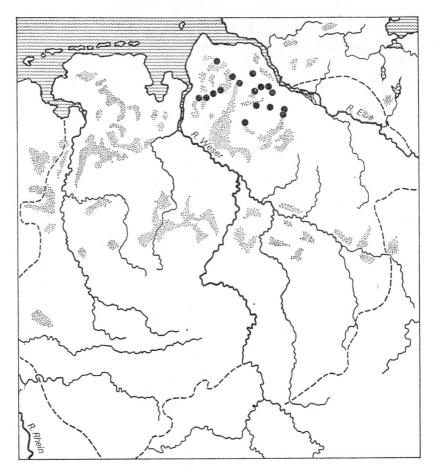

Fig.6.10. The distribution of a sword type in north Germany.
Source: Bergmann 1970, map 29.

indication of the V coefficient value for each pair of distributions is given. The distributions are ordered along the margins according to the class of object. Of the axes, only two show any close association with the range of ornaments. This is because the axes have concentrations of their distributions in areas (C group and at a number of other points) different from those of the ornaments and because they are much more widely spread. Spearheads and swords are also not closely associated with types of ornaments, while the ceramic traits have diffuse and scanty distributions. What is perhaps misleading, is that a number of pin types do not appear to be closely associated with the other ornaments. These are small samples of three or four examples sometimes spread widely. Other pin types have very localised distributions, and these are closely associated with the wide range of ornament types found mainly in the A and B regions. The difference between wide-

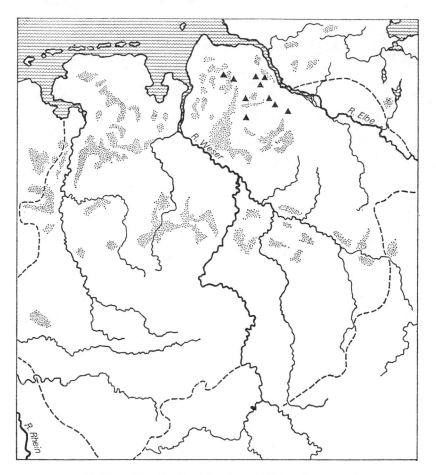

Fig.6.11. The distribution of a sword type in north Germany.
Source: Bergmann 1970, map 30.

spread and localised distribution, may be partly due to the level of
definition of the types involved (p. 29). Certainly the axes are of fairly
simple forms and are perhaps not easy to define closely. The concept
of range and value (section 5.6) may also be of importance in the study
of patterns of interaction in this area in the early Bronze Age.

A second study is based on some middle Bronze Age distributions in
the Carpathian Basin (Hänsel 1968). Hänsel was able to distinguish a
number of phases in this period. In his first phase (MB.I) cultural
groupings in the material were thought to be most evident. However,
only very broad groupings, one west and one east of the Danube, could
be distinguished among the great complexity of overlapping distributions. We shall see that considerable refinement of this is possible. The
metal types are well defined.

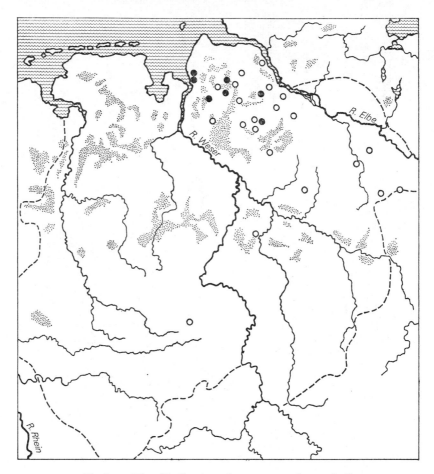

Fig.6.12. The distribution of an axe type in north Germany.
○, Single finds not from graves or hoards; ●, finds from
hoards and graves. Source: Bergmann 1970, map 38.

It is clear from Hänsel's distribution maps that, as with Bergmann's
data, localised groupings can be defined by ornament types, while
swords and axes, although they often have the same centres of distribution as ornament types, are spread more widely. To examine the pattern
of association between the distributions in MB.I, their modal centres
were obtained. Any tendency for these centres to cluster in particular
areas can then be identified. The centres are shown on the base lattice
in fig.6.14*b*. They cluster in the two areas of highest density of finds
indicated in fig.6.14*a*. Since these are the areas of highest densities of
finds it is not surprising that most modal centres occur in them (6.14*b*).
However, it is clear in the patterns in fig.6.14*c*, *d* and *e* that types
are often restricted to one or other of the density groups. Other types

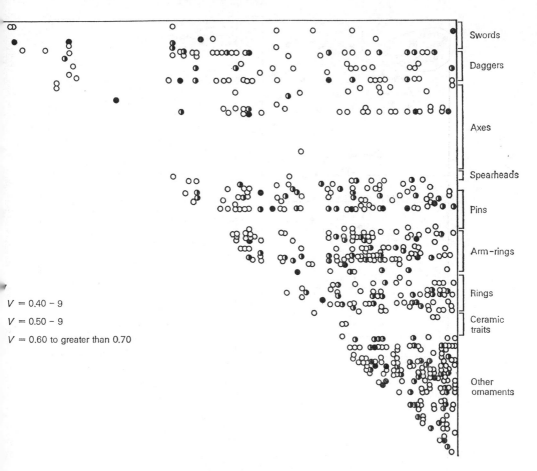

Fig.6.13. The matrix of V coefficients for Bergmann's data.

are found more widely but with marked concentrations in one of the groups, as opposed to having marked concentrations in both.

If axe types are considered, on the other hand, much wider distributions are found (for example fig.6.14f). These are complex decorated artifacts, more capable of close description and definition than in the previous example.

The pattern, therefore, seems to be one of association groups of ornament types occurring in areas of higher densities of finds, and perhaps of settlement. Outside a core area, a type is found with decreasing frequency as distance increases. In the peripheral area of its distribution a type may retain a low frequency even though other types occur densely. The maximum distance over which an artifact is

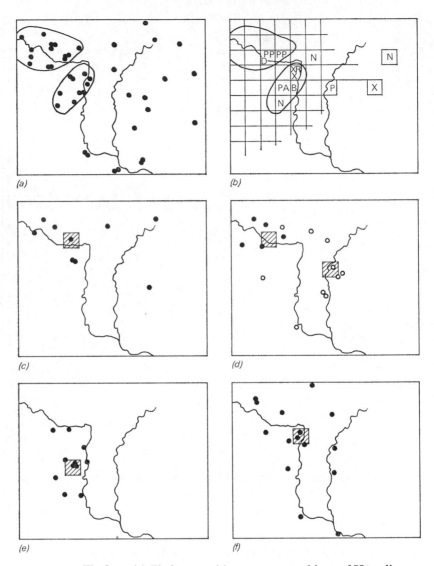

Fig.6.14. (*a*) Find spots with two or more objects of Hänsel's period 1. The two areas of highest density are indicated. (*b*) Location of modal centres. P, pin; D, dagger; N, pendant; X, axe; R, arm-ring; A, arm-spiral; B, belt piece. (*c*) The distribution of pin type 67, modal centre shaded. (*d*) The distribution of pin type 71 (○) and 76 (●). (*e*) The distribution of the pendant type 128. (*f*) The distribution of axe type 58.

found depends to some extent on the type of object. Thus, types such as axes and swords probably had a comparatively low level of local demand, and whether they were manufactured in one centre or not, these types are more widely spread than the ornaments. They may relate to interaction at a high level in the social hierarchy (Dalton 1969).

As a further illustration of the application of methods of spatial analysis to archaeological data, the two versions of the Runs test described in section 6.1 were applied to the distributions shown in figs.6.2 and 6.3. For fig.6.2 we have

$$n = \ 9 \ (\text{type } 67)$$
$$m = 11 \ (\text{type } 69)$$
$$l = \ 5 \ (\text{type } 76)$$

Referred to the north–south axis, the number of runs for each pair of types is

$$d(n, m) = 9$$
$$d(m, l) = 8$$
$$d(l, n) = 9$$

where $d(n, m)$ is the number of runs for types 67 and 69, etc. The corresponding values when referred to the east–west axis are 10, 6 and 8 respectively. None of these values give any reason to reject the null hypothesis that all three distributions can be thought of as 'samples' from the same parent distribution. In other words, taking the overall pattern of find spots as 'given', the three patterns relating to the three individual types are not distinguishable (with regard to the properties that have been examined) from three random samples taken from the overall pattern. This is only the case for the observed distributions and the situation may change as further artifacts of these types are found.

When the 'circular' test (described on p. 210) is applied (with the overall arithmetic mean centre as origin), the values for d are 12, 4 and 8. The probability of a value at least as small as 4, if there were really no difference between the distributions of types 76 and 69, is about 9%. Even this value is not small enough to cause us to reject the null hypothesis: we have been considering three pairwise comparisons, and a level of 9% for *one* of them is not as significant as it would be if only one pair had been under consideration.

For fig.6.3 the values of m and n are 5 and 11 (types 76 and 128), and referred to the north–south axis the value of d is 2. In this case

$$h(d) = 2 \ \frac{\binom{4}{0}\binom{10}{0}}{\binom{16}{5}} = 0.05\%$$

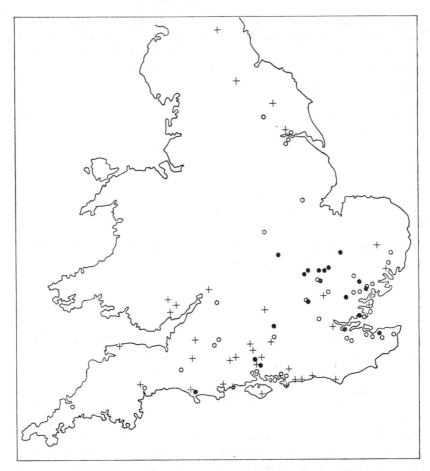

Fig.6.15. The distibution of Terra Rubra (TR) and Terra Nigra (TN) pottery in Britain. ○, Stamps; ●, stamps in burials; +, unstamped sherds. Source: Rigby 1973.

and the null hypothesis is rejected in favour of north–south segregation. Referred to the east–west axis, the value of d is 6, which is not significant. The circular test, with overall arithmetic mean as origin, gives $d = 6$, again not significant.

As an example of the approximate methods applicable for larger numbers, the distributions of stamped and unstamped Terra Rubra and Terra Nigra given by Rigby (1973, 22) were studied (see fig.6.15). In this example $m = 54$ ('stamps' plus 'stamps in burials') and $n = 35$ ('unstamped sherds'). Then $N = 89$, $\alpha = 0.61$, $\beta = 0.39$. The number of runs, d, is thus approximately Normally distributed with mean $2N\alpha\beta = 42$ and variance $4N\alpha^2\beta^2 = 20$ and standard devation $\sqrt{20} = 4.45$. Referred to the north–south axis, the value of d is 34, while it is 36 when referred to the east–west axis, and 37 in the circular test (overall arithmetic mean centre as origin). None of these values is significant, the nearest is the first with a deviation of 8, or 1.8 standard deviations. There is perhaps some suggestion of a north–south segregation, but no convincing evidence. This result is only relevant to the presently available data and the degree of association between the distributions may alter as further material is excavated. This is an important proviso relevant to all the tests described in this chapter. It is also possible that more detailed measures and tests of association will be developed in the future (Hodder 1975) which will allow greater sensitivity in the detection of patterns of association between distributions, such as the pattern in fig.6.15.

7
The relationship between sites and other features

7.1 Methods and applications

We have already seen (section 4.4) how settlement patterns can be affected by a 'background' variable (e.g. soil type), in the context of studying possibly aggregated patterns (p. 85). The relationship between a point-pattern, whether of settlements or of finds, and a variable which in some sense describes the environment of the pattern – e.g. soil type, altitude, distance from nearest river, can also be studied directly. In this chapter methods of studying such relationships with different types of variables will be described.

7.1.1 Qualitative variables

First we deal with essentially non-numerical variables – for example soil type, vegetation type, or a similar variable which classifies all the land of an area into two or more categories. Although the categories could be numbered, the numbering would be arbitrary and a re-numbering would not change the sense of the classification. Suppose that the total area under consideration is A, and that in this total area, an area a_1 is classified to type 1, an area a_2 is classified to type 2 and so on up to a_k, k being the number of categories. Suppose also there are N sites, of which n_1 are on land classified to type 1, n_2 on land classified to type 2 and so on up to n_k.

Then $$\sum_{i=1}^{k} a_i = A,$$

and $$\sum_{i=1}^{k} n_i = N.$$

Under the null hypothesis of no association between sites and land types – i.e. that the sites are equally likely to occur on all land types, we can calculate the 'expected' number of sites for each type, by the equation: expected number of sites on land

$$\text{type } i = r_i = N \frac{a_i}{A}.$$

In other words, if a particular land type has a certain percentage of the land area, under the null hypothesis we would expect it to have the same percentage of the sites. The differences between the observed values n_i and the expected values r_i can be tested by calculating the goodness-of-fit statistic,

$$\chi^2_{k-1} = \sum_{i=1}^{k} \frac{(n_i - r_i)^2}{r_i}$$

and declaring it significant at the $\alpha \%$ level if it exceeds the $(100 - \alpha)$ percentile of the distribution of χ^2 with $k - 1$ degrees of freedom.

A study of this general form is Davey's (1971) analysis of the distribution of later Bronze Age metalwork in Lincolnshire. Davey divides Lincolnshire into a number of physiographic regions such as the limestone and chalk uplands of the Lincoln Edge and the Wolds and the low lying area of the Isle of Axholme, the Fen and the Marsh. The distribution of later Bronze Age metalwork in Lincolnshire is suggested as being uneven, and Davey wishes to examine the relationship between local variation in the metalwork distribution and physiographic factors.

The percentage of the total area covered by each physiographic type is calculated. The expected number (E) of finds in each physiographic area is obtained from these percentages and compared with the observed number (O) using

$$\chi^2 = \frac{\Sigma(O - E)^2}{E}.$$

The χ^2 value of 44.1 allowed Davey to reject the null hypothesis of no significant difference between the physiographic region in the distribution of the bronzes at $p = 0.01$. 'Natural regions must therefore be considered as an important factor in the distribution of bronzes, and the differences between the regions to merit further analysis' (*ibid.*, 97). Although a discussion is conducted of the relationship between the distribution of metalwork and physiographic regions, Davey's quoted conclusion, does not necessarily follow from his analysis, since many factors could have resulted in the observed relationship. There need be no direct or causal link between the distributions even though they are similar. Additional or intermediary factors may have been involved in producing the relationship.

A study by Green (1973) examines the relation between the spatial distribution of Mayan sites in Northern Belize and the distribution of soils, vegetation, water supplies etc. The amount of each land type in the study area was compared with the number of sites on that land type. The significance of the difference between the observed and expected number of sites on the land types was tested by the binomial test and the 't' test.

7.1.2 *Quantitative data*

In some circumstances, the categories in which the land is divided can be ranked in a definite order. For example, the classifying variable might be altitude – less than 16 m, 16–32 m, 32–48 m etc., or distance from, for example, the nearest river or large town. Although the χ^2 goodness-of-fit test can still be used, it is possible to improve on it by using the additional information contained in the ordering of the categories. This can be done by comparing the cumulative frequency distribution of the sites (e.g. proportions of sites at less than 16 m, less than 32 m, less than 48 m etc.) with the cumulative density of the land area (e.g. proportion of area at less than 16 m, proportion at less than 32 m etc.). In this way small but systematic differences, which might not be significant in a goodness-of-fit test, can add up to a large cumulative difference. Such a difference can be tested by means of the Kolmogorov–Smirnov test (Lindgren 1960, 300), in which the greatest cumulative difference (D_{max}) is compared with a critical value which depends on the number of sites. Tables are given by Massey (1951). If the exact altitude (or relevant variable) of each site is known, the test can be applied exactly, but if the data are grouped (e.g. 100–200 m), the test can still be applied but levels of significance will be understated – the understatement being more serious the coarser the grouping.

As an example of this sort of problem, we studied the relationship between late Iron Age inscribed or 'dynastic' coins and Roman roads in central and southern England. The distributions are shown in fig.7.1. The Isle of Wight was excluded. The distances of the coins from the nearest road were measured (to the nearest millimetre as measured on the O.S. Map of Roman Britain) and tabulated. The land area of the map was divided up by drawing 'contours' at distances 2 mm, 5 mm and 10 mm from the nearest road, and the area in each zone measured. From this information a cumulative frequency distribution was drawn, and compared with the corresponding distribution of the coins (fig.7.2). In this figure, the number of coins (n) is 173, the value D_{max} is 0.189, and the critical values are $1.36/\sqrt{n}$ (at 5 % level) and $1.63/\sqrt{n}$ (at 1 % level). This gives critical values of 0.104 and 0.124. The difference between the two distributions is significant at well below the 1 % level. Alternatively, the χ^2 test can be used. A full cumulative

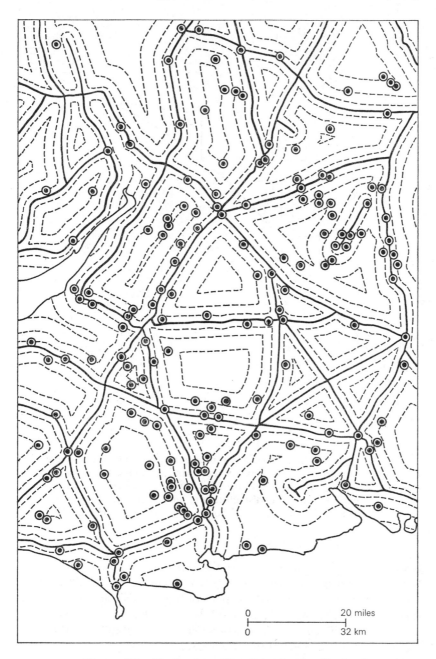

Fig.7.1. The distribution of late Iron Age inscribed coins and
Roman roads in central and southern England.

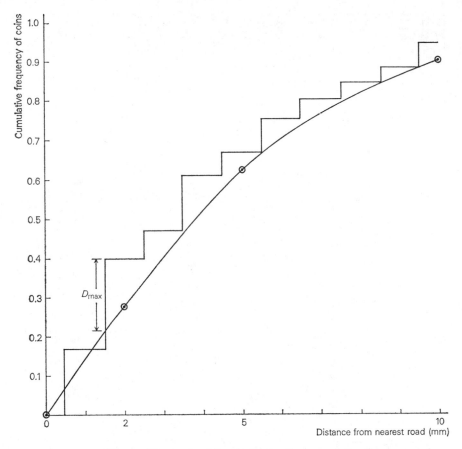

Fig.7.2. The stepped line indicates the cumulative frequency of
late Iron Age coins at distances from the nearest Roman road
(see fig.7.1). The smoothed line is the frequency of coins
expected from the distribution of land area. Information was
obtained at the encircled points. For further description see text.

frequency distribution was interpolated from the areas within the
'contours', and the 'expected' numbers of coins were then calculated.
A value of $\chi^2 = 52.9$ with 10 degrees of freedom is obtained, well in
excess of the 1 % significance level of 23.2. Thus both techniques
indicate a significant association between the distribution of the Iron
Age coins and the routes of the Roman roads.

At a purely technical level, difficulty may be encountered in measuring the area of irregularly shaped zones. This can be done by trans-
ferring the map to tracing paper, placing it over graph paper and
counting the number of squares covered by each zone (incomplete
squares count as one if more than half, otherwise discounted).

Although a relationship has been demonstrated between the lines taken by Roman roads and the supposedly pre-Roman distribution of Iron Age coins, this does not necessarily entail a direct causal relationship. It is the case that the coins were often retained into the early Romano-British period (as is suggested in a number of hoard and settlement site associations) so that the observed relationship between coins and roads may reflect the attraction of early Romano-British settlement to these important routes. However, further research is needed before this can be asserted with any confidence. The observed relationship between the coins and the roads could be due to a variety of yet other or indirect factors. For example, Roman roads may have followed Iron Age routes or both Iron Age and Roman roads may have followed natural features of the countryside. Detailed further research is clearly needed into (*a*) the use and function of the Iron Age coins, (*b*) the extent of their use by Roman troops in the Julio-Claudian period and (*c*) the distribution of pre-Roman settlements in the areas mapped. The value of demonstrating a spatial relationship of the above sort is simply to raise questions. No answers about the cause of the relationship are provided by this type of analysis.

7.2 *A model for the relationship between a site and its environment*

An important model for agricultural activity was proposed by von Thünen (1875) in *Der Isolierte Staat*. This was based on observations of movements in Mecklenberg in the early nineteenth century. Von Thünen suggested that concentric rings of land use (table 7.1) would occur around a city or market centre so that more intensive and profitable land use was nearer the centre. This model was developed under the following assumptions (Henshall 1967, 444); (1) the existence of an 'Isolated state', (2) one central city as the sole market, (3) a uniform plain surrounding the city, (4) only one mode of transport, horse and cart, (5) the plain inhabited by farmers supplying the city, and (6) the maximising of profits by the farmers with automatic adjustment to the needs of the central market. However, some of the assumptions of the 'Isolated state' were modified (fig.7.3) by allowing (1) a navigable river on which transportation was speedier and costs less than land transport, (2) a minor competing market centre, and (3) local differences in the agricultural productivity of the plain around the city.

Chisholm (1962) has looked at land use around hamlets or farms in terms of Von Thünen's concentric ring model. The distance from farmhouse to field affects the amount of labour that can be put into the land use of that field. Distance therefore affects the type of land use attempted in concentric rings around the farmhouse. 'There are several cases cited in geographical literature where land use around a

Table 7.1. *Der Isolierte Staat (1826): Thünen's land-use 'rings'*

Zone	Area per cent of state area	Relative distance from central city	Land-use type	Major marketed product	Production system
0	Less than 0.1	−0.1	Urban-industrial	Manufactured goods	Urban trade centre of state; near iron and coal mines
1	1	0.1–0.6	Intensive agriculture	Milk; vegetables	Intensive dairying and trucking; heavy manuring; no fallow
2	3	0.6–3.5	Forest	Firewood; timber	Sustained-yield forestry
3a	3	3.6–4.6	Extensive agriculture	Rye; potatoes	Six-year rotation: rye (2), potatoes (1), clover (1), barley (1), vetch (1); no fallow; cattle stall-fed in winter
3b	30	4.7–34	Extensive agriculture	Rye	Seven-year rotation system; pasture (3), rye (1), barley (1), oats (1), fallow (1)
3c	25	34–44		Rye: animal products	Three-field system: rye, etc. (1), pasture (1), fallow (1)
4	38	45–100	Ranching	Animal products	Mainly stock-raising some rye for on-farm consumption
5	—	Beyond 100	Waste	None	None

Source: Haggett 1965, 165.

settlement is directly related to distance from the settlement (for Africa by Prothero 1957, and Steel, Fortes and Ady 1947; for India by Ahmad 1952; for Brazil by Waibel 1958)' (Henshall 1967, 445).

Chisholm's (1962) work on agricultural communities, Lee's (1969) comparable analysis of the !Kung bushman hunter–gatherer subsistence, and the Von Thünen concentric ring model have assumed considerable importance in archaeology as a result of site-catchment analysis (Higgs and Vita-Finzi 1972; Jarman 1972; Vita-Finzi and Higgs 1970). 'Human populations, are generally only able to exploit resources that exist within a certain distance of their occupation site, be this a camp, cave, village or town' (Jarman 1972, 706). 'The further the area is from the site, the less it is likely to be exploited' (Vita-Finzi and Higgs 1970, 7). Thus the main area exploited for food will be

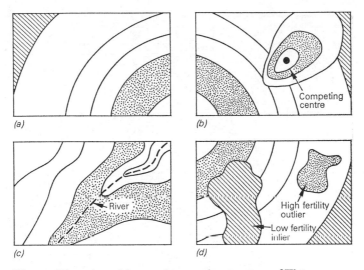

Fig.7.3. Distortion of the regular annular structure of Thünen landscape (*a*) by a second competing centre (*b*), alternative transfer routes (*c*), and areas of different productivity (*d*). Source: Haggett 1965.

close to the site being considered. The analysis of subsistence activities must concentrate on this localised area rather than on the broad physiographic, vegetational, climatic etc. zones within which the site rests (Vita-Finzi and Higgs 1970, 1). Such zones may be too broad to tell us about the area actually exploited. In reconstructing the area of exploitation around a site, 'even the use of detailed maps will not give a satisfactory estimate of the important time/effort factor in delineating the exploitation territory, as this is often critically affected by minor features of topography' (Jarman 1972, 712). Thus the 'catchment area' around a site is determined by walking outwards from it in at least four directions (Higgs and Vita-Finzi 1972, 33). The total distance or time of the walks is derived from the studies of Chisholm and Lee for agricultural and hunter-gatherer communities. The type of land use or possible land use is also noted on the line of each walk. In classifying land use, three basic economic potential categories of land are used – (1) arable/potential arable, (2) rough grazing, (3) marsh, bare rock etc. – although these categories are often subdivided (Jarman 1972, 715). The relative importance of these categories of land types in the catchment area (fig.7.4) is used to reconstruct the economic pattern of the site, for example as being mainly pastoral or arable farming.

One of the most important aspects of site-catchment analysis is that it has focused attention on the micro-environment associated with a site. The underlying model would certainly seem to be most fruitful in analysing archaeological data. However, the methods used at the moment suffer from a few features which are perhaps worth discussing.

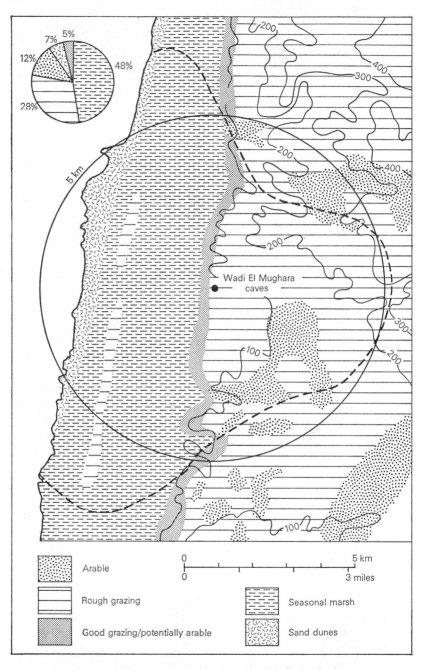

Fig.7.4. Classification of land use at Wadi el Mughara.
Dashed line = estimated boundaries of exploitation territories.
Source: Higgs and Vita-Finzi 1972.

An important consideration is that the model on which site-catchment analysis is based may be less widely applicable than was assumed initially by geographers and archaeologists. In many areas, von Thünen's and Chisholm's arguments have not been adequately tested. But in a survey of observations on land use in rural Africa, Jackson (1972) found that '(a) cultivation zones of concentric rings are uncommon in Africa, (b) where they do exist they are often far from true exemplars of the models of Chisholm based on von Thünen's method of analysis' (*ibid.*, 261). Thus the rings of land nearest a village or farmstead often consist of poor, denuded and uncultivated soil. Certainly there are many cases in which, without the need for efficient commercial production of surplus food, the main areas of cultivated land are some distance from the settlement. More work, perhaps, needs to be done on the basic model before it can be widely applied in prehistory with any confidence.

A further problem is that in site-catchment analysis, late palaeolithic or neolithic land potential is frequently derived from modern land use patterns. In a study of the Mt Carmel area in Israel, 'the land use capability classes shown on the maps are based on the present-day situation, and pay insufficient regard to changes in land potential produced by geological and other agencies; this is a deficiency that more detailed studies should correct' (Vita-Finzi and Higgs 1970, 8). The importance of study at the micro-scale has already been mentioned and it is often extremely difficult to reconstruct local features and soil conditions after 8000 or 10 000 years, especially since the very presence of land use by man may have caused soil degradation and erosion. Jarman (1972, 714–15) states that past erosion and soil changes can often be assessed, although there often seems to be little analysis of this aspect (*ibid.*, 718).

It is also often assumed that patterns of exploitation have varied little. 'Where the geographical distribution of essential resources and the technology by which they are exploited have changed little, the pattern of human response might be expected to persist' (Vita-Finzi and Higgs 1970, 4). Modern patterns of transhumance are frequently suggested to have existed in early times (Higgs *et al.* 1967; Jarman 1972; Noy, Legge and Higgs 1973; Vita-Finzi and Higgs 1970). Such a deterministic relationship between economic strategy, resources and technology would certainly be more convincing if detailed studies of the intervening millenia in the areas examined were carried out.

Another feature of site-catchment analysis which would pay further examination is the relative importance of the economy or of subsistence activities in early society. For example, Vita-Finzi and Higgs (1970, 4–5) assume that population will have risen to take full advantage of all resources, even though 'this view would appear to conflict with those modern ethnographic studies that indicate a comfortable gap between the needs of hunter–gatherer populations and their resources' (*ibid.*, 5). This ethnographic evidence is discounted because it relates to modern hunter–gatherers who are assumed to be atypical, and because it does not relate to the long term of archaeological trends. 'In time, intra-specific competition will bring selective pressure to bear upon the groups practising the less productive economies, to their detriment in the archaeological record' (*ibid.*, 6). It may be, however, that as in the ethnographic studies, subsistence activities are not of prime importance in many primitive contexts. Other factors of equal or greater importance in the location of sites are defence, proximity to building materials and water, nearness to other sites with which social ties exist (p. 86, and Green 1973), and nearness to routes or religious centres. Therefore, given an overall view, it would not necessarily be considered suboptimal to locate a site on apparently poor soil. In certain situations it may have been considered worthwhile to have the main food supply source away from the site (that is outside the hypothetical bounds of the site catchment area) if other factors of site location were in this way satisfied. Certainly no proof is presented by those conducting site-catchment analysis that 'in most cases economic considerations of resource availability and population size will be the primary factors controlling site location' (Webley 1972, 169).

The importance of subsistence activities is often assumed in site catchment analysis to be such that the pattern of economic exploitation can be derived directly from percentages of land use types in the catchment area.

> We have made the modest assumption that a human group will in the long run make use of those resources within its territory that are economic for it to exploit and that are within reach of the available technology. On this assumption, a site placed in a territory largely composed of grazing country will have been inhabited by human groups intent on the exploitation of grazing animals. Similarly, provided a suitable technology was available, agriculture will have been a prime concern in territories largely suitable for arable cultivation. ... It is, of course, possible and indeed probable that some culture influence, rather than the economic, would have persuaded some human groups to exploit an area in an unsuitable and uneconomic way, particularly in periods of rapid technical change, but we think these occurrences would have been irrelevant to the general trend which, on an archaeological time scale, we are able to perceive [Vita-Finzi and Higgs, 1970, 2].

It would, however, appear to be difficult to determine the relative importance of economic activities such as animal grazing and cereal cropping first because the size of the catchment area is often, in practice, chosen arbitrarily (*ibid.*, 16) and so percentages of land type within the catchment area can only be approximations to the relative importance of different types of land use. Second, there is no reason why the percentage of land use types in an area should directly and accurately reflect the relative importance of land usage in that area. Some soil types are likely to have been exploited preferentially for a variety of reasons. Third, although the relative importance of land suitable for providing plant and animal food is used to reconstruct some site exploitation strategies (Noy *et al.* 1973) and may be used to determine whether enough land of a particular type existed around a site to support sedentism (Vita-Finzi and Higgs 1970, 18–20), it is difficult to see how such hypotheses can be tested by archaeological data, as is suggested by Vita-Finzi and Higgs (1970, 2). The relative amounts of excavated bones and seeds from a site depend to a considerable degree on the methods of collection, the survival conditions of the soil, and the social determinants of refuse deposition.

'The Thünian model does not take into account the influence of non-economic factors and thus is limited in its scope' (Henshall 1967, 445). It is apparent from the above discussion that much the same can be said for site-catchment analysis. In addition, the latter form of analysis has paid little attention to whether subsistence activities might have been influenced by trade in neolithic and later periods. In a study of the Nahal Oren site in Israel (Noy *et al.* 1973, 95), 'the presence of flint from the Menashe hills, particularly in the "pre-pottery Neolithic" layers, and of dentalium shells, suggests that the catchment area was larger than the territory. Such anomalous finds may be readily explained by sporadic extra-territorial exploitation, transhumance or exchange'. However, in such a context, the possibility of the exchange of foodstuffs must be considered (p. 77). Also, sites may have been located relative to trade routes rather than simply to soil types.

A final consideration concerning site catchment analysis is that it suffers from the same difficulty as Von Thünen's 'isolated state'. This is that the sites and their catchment areas are considered in isolation. The soil or land use pattern within a given area of the site is studied, but we are seldom given any idea of broader soil patterns. Thus, in a study by Vita-Finzi and Higgs (1970), coastal Natufian sites are found to have less arable land in their catchment areas than inland upland sites with Natufian assemblages. We are not shown the overall soil pattern, so that it may be the case that there is generally less arable land near the coast than inland in this region. If so, whatever may have been the reasons for site locations, there will be less agricultural land around coastal sites. This does not necessarily indicate less arable farming at the coastal sites. If, on the other hand, it could be shown that, within the overall pattern of land use distribution, certain sites preferred certain land use types or combinations of these, interpretations of economic strategies would have a better basis. The association between the overall pattern of land use types, and land use types in the areas around sites could be studied with the techniques outlined in section 7.1. If the sites are examined in isolated catchment areas, this is not possible (see, however, Webley 1972).

It would certainly be possible to develop site-catchment analysis by employing more detailed studies of past environments and soil conditions. Also, hypotheses about early subsistence activities in an area and their relationship to present-day activities would have a better basis, if the patterns of land use in that area were studied through later prehistoric and historic periods. A fruitful approach would be to conduct detailed surveys of sites in small areas (e.g. Kruk 1973) so that the total site pattern could be related to the total soil pattern in each studied area. Excavation results at a number of the sites and the results of site-catchment analysis could be used together to reconstruct subsistence activities and to suggest reasons for site locations. Computer simulation would be a valuable tool for testing such hypotheses. Given a soil pattern in an area, the location and spread of sites in that area could be simulated according to different hypotheses concerning economic strategies. The degree of similarity between the observed and simulated site patterns would be informative.

8
Conclusion

In the foregoing chapters it has been apparent that spatial analytical techniques are of general relevance in archaeology because the distributions of sites and artifacts, and the distributions of variables such as the percentage of a pottery type, are important types of archaeological data. From the maps and their relationships we can hope to throw light on many aspects of past human behaviour. However, in chapter 1 it became clear that previous work on this subject has lacked a rigorous approach, so that the application of explicit procedures of analysis is appropriate. There are some serious general problems involved in this type of analysis, which may be considered under three headings – problems resulting from the nature of the archaeological data, particular methodological problems of using the techniques in archaeology, and the problems of the relationship between spatial form and process.

8.1 *Some general problems of the application of spatial analysis in archaeology*

As far as the *problems connected with the data* are concerned, perhaps one of the most serious is spatial variation in site survival. The numerous factors affecting site survival, such as motorway and housing construction and modern methods of agriculture, have been discussed in chapter 2. Much of the patterning of site distributions is probably the result of the pattern of site erosion and destruction and also of local archaeological interest. This is clearly an extremely difficult problem to overcome in reference to archaeological sites, the only answer seeming to be very detailed examination of past and recent research activities and practices of land use. In this way perhaps some idea of the possible distortions of the maps may be gained. Kruk's (1973) work in this field would seem to be a promising development.

In terms of artifact distributions, survival problems can to some extent be alleviated by comparing the distribution under study with other distributions. For example, in a study of the distribution of a neolithic axe type (p. 107), the distribution was found to be different in nature from that of similar objects in the same area. Since it is likely that, in a small area, both types of object have had equal chances of survival and recovery, their difference in distribution is informative. Similarly, it is useful to plot 'negatives' on distribution maps – that is contemporaneous sites without the variable being mapped. If this is done, then it can often be shown whether a 'blank' area on a map is the result of a lack of excavated sites or of a real absence of the variable from sites in that area.

If patterning on distribution maps is expected to be the result of uneven research interests and activities then it is up to the archaeologist to test this possibility by further detailed fieldwork. But the importance of survival and recovery effects varies very much from region to region and depends on the scale at which the distributions are being considered. It became clear in section 2.2, that as more detailed spatial patterning is investigated so the distortion effects of survival and recovery must loom larger in the consideration of the researcher. But it is perhaps at the local level that survival and recovery factors can best be investigated in detail (Kruk 1973) and compensated for in discussing the distributions. At wider scales it may be difficult to gain a reliable impression of the effects of different research interests and intensities of work, so that it is correspondingly less easy to assess the distribution maps.

As well as the problems connected with the survival and recovery of archaeological data, there is the particular difficulty resulting from the inability to date prehistoric sites accurately. In many areas excavations of large numbers of sites were carried out before systematic excavation methods were widely in use, and in many areas local typological development is not yet fully understood. In such cases it is extremely difficult to produce a map on which all the sites can confidently be said to be exactly contemporaneous. In earlier periods especially, phases based on typological development are fairly long and it is difficult to know how frequently settlements moved within them. Thus to say that two sites are precisely contemporaneous is a difficult task. Such problems can only be overcome by the application of more accurate dating techniques and more detailed studies of local cultural development.

It is important that most of the techniques discussed in the preceding chapters demand good data. Although bodies of reliable information are beginning to be collected and many have been used in the foregoing pages, it is to be hoped that archaeologists will be stimulated by the possibilities offered by the techniques to collect in the future more data of high standard.

But even with good data, there are *problems connected with the methods and techniques* themselves. These have been fully discussed, but one general problem resulting from their application in archaeology should be emphasised. Many of the statistical tests which have been used demand certain assumptions to be made about the data. For example, in discussing regression analysis and trend surface analysis, it was noted that the data should be normally distributed if tests of significance are to be applied. In many cases in archaeology it is impossible to make the necessary assumptions. As a result, the tests cannot be used with the rigour possible in other disciplines and they should be regarded with special care and caution when applied to archaeological data. Perhaps one promising answer to this problem of significance tests is to randomise the data and then to re-apply the statistical tests using the randomised information. This is the approach which has been used for the tests of spatial autocorrelation, and for the regression analysis which was applied to the middle Bronze Age palstaves. If measures such as the correlation coefficient can be recalculated after a large number of randomisations of the data, then a good idea can be obtained of the likelihood of getting the observed value of the statistic 'by chance'. This approach will often, of course, imply the use of high speed computers. But perhaps the most satisfactory way of testing the reliability of observed patterns is to collect further data, where this is possible, in order to see whether the new data fit in with the observed trends. For example, the significance of the difference in type of fall-off curve corresponding to different artifact types, which has been discussed in section 5.2 and by Hodder (1974*a*), can only be tested or shown to have validity by the collection and analysis of further data.

The *third general problem* to be discussed here is that different spatial processes may produce the same spatial form. Thus an association might be demonstrated between two distributions, but this provides no explanation as to the reason for the association. There may be no direct causal link between the two distributions, for both may be the result of some third factor or the association may be the result of the pattern of site survival and recovery. In fact a large number of processes could have produced the observed association and it is often impossible to distinguish between them from the form of the association itself. Similarly, a number of different dispersal processes can produce similar forms of fall-offs and this has been shown in section 5.3 by the simulation of different types of random walks. There would seem to be two main approaches to this problem of interpreting process from form. One is by simulation. The simulation of random walks, although showing that different processes could produce similar fall-off curves, also showed that, in certain cases, different processes could be identified. Intensive local and direct contact with a centre produces fall-off patterns rather different from indirect contact in which objects move several times before reaching their final destination. These different processes have been found to relate to different types of archaeological material – on the one hand low-value objects, and, on the other, 'expensive' or highly valued products. Also, by simulating the spread of Bandkeramik settlement it has been shown that we can experiment with hypotheses about how that spread occurred (Hodder 1975). There is certainly a potential here for much further work.

Another approach to the problem of discerning between different processes which produce similar patterns is to employ very detailed analytical procedures in examining the patterns. For example, detailed analysis of early settlement in south Poland (p. 89) showed that it was possible to discover whether a distribution of sites had resulted from a process of spread or from density variation due to environmental, survival and recovery factors. In this case, the process which produced the distribution could be suggested. However, in other cases, the archaeological evidence may be inferior, or the different processes being considered may not result in very different forms of distribution. In such cases it may be impossible to differentiate between different processes, even after detailed analysis. This was the conclusion reached after an examination of the distribution of the Romano-British walled towns (section 4.3).

A related problem to that of differentiating spatial processes from spatial forms should be discussed. This concerns the fitting to the archaeological data of theoretically derived functions such as regression curves, polynomial trend surfaces and the negative binomial distribution. There seems little point in doing this if the functions and curves are chosen arbitrarily. A value only becomes apparent if the functions chosen can be shown to be the result of relevant theoretical processes or have been found empirically to represent specific processes. For example, the negative binomial model used in section 4.4 concerns processes of either contagious spread, or the random allocation of points in an area but with the mean density varying from place to place. Also, the various types of regression curves fitted in section 5.2 to a wide range of archaeological data have been noted in various studies outside archaeology to represent different processes of spread. This work in human geography and plant ecology has been fully summarised in section 5.3. There is, therefore, some basis for the use of similar curves in archaeology.

If an *ad hoc* choice of curve has to be made, this seriously limits the value of the results of the analysis, since it is probable that many curves could be found which fit the data equally well. This is a problem concerning the use of trend surface analysis (section 5.4). Archaeologists, if they use this type of analysis, are forced, as are human geographers and geologists, to do what amounts to fitting trends of an arbitrary nature to their data. However, the polynomials which are usually used in trend surface analysis are flexible and can conform to complex surfaces (p. 162). They have been very widely applied in geology and human geography with many valuable results (Chorley and Haggett 1965). The advantages of and difficulties with the method have been made clear before its use in archaeology. Nevertheless it must be remembered that the fitted surfaces do not have any theoretical basis and the polynomial functions are only used as approximations to the results of prehistoric spatial processes. It is for this reason that the curve-fitting processes mentioned in the previous paragraph are of considerably greater value.

8.2 *The value and relevance of spatial analysis in archaeology*

One of the applications in archaeology of the techniques discussed in the preceding chapters is to enable us to examine different processes which may have produced similar distribution maps. The value and relevance of spatial analytical techniques in archaeology will be further considered. A quantitative approach would seem to provide a clarity in the demonstration of spatial trends, patterns and relationships. It also provides a certain objectivity in the analysis of these patterns. The techniques also often lead to the discovery of patterns not revealed by usual archaeological analysis, and thus provide something for the archaeologist to explain. The methods aid the testing of hypotheses about spatial processes, allow large amounts of data to be handled, and enable predictions to be made about the location, importance and functioning of sites.

Clarification would seem to be an important function of the quantified approach which has been suggested. Trends in the data can be demonstrated more clearly if the data are in a quantified form. A good example of this is provided by fig.2.4 in which the percentages of fine Romano-British pottery are shown. By providing such information on a map it is easier to assess whether there is a relationship between the pottery and the Roman roads. This is further facilitated by providing different symbols for evidence of different qualities, and by including 'negatives'. A clear pattern is shown in fig.5.73 in which a type of Romano-British pottery extends markedly up one Roman road. By producing detailed quantified maps, then, we are in a better position to decide whether spatial data show trends or patterns which may be of interest. In discussing the distribution of the Bagterp spearheads (5.4.2), localised manufacture and dispersal was evident in the pattern of residuals from a fitted trend surface. Although localised workshops had already been suspected, this was clarified by a more detailed analysis.

In chapter 1 it was shown that objectivity is a desirable quality to inject into the analysis of distribution maps because such maps are very susceptible to subjective impressions. It is often easy to see the patterning that is desired in a particular map. Techniques are therefore necessary to allow map pattern to be assessed rigorously. Measures of spatial autocorrelation are especially valuable in the initial stages of map analysis. They provide an objective way of discerning whether structured patterning exists in the distribution of some variable. This would be a useful preliminary procedure to carry out in many spatial studies. Often, however, the level of objectivity obtainable in archaeology is less than in other disciplines for the reasons already discussed. But a certain degree of objectivity may always be obtained by using explicit well-defined and repeatable procedures. For example two trend surface analyses of the regression type, if applied to the same data, will always produce the same results and the procedure is explicit and well defined. This is not the case with a subjective contouring of some mapped variable. Different people are likely to produce different results. Similarly, the residual patterning resulting from the regression analysis of palstave similarities (p. 124) suggested local styles which were not only clearer and easier to distinguish than those produced by other methods, but which were also derived by an explicit and well-defined procedure. In the analysis of point distributions, the subjective approach to searching for pattern has been shown (chapter 1) to be inadequate. Methods such as nearest-neighbour analysis allow patterning in such data to be defined in reference to random patterns. The degree of departure of the observed distribution from this convenient base can be measured and, although the types of pattern which can be identified in this way are limited, more detailed techniques are available such as that used in the analysis of the Mayan site distribution (section 3.2). All these techniques describe pattern in a way that is impossible subjectively.

A further value of applying spatial analytical techniques in archaeology is that problems and patterns may be discovered which have not been revealed by usual archaeological methods. If new structured patterning is obtained, then this gives the archaeologist something more to work with and explain. For example, the identification of spatial autocorrelation in a set of spatial data immediately gives us something to explain and interpret. Also association analysis, applied in section 6.2 to the distributions of Bronze Age artifacts in northwest Germany, was able to identify small localised groupings which had not been distinguished as a result of normal archaeological procedures. Similarly, more detailed groupings of material resulted from the analysis of Hänsel's middle Bronze Age data. In both cases too, some idea of the structure of the association groupings could be obtained. This all provides additional information which may play an important part in the interpretation of the data.

In many cases an explanation of the newly revealed patterning may be immediately apparent. For example, localisations of artifact types in a settlement *may* suggest different activity areas, and differing associations *may* indicate 'tool kits'. The analysis of sites such as Iron Age hillforts and Mayan ceremonial centres, which are regularly spaced, may indicate a competitive relationship which could not have been otherwise demonstrable from their spatial distributions. Competition between sites tells us something about the society in which the phenomenon occurs. A further example of the additional information which may be provided as a result of the application of spatial analytical techniques, is provided by the examination of fine Romano-British pottery from the Oxford and New Forest kilns (sections 5.2, 5.4.2, 5.6.2). When the Oxford pottery was analysed in detail, the regression residuals from the fitted model (section 5.2) had a structure which could immediately be explained in terms of pottery transport along waterways, and in terms of the competing centre in the New Forest. Similarly, as better data become available from a large number of well-excavated Romano-British sites, it is possible that areas of positive regression residuals from fitted trend surfaces will be shown to occur around certain nodal centres. These nodes could then be interpreted in terms of market centres and the patterning would add much to our understanding of the Romano-British economy.

Often, however, the explanation for a newly identified trend or pattern may not be immediately obvious. It is important, nevertheless, that the patterning which does exist should be discovered. The regression analysis of palstave similarities (p. 124) indicated local styles in palstave manufacture. But it is difficult to know how these should be interpreted – whether in terms of social groupings, marketing patterns, or the work of one family of travelling smiths. This problem leads on to a further value of applying spatial analysis in archaeology. This is that it aids the testing of hypotheses.

Hypotheses can often be tested or examined in a formal way if they are couched in quantified terms. In such cases a hypothesis can be compared directly with the data, although we are often left with the problem of deciding how well it fits the data. But the general value of this approach was apparent in the analysis of the Romano-British walled towns (section 4.3), because in this way the relative importance of different hypotheses for the location of the towns could be judged. Although, in this case, the results were not clear-cut, the procedure would seem to be worthwhile if we wish to examine hypotheses critically. The construction of mathematical or statistical models or hypotheses also allows direct comparison with the data. A good example of the value of applying such models is provided by the gravity models (section 5.6.2). By comparing artifact distributions around centres with the predictions of these models, we can throw light on hypotheses concerning the functioning of central places, competition with other centres, and the reasons for the form of the artifact distributions. For example, in an examination of Romano-British pottery from the Rowlands

Castle kilns (5.6.2), a reason for the rather lop-sided distribution could be suggested as a result of applying the gravity model, and the part played by the town at Chichester in the distribution could also be hypothesised. Similarly, the distributions of Oxford and New Forest pottery differ in extent (5.6.2) and a hypothesis that this was due to competition between kiln centres of different sizes could be examined by applying the gravity model. The close correspondence between the actual distributions and those predicted by the gravity model does not prove that the hypothesis is correct. It simply adds weight to the suggested relationship between the two centres.

A value of applying spatial and computerised analytical procedures in archaeology is that large amounts of data can often be handled more easily. The analysis of a large number of distributions from the early Bronze Age in northern Germany (6.2) was made possible by the existence of well-defined methods which could be used on computers. In the same way, use of a high speed computer allowed a large number of different techniques and analyses to be applied to the middle Bronze Age palstave data (p. 119), so that more detailed information could be gained. A regression analysis of a data set containing 4950 palstave similarities would have been practically impossible by any other means.

Our final point concerning the value of the application of spatial analysis in archaeology is less apparent and its relevance is uncertain. The possibility exists that the methods and models could be used ultimately to predict the location of undiscovered sites. Equally, it would be possible, for example, to predict the relative importance of known sites. Any such predictions would, of course, have to be tested by fieldwork, but they may be of value to those concerned with survey and excavation strategy in an area. If there is limited money and time to examine the archaeology of a region, then the application of spatial techniques could be used to predict which sites were most important (for instance, by the application of some re-formulation of the gravity models), or to suggest which sites should be excavated if the fullest possible understanding of the settlement pattern is to be gained with the allotted resources. The location of kilns could, for example, be predicted by the high point on fitted trend surfaces. It would be difficult to do this with a high degree of accuracy, since the results have been shown (section 5.4.1) to depend to some extent on the methods used. The analysis might, however, suggest the best areas to investigate.

Some of the values of applying spatial analytical methods in archaeology have been summarised, but the realisation of the full potential of these techniques in archaeology will go hand-in-hand with the collection of better data. If the archaeologist working in the field can recognise the value of collecting very detailed information about spatial patterns then the quality of data necessary for the better understanding of spatial processes will begin to be amassed. Careful excavation of sites with detailed recording of percentages of types present will allow a better idea of inter-site relationships. Painstaking recording on sites of the position of artifacts and their relationship to other features will provide data for the analysis of within-site patterns. Some of the additional types of information which could be collected have been discussed in chapter 2, but it is really the slow collection of large bodies of reliable data, whether these concern neolithic axes or Romano-British pottery, that will allow spatial processes to be better understood. If interest in spatial processes increases, it is hoped that the discussion of techniques provided in this work will be of some value.

APPENDIX

Note on the Clark and Evans test of spatial randomness

PETER J. DIGGLE

Department of Statistics,
University of Newcastle upon Tyne

Clark and Evans (1954) propose a simple test of spatial randomness based on a complete census of nearest-neighbour distances in a population of moderate size, n. Noting that, in a completely randomly distributed population of infinite extent and density ρ individuals per unit area, the distance, X, from a randomly selected individual to its nearest neighbour has mean $1/2\sqrt{\rho}$ and variance $(4 - \pi)/4\pi\rho \simeq 0.0683/\rho$, they define an 'index of non-randomness',

$$R = 2\sqrt{\rho} \sum_{i=1}^{n} x_i/n = 2\sqrt{\rho}\bar{x}, \qquad (A.1)$$

which should be approximately equal to one in a completely random population, small values suggesting aggregation, and large values regularity. They further suggest that the statistic

$$C = [\bar{x} - 1/(2\sqrt{\rho})]\sqrt{(0.0683/n\rho)} \qquad (A.2)$$

will be approximately Normally distributed, with zero mean and unit variance, in a completely random population. In both the above formulae, ρ is to be intepreted as the *actual* number of individuals per unit area in the population.

The test has recently found favour with archaeologists since it permits full utilisation of comparatively scarce data. However, the use of a complete census of n individuals, rather than an independent random sample of size n from a very much larger population, raises a number of questions. The problem of edge-effects was recognised by Clark and Evans, who recommended that measurements should be taken only from individuals within a centrally located subsection of the population. Note, however, that the alternative procedure of simply ignoring any measured distance greater than the distance from the corresponding individual to the edge of the population leads to bias in favour of the retention of small nearest-neighbour distances. Thus, the centrally located subpopulation should be chosen somewhat con-

Table A.1.   *The results of the Monte Carlo experiment*

n	Estimate of $n\rho$ Var $(\bar{x})$ (standard error in brackets)	1. p	2. Size of nominal 5% equal-tailed test (%)
25	0.0756 (0.0038)	0.010	6.2
30	0.0740 (0.0033)	0.033	6.0
40	0.0703 (0.0031)	0.254	5.4
50	0.0687 (0.0031)	0.444	5.0
60	0.0749 (0.0034)	0.017	6.2
70	0.0706 (0.0032)	0.224	5.4
80	0.0786 (0.0035)	0.001	6.8

1. p = probability of obtaining a value for $n\rho$ Var $(\bar{x})$ as great as or greater than the tabulated value, assuming the value 0.683 to be correct.
2. Refers to the actual size of a nominal 5% equal-tailed test, assuming the tabulated value of $n\rho$ Var $(\bar{x})$ to be correct.

servatively, and the available population size may be reduced considerably.

A second problem is that of non-independence of the different nearest-neighbour distances. For example, Pielou (1969, 121) has shown that, in a completely random population, two individuals will be closer to one another than to any third individual with probability approximately 0.62, and while Clark and Evans state that 'such double distances introduce no bias and both measurements should be used in the calculations', the rather complex correlation structure among the different x_i may adversely affect the Normal approximation to the distribution of $\bar{x}$, and will almost certainly increase its variance.

To investigate this second difficulty, a Monte Carlo experiment was carried out in which n individuals were positioned independently and uniformly at random within a circle, surrounded by a 'buffer-zone' of randomly distributed individuals. For each of several values of n, 1000 replications of the experiment were performed, and estimates of the moments of $\bar{x}$ obtained. The third and fourth moments gave no indication of non-Normality for $\bar{x}$, but the estimated variance was consistently larger than the value of $0.0683/np$ assumed by Clark and Evans, suggesting that the test is liable to give spuriously significant results; the element of inaccuracy so introduced is, however, of a comparatively minor nature (see table A.1).

We conclude that the use of the Clark and Evans test is not unreasonable, with the provisos that nominal significance levels will tend to be slightly optimistic and, more seriously, that little information appears to be available concerning the power of the test against alternatives to complete spatial randomness. As regards rival tests, Diggle, Besag and Gleaves (1975) discussed the use of distance methods for the analysis of spatial point patterns and compared a number of tests designed primarily for use in large populations, with particular reference to their respective powers against plausible alternatives. In contrast, Mead (1974) proposed a series of tests based on data from a grid of contiguous quadrats, which may be more suitable in the present context, although an objective investigation of power has again not yet been undertaken.

BIBLIOGRAPHY

This includes relevant works of general interest
not cited in the text.

Abbreviations
A.A.A.G.   *Annals of the Association of American Geographers*
C.B.A.   Council for British Archaeology
P.P.S.   *Proceedings of the Prehistoric Society*

Abler, R., Adams, J. and Gould, P. (1971). *Spatial organisation*. Prentice
Hall, Englewood Cliffs, N.J.
Ahmad, E. (1952). Rural Settlement types in the Uttar Pradesh (United
Provinces of Agra and Oudh). *A.A.A.G.*, **42**, 223–46.
Allen, D. F. (1944). The Belgic dynasties of Britain and their coins.
Archaeologia, **90**, 1–46.
   (1958). The origins of coinage in Britain: a reappraisal. In Frere, S. S. (ed.),
Problems of the Iron Age in southern Britain. Institute of Archaeology,
London.
   (1961). A study of the Dobunnic coinage. In Clifford, E. M., *Bagendon:
A Belgic oppidum*, pp. 75–149. Heffer, Cambridge.
Alonso, W. (1964). Location theory. In Friedmann, J. and Alonso, W. (eds.),
Regional development and planning: a reader, pp. 78–106. Massachusetts
Institute of Technology.
Ammerman, A. J. and Cavalli-Sforza, L. L. (1972). Measuring the rate of
spread of early farming in Europe. *Man*, **6**, 674–88.
   (1973a). A population model for the diffusion of early farming in Europe.
In Renfrew (1973a), pp. 343–57.
   (1973b). Bandkeramik simulation models: a preliminary report,
(circulated privately).
Annable, F. K. (1962). A Romano-British pottery in Savernake Forest.
Kilns 1–2. *Wiltshire Archaeological and Natural History Magazine*, **58**,
143–55.
Anscombe, F. J. (1950). Sampling theory of the negative binomial and
logarithmic series distributions. *Biometrika*, **37**, 358–82.
Atkin, R. H. (1972). Research Report I, Urban structure Research Project.
University of Essex, Colchester.
   (1973a). Research Report II, Urban Structure Research Project.
University of Essex, Colchester.
   (1973b). Research Report III, Urban Structure Research Project.
University of Essex, Colchester.
Atkinson, R. J. C. (1972). The demographic implications of fieldwork. In
Fowler, E. (ed.), *Field survey in British archaeology*, pp. 60–6. C.B.A.,
London.

Azoury, I. and Hodson, F. R. (1973). Comparing paleolithic assemblages; Ksar Akil, a case study. *World Archaeology*, **4**, 292–306.

Barnard, G. A. and Pearson, E. S. (1947). Significance tests for 2 × 2 tables. *Biometrika*, **34**, 123–38; The choice of statistical tests illustrated on the interpretation of data classed in a 2 × 2 table. *Ibid.*, **34**, 139–67.

Barnes, J. A. (1972). *Social networks*. Addison-Wesley Module in Anthropology, **26**, 1–29.

Bartlett, M. S. (1960). *Stochastic population models in ecology and epidemiology*. Methuen, London.

Bateman, A. J. (1962). Data from plants and animals. In Sutter, J. (ed.), *Human displacements*, pp. 85–90. Hachette, Paris.

Benet, F. (1957). Explosive markets: the Berber highlands. In Polanyi, K., Arensberg, C. M. and Pearson, H. W. (eds.), *Trade and Market in the early empires*, pp. 188–217. Free Press, Glencoe, Ill.

Benson, D. and Miles, D. (1974). *The Upper Thames valley*. Oxford Archaeological Unit, Survey No. 2. Oxford.

Bergmann, J. (1968). Ethnosoziologische Untersuchungen an Grab- und Hortfundgruppen der älteren Bronzezeit in Nordwestdeutschland. *Germania*, **46**, 224–40.

(1970). *Die ältere Bronzezeit Nordwestdeutschlands*. Elwert, Marburg.

Berry, B. J. L. (1961). City size distributions and economic development. *Economic development and cultural change*, **9**, 573–88.

(1967). *The geography of market centres and retail distribution*. Prentice Hall, Englewood Cliffs, N.J.

Berry, B. J. L. and Garrison, W. L. (1958a). A note on central place theory and the range of a good. *Economic geography*, **34**, 304–11.

(1958b). Recent developments in central place theory. *Papers and proceedings, regional science association*, 1958, 107–20.

Berry, B. J. L. and Pred, A. (1961). *Central place studies*. Regional Sciences Research Institute, Bibliography series, no. 1. Philadelphia.

Berry, B. J. L., Simons, J. W. and Tennant, R. J. (1963). Urban population densities: structure and change. *Geographical Review*, **53**, 389–405.

Bessac, F. (1968). Cultunit and ethnic unit – processes and symbolism. In *Essays on the problem of tribe*, pp. 58–71. American Ethnological Society, University of Washington Press, Seattle.

Binford, L. R. (1963). 'Red Ocher' caches from the Michigan area: a possible case of cultural drift. *Southwestern Journal of Anthropology*, **19**, 89–108.

(1972). *An archaeological perspective*. Seminar Press, New York.

Blalock, H. M. (1960). *Social statistics*. McGraw Hill, New York.

Bohannan, P. (1954). The migration and expansion of the Tiv. *Africa*, **24**, 2–16.

Bohannan, P. and Dalton, G. (eds.) (1962). *Markets in Africa*. Northwestern University Press, Ill.

Bohmers, A., Bruijn, A., Modderman, P. J. R. and Waterbolk, H. T. (1959). Zusammenfassende Betrachtungen über die Bandkeramik in den Niederlanden. *Palaeohistoria*, **6–7**, 225.

Bordes, F. (1973). *A tale of two caves*. Harper and Row, New York.

Bracey, H. E. (1956). A rural component of centrality applied to six southern counties in the United Kingdom. *Economic Geography*, **32**, 39–50.

Bradley, R. (1970). The excavation of a Beaker settlement at Belle Tout, East Sussex, England, *P.P.S.*, **36**, 312–79.

(1971). Trade competition and artefact distribution. *World Archaeology*, **2**, 347–52.

Branigan, K. (1967). Romano-British rural settlement in the western Chilterns. *Archaeological Journal*, **124**, 129–59.

Bray, J. R. (1956). A study of mutual occurrence of plant species. *Ecology*, **37**, 21–8.

Bretz-Mahler, D. (1971). *La civilisation de la Tène I en Champagne*. Centre National de la Recherche Scientifique.

Brown, L. A. and Moore, E. G. (1969). Diffusion research in geography: a perspective. *Progress in Geography*, **1**, 121–57.

Brownlee, J. (1911). The mathematical theory of random migration and epidemic distribution. *Proceedings of the Royal Society of Edinburgh*, **31**, 262–89.

Brush, J. E. (1953). The hierarchy of central places in Southwestern Wisconsin, *Geographical Review*, **43**, 380–402.

Brush, J. E. and Bracey, H. E. (1955). Rural service centres in southwestern Wisconsin and southern England. *Geographical Review*, **45**, 559–69.

Bulleid, A. and Gray, H. St. G. (1948). *The Meare lake village*. Taunton.

Bunge, W. (1966). *Theoretical geography*. Lund studies in geography, *C*, **1** (2nd edn).

Bylund, E. (1960). Theoretical considerations regarding the distribution of settlement in inner north Sweden. *Geografiska Annaler*, B, **42**, 225–31.

Calkin, J. B. (1948). The Isle of Purbeck in the Iron Age. *Proceedings of the Dorset Natural History and Archaeological Society*, **70**, 53–4.

Carroll, J. D. and Bevis, H. W. (1957). Predicting local travel in urban regions. *Papers and proceedings of the Regional Science Association*, **3**, 183–97.

Carrothers, G. A. P. (1956). An historical review of the gravity and potential concepts of human interaction. *Journal of the American Institute of Planners*, **22**, 94–102.

Carter, H. (1955). Urban grades and spheres of influence in south west Wales: an historical consideration. *Scottish Geographical Magazine*, **71**, 43–58.

Catana, A. J. Jr (1963). The wandering quarter method of estimating population density. *Ecology*, **44**, 349–60.

Chaney, R. P. and Ruiz Revilla, R. (1969). Sampling methods and interpretation of correlation: a comparative analysis of seven cross-cultural samples. *American Anthropology*, **71**, 597–633.

Chang, K. C. (1972). *Settlement patterns in archaeology*. Addison–Wesley Module in Anthropology, **24**, 1–26.

Childe, G. (1951). *Social evolution*. C. A. Watts, London.

Chisholm, M. D. I. (1962). *Rural settlement and land use: an essay in location*. Hutchinson, London.

Chisholm, M. and O'Sullivan, P. (1973). *Freight flows and spatial aspects of the British economy*. Cambridge University Press, London.

Chorley, R. J. and Haggett, P. H. (1965). Trend-surface mapping in geographical research. *Transactions of the Institute of British Geographers*, **37**, 47–67.

Chorley, R. J. and Kennedy, B. A. (1971). *Physical geography. A systems approach*. Prentice Hall, London.

Christaller, W. (1933). *Die zentralen Orte in Suddeutschland*. Jena.

Claeson, C. F. (1968). Distance and human interaction. *Geografiska Annaler B*, **50**, 142–61.

Clark, G. (1957). *Archaeology and society* (3rd edn). Methuen, London.
(1965). Traffic in stone axe and adze blades. *Economic History Review*, 2nd series, **18**, 1–28.

Clark, P. J. and Evans, F. C. (1954). Distance to nearest neighbour as a measure of spatial relationships in populations. *Ecology*, **35**, 445–53.

Clarke, D. L. (1968). *Analytical Archaeology*. Methuen, London.

(1972). Models and paradigms in contemporary archaeology, and A provisional model of an Iron Age society and its settlement system. In Clarke, D. L. (ed.), *Models in archaeology*, pp. 1–60, and 801–70. Methuen, London.

Cliff, A. D. (1968). The neighbourhood effect in the diffusion of innovations. *Transactions of the Institute of British Geographers*, **44**, 75–84.

Cliff, A. D., Haggett, P. and Ord, J. K. (1974). *Elementary regional structure: some quantitative approaches to the spatial organisation of static and dynamic regional systems*. Cambridge University Press, London.

Cliff, A. D., Martin, R. L. and Ord, J. K. (1974). Evaluating the friction of distance parameter in gravity models. *Regional Studies*, **8**, 281–6.

Cliff, A. D. and Ord, J. K. (1973). *Spatial autocorrelation*. London.

(1974). The quantitative approach in human geography: a review, an interpretation and some new results, (privately circulated).

Clifford, E. M. (1955). Stamped tiles found in Gloucestershire. *Journal of Roman Studies*, **45**, 68–72.

Cochran, W. G. (1952). The χ^2 Test of goodness of fit. *Annal of Mathematical Statistics*, **23**, 315–45.

Cohen, J. E. (1966). *A model of simple competition*. Harvard University Press.

Cohen, R. and Schlegel, A. (1968). The tribe as a socio-political unit: a cross-cultural examination. In *Essays on the problem of tribe*, American Ethnological Society, pp. 120–49. University of Washington Press, Seattle.

Cottam, G. and Curtis, J. T. (1949). A method for making rapid surveys of woodlands by means of pairs of randomly selected trees. *Ecology*, **30**, 101–4.

Cox, D. R. and Miller, H. D. (1965). *The theory of stochastic processes*. Methuen, London.

Croxton, F. E. (1953). *Elementary statistics with applications in medicine and the biological sciences*. Dover Pubns.

Cummins, W. A. (1974). The neolithic stone axe trade in Britain. *Antiquity*, **48**, 201–5.

Cunliffe, B. W. (1966). Regional groupings within the Iron Age of southern Britain. Ph.D. thesis, University of Cambridge.

(1971*a*). Some aspects of hillforts and their cultural environments. In Jesson, M. and Hill, D., *The Iron Age and its hillforts*, pp. 53–69. Southampton University Press.

(1971*b*). *Excavations at Fishbourne: 1961–1969*, vol. 2. Reports of the Research Committee of the Society of Antiquaries of London, no. 27.

(1972). Saxon and medieval settlement-pattern in the region of Chalton, Hampshire. *Medieval Archaeology*, **16**, 1–12.

Cunliffe, B. W. and Phillipson, D. W. (1968). Excavations at Eldon's Seat, Encombe, Dorset, *P.P.S.*, **34**, 191–237.

Cunnington, M. E. (1909). Notes on a late Celtic rubbish heap near Oare. *Wiltshire Archaeological Magazine*, **36**, 125–39.

(1923). *The early Iron Age inhabited site at All Cannings Cross farm, Wiltshire*. Devizes Museum.

Curry, L. (1964). The random spatial economy: an exploration in settlement theory. *A.A.A.G.*, **54**, 138–46.

(1967). Central places in the random spatial economy. *Journal of Regional Science*, **7** (supplement), 217–38.

Dacey, M. F. (1963). Order neighbour statistics for a class of random patterns in multidimensional space. *A.A.A.G.*, **53**, 505–15.
  (1964). Modified Poisson probability law for point pattern more regular than random. *A.A.A.G.*, **54**, 559–65.
  (1967). An empiric study of the areal distribution of houses in Puerto Rico. *Transactions of the Institute of British Geographers*, **45**, 51–69.
  (1973). Statistical tests of spatial association in the locations of tool types. *American Antiquity*, **38**, 320–8.
Dacey, M. F. and Tung, T. (1962). The identification of randomness in point patterns. *Journal of Regional Science*, **4**, 83–96.
Dalton, G. (1969). Theoretical issues in economic anthropology. *Current Anthropology*, **10**, 63–102.
Daniel, G. (1962). *The idea of prehistory*. Penguin, London.
Davey, P. J. (1971). The distribution of later Bronze age metalwork from Lincolnshire. *P.P.S.*, **37**, 96–111.
David, N. (1972). On the life span of pottery, type frequencies and archaeological inference. *American Antiquity*, **37**, 141–2.
Davies, O. L. (1961). *Statistical methods in research and production*. Oliver and Boyd, Edinburgh.
Davies, O. L. and Goldsmith, P. L. (1972). *Statistical methods in research and production*. Oliver and Boyd, Edinburgh.
Davis, J. C. (1973). *Statistics and data analysis in geology*. Wiley, New York.
Deetz, J. (1967). *Invitation to archaeology*. Natural History Press, New York.
De Navarro, J. M. (1925). Prehistoric routes between northern Europe and Italy defined by the amber trade. *Geographical Journal*, **66**, 481–507.
Dice, L. R. (1945). Measures of the amount of ecologic associations between species. *Ecology*, **26**, 297–302.
Dickinson, R. E. (1932). The distribution and functions of the smaller urban settlements of East Anglia. *Geography*, **17**, 19–31.
Dicks, T. R. B. (1972). Network analysis and historical geography. *Area*, **4**, 4–9.
Diggle, P. J., Besag, J. and Gleaves, J. T. (1975). On the statistical analysis of spatial point patterns by means of distance methods. *Biometrics* (in press).
Dixon, J. R., Cann, J. R. and Renfrew, C. (1968). Obsidian and the origins of trade. *Scientific American*, **218**, 38–46.
Doran, J. (1969). Systems theory, computer simulations and archaeology. *World Archaeology*, **1**, 289–98.
Douglas, M. (1962). Lele economy compared with the Bushong. In Bohannan and Dalton (eds.), *Markets in Africa*, pp. 211–33. Northwestern University Press, Ill.
Doveton, J. H. and Parsley, A. J. (1970). Experimental evaluation of trend surface distributions induced by inadequate data-point distributions. *Transactions, Section b, Institute of Mining and Metallurgy*, B197–B208.
Draper, N. R. and Smith, H. (1966). *Applied regression analysis*. Wiley, New York.
Driver, H. E. (1961). Introduction to statistics for comparative research. In Moore, F. W. (ed.), *Readings in cross-cultural methodology*, pp. 303–31. Hraf Press, New Haven.
Driver, H. E. and Massey, W. C. (1957). Comparative studies of North American Indians. *Transactions of the American Philosophical Society*, **47**, 166–456.
Drury, P. J. (1972). Preliminary report. The Romano-British settlement at Chelmsford, Essex: *Caesaromagos*. *Transactions of the Essex Archaeological Society*, no. **4**.

Edmonson, M. S. (1961). Neolithic diffusion rates. *Current Anthropology*, **2**, 71–102.

Ellison, A. and Harriss, J. (1972). Settlement and land use in the prehistory and early history of southern England: a study based on locational models. In Clarke, D. L. (ed.), *Models in archaeology*, pp. 911–62. Methuen, London.

Evans, J. D. (1973). Sherd weights and sherd counts – a contribution to the problem of quantifying pottery studies. In Strong, E. D. (ed.), *Archaeological theory and practice*, pp. 131–49. Seminar Press, London.

Evens, E. D., Grinsell, L. V., Piggott, S. and Wallis, F. S. (1962). Fourth report of the sub-committee of the southwestern group of museums and art galleries on the petrological identification of stone axes. *P.P.S.*, **28**, 209–66.

Firth, R. (ed.) (1967a). *Themes in economic anthropology*. Tavistock Pubns., London.

(1967b). Themes in economic anthropology: a general comment. In Firth (1967), pp. 1–28.

Foster, G. M. (1966). The sociology of pottery: questions and hypotheses. In Matson, F. R. (ed.), *Ceramics and man*. Viking Fund Publications in Anthropology, no. 41.

Fowler, P. J. (ed.) (1969). M5, M4 and archaeology. *Archaeological Review*, **4**, 13–20.

Fox, C. (1943). *The personality of Britain*. National Museum of Wales, Cardiff.

Frere, S. S. (1967). *Britannia*. Routledge, London.

Friedman, J. and Rowlands, M. (1974). Notes towards an epigenetic model of the evolution of 'civilisation'. *Seminar on the evolution of social systems*, Research seminar on archaeology and related subjects. Institute of Archaeology, London University.

Fulford, M. G. (1973a). A fourth century colour-coated fabric and its types in south-east England. *Sussex Archaeological Collections*, **111**, 41–4.

(1973b). The distribution and dating of New Forest pottery. *Britannia*, **4**, 160–78.

(1973c). The New Forest Roman pottery industry. Ph.D. thesis, University of Southampton.

Fulford, M. G. and Hodder, I. R. (1974). A regression analysis of some late Romano-British fine pottery: a case study. *Oxoniensia*, **39**, 26–33.

Garner, B. J. (1967). Models of urban geography and settlement location. In Chorley, R. J. and Haggett, P. H. (eds.), *Models in geography*, pp. 303–60. Methuen, London.

Geary, R. C. (1954). The contiguity ratio and statistical mapping. *The Incorporated Statistician*, **5**, 115–41.

Getis, A. (1964). Temporal land-use pattern analysis with the use of nearest neighbour and quadrat methods. *A.A.A.G.*, **54**, 391–9.

Gifford, E. W. and Kroeber, A. L. (1937). *Culture element distributions: IV, Pomo*. University of California, Publications in American Archaeology and Ethnology, **37**, 117–255.

Gleave, D. J. (1970). *Trends in journey to work to Newcastle-upon-Tyne, 1925–1966*. University of Newcastle-upon-Tyne, Department of Geography, Seminar papers, no. 13.

Godlund, S. (1956). *The function and growth of bus traffic within the sphere of urban influence*. Lund studies in geography, *B*, no. 18.

Golledge, R. G. (1967). Conceptualising the market decision process. *Journal of Regional Science*, **7** (supplement), 239–58.

Gould, P. R. (1969). *Spatial diffusion*. Association of American Geographers, Resource paper, no. 4.

Gower, J. C. (1971). A general coefficient of similarity and some of its properties. *Biometrics*, **27**, 857–74.

Gray, J. M. (1972). Trend surface analysis. *Area*, **4**, 275–9.

Green, E. L. (1973). Location analysis of prehistoric Maya sites in Northern British Honduras. *American Antiquity*, **38**, 279–93.

Gregory, S. (1963). *Statistical methods and the geographer*. Longman, London.

Greig-Smith, P. (1952). The use of random and contiguous quadrats in the study of the structure of plant communities. *Annals of Botany, London*, **16**, 293–316.

  (1964). *Quantitative plant ecology*. Methuen, London.

Hägerstrand, T. (1953). *Innovation diffusion as a spatial process*. (Translated by Pred, A., 1967. Chicago.)

  (1957). Migration and area. In Hennerberg, D., Hägerstrand, T. and Odeving, B. (eds.). *Migration in Sweden, a symposium*. Lund studies in geography, *B*, no. **13**.

  (1967). On Monte Carlo simulation of diffusion. In Garrison, W. L. and Marble, D. F. (eds.). *Quantitative geography*, **1967**, 1–32.

Haggett, P. (1965). *Locational analysis in human geography*. E. Arnold, London.

  (1972). *Geography: a modern synthesis*. Harper and Row, New York.

Hammond, N. D. C. (1972). Locational models and the site of Lubaantun: a Classic Maya centre. In Clarke, D. L. (ed.), *Models in Archaeology*, pp. 757–800. Methuen, London.

Hänsel, B. (1968). *Beitrage zur Chronologie der mittleren Bronzezeit im Karpathenbecken*. Beiträge zur Ur- und Fruhgeschischtlichen Archäologie des Mittelmeer-Kulturraumes, 7 and 8. Rudolf Habelt, Bonn.

Harding, D. W. (1972). *The Iron Age in the upper Thames basin*. Clarendon Press, Oxford.

Hartley, K. F. (1973). The marketing and distribution of mortaria. *C.B.A. Research Report*, **10**, 39–51.

Harvey, D. (1968). Some methodological problems in the use of the Neyman Type A and the negative binomial probability distributions for the analysis of spatial point patterns. *Transactions and Papers of the Institute of British Geographers*, **44**, 85–95.

  (1969). *Explanation in geography*. E. Arnold, London

Hawkes, C. (1973). Innocence retrieval in archaeology. *Antiquity*, **47**, 176–8.

Helvig, M. (1964). *Chicago's external truck movements*. University of Chicago, Department of Geography research paper, no. **90**.

Henshall, J. D. (1967). Models of agricultural activity. In Chorley, R. J. and Haggett, P. H. (eds.) *Models in Geography*, pp. 425–58. Methuen, London.

Higgs, E. S. and Vita-Finzi, C. (1972). Prehistoric economies: a territorial approach. In Higgs, E. S. (ed.), *Papers in economic prehistory*, pp. 27–36. Cambridge University Press.

Higgs, E. S., Vita-Finzi, C., Harriss, D. R. and Fagg, A. E. (1967). The climate, environment and industries of stone age Greece: part III. *P.P.S.*, **33**, 1–29.

Hill, J. N. (1966). A prehistoric community in Eastern Arizona. *Southwestern Journal of Anthropology*, **22**, 9–30.

  (1968). Broken K. Pueblo: patterns of form and function. In Binford, S. R. and Binford, L. R. (eds.), *New perspectives in archaeology*, pp. 161–70. Aldine Publishing Co., Chicago.

Hindle, B. P. (1972). Networks and Roman roads. Comments. *Area*, **4**, 138–9.

Hodder, B. W. (1963). Markets in Yorubaland. Ph.D. thesis, University of London.
(1965). Some comments on the origins of traditional markets in Africa south of the Sahara. *Transactions of the Institute of British Geographers*, **36**, 97–105.
(1967). West Africa. In Hodder and Harris (1967), pp. 221–58.
Hodder, B. W. and Harris, D. R. (eds.) (1967). *Africa in transition.* Methuen, London.
Hodder, B. W. and Ukwu, U. I. (1969). *Markets in West Africa.* Ibadan University.
Hodder, I. R. (1971). The use of nearest neighbour analysis. *Cornish Archaeology*, **10**, 35–6.
(1972). Locational models and the study of Romano-British settlement. In Clarke, D. L. (ed.) *Models in archaeology*, pp. 887–909. Methuen, London.
(1974a). A regression analysis of some trade and marketing patterns. *World Archaeology*, **6**, 172–89.
(1974b). The distribution of Savernake ware. *Wiltshire Archaeological and Natural History Magazine*, **69**, (in press).
(1974c). The distribution of two types of Romano-British coarse pottery in the west Sussex region. *Sussex Archaeological Collections*, **112**, 1–11.
(1974d). Some marketing models for Romano-British coarse pottery. *Britannia*, **5**, 340–59.
(1975). Some new directions in the spatial analysis of archaeological data. In Clarke, D. L. (ed.), *New directions in archaeology*, (in press).
Hodder, I. R. and Hassall, M. (1971). The non-random spacing of Romano-British walled towns. *Man*, **6**, 391–407.
Hodder, I. R. and Orton, C. R. (1974). A note in 'The distribution of Late Classic Maya major ceremonial centres in the Central Area' by N. Hammond. In Hammond, N. (ed.), *Mesoamerican archaeology. New approaches.* Duckworth, London.
Hodson, F. R. (1962). Some pottery from Eastbourne, the 'Marnians' and the Pre-Roman Iron Age in southern England. *P.P.S.*, **28**, 140–55.
(1964). Cultural grouping within the British pre-Roman Iron Age. *P.P.S.*, **30**, 99–110.
(1969a). Searching for structure within multivariate archaeological data. *World Archaeology*, **1**, 90–105.
(1969b). Cluster analysis and archaeology: some new developments and applications. *World Archaeology*, **1**, 299–320.
Hodson, F. R., Sneath, P. H. and Doran, J. E. (1966). Some experiments in the numerical analysis of archaeological data. *Biometrica*, **53** (3 and 4), 311–324.
Hogg, A. H. A. (1971). Some applications of surface fieldwork. In Jesson, M. and Hill, D. (eds.), *The Iron Age and its hillforts*, pp. 105–25. Southampton University.
Holgate, P. (1965). Some new tests of randomness. *Journal of Ecology*, **53**, 261–6.
Hsu, S. and Tiedemann, C. E. (1968). A rational method of delimiting study areas for unevenly distributed point phenomena. *Professional Geographer*, **20**, 376–81.
Hudson, J. C. (1969). A location theory for rural settlement. *A.A.A.G.*, **59**, 365–81.
Huff, D. L. (1964). Defining and estimating a trading area. *Journal of Marketing*, **28**, 34–8.

Hutchinson, P. (1972). Networks and Roman roads. *Area*, **4**, 279–80.

Isaac, G. Ll. (1972). Early phases of human behaviour: models in Lower Palaeolithic archaeology. In Clarke, D. L. (ed.), *Models in archaeology*, pp. 167–200. Methuen, London.

Jackson, R. T. (1971). Periodic markets in southern Ethiopia. *Transactions of the Institute of British Geographers*, **53**, 31–42.

Jackson, R. (1972). A vicious circle? – The consequences of von Thünen in tropical Africa. *Area*, **4**, 258–61.

Jacob-Friesen, K. K. (1967). *Bronzezeitliche Lanzenspitzen Norddeutschlands und Skandinaviens*. Veröffentlichungen der urgeschichtlichen Sammlungen des Landesmuseums zu Hannover, 17, Hildesheim.

Jarman, M. R. (1972). A territorial model for archaeology: a behavioural and geographical approach. In Clarke, D. L. (ed.), *Models in archaeology*, pp. 705–34. Methuen, London.

Johnson, G. A. (1972). A test of the utility of Central Place Theory in archaeology. In Ucko, P. J., Tringham, R. and Dimbleby, G. (eds.), *Man, settlement and urbanism*, pp. 769–85. Duckworth, London.

Johnston, M. E. (1963). *Econometric methods*. McGraw-Hill, New York.

Jones, A. H. M. (1964). *The Later Roman Empire*, 4 vols. Blackwell, Oxford.

Jope, E. M. (1963). The regional cultures of medieval Britain. In Foster. I. L. and Alcock, L. (eds.), *Culture and environment*, pp. 327–50. Routledge, London.

(1972). The transmission of new ideas: archaeological evidence for implant and dispersal. *World Archaeology*, **4**, 368–73.

Kariel, H. G. (1970). Analysis of the Alberta settlement pattern for 1961 and 1966 by nearest neighbour analysis. *Geografiska Annaler, B*, **52**, 124–31.

Keen, L. and Radley, J. (1971). Report on the petrological identification of stone axes from Yorkshire. *P.P.S.*, **37**, 16–37.

Kenyon, K. M. (1955). Excavations at Sutton Walls, Herefordshire, 1948–1951. *Archaeological Journal*, **110**, 62.

Kershaw, K. A. (1964). *Quantitative and dynamic ecology*. E. Arnold, London.

King, L. J. (1962). A quantitative expression of the pattern of urban settlements in selected areas of the United States. *Tijdschrift voor Economische en Sociale Geografie*, **53**, 1–7.

(1969). *Statistical analysis in geography*. Prentice Hall, Englewood Cliffs, N.J.

Klir, J. and Valach, M. (1967). *Cybernetic modelling*. Iliffe, London.

Kluckhohn, C. (1939). On certain recent applications of association coefficients to ethnological data. *American Anthropologist*, **41**, 345–77.

Kluckhohn, R. (1962). The Konso economy of southern Ethiopia. In Bohannan, P. and Dalton, G. (eds.), *Markets in Africa*, pp. 409–28. Northwestern University Press.

Kolb, J. H. and Brunner, E. de S. (1946). *A study of rural society*. Houghton Mifflin, Boston.

Kowalski, C. J. (1972). Non-normality and the correlation coefficient distribution. *Applied Statistics*, **21**, 1–12.

Kruk, J. (1973). *Studia osadnicze nad neolitem wyzyn lessowych*. Polska akademia nauk insytut historii kultury materialnej.

Kulldorf, G. (1955). *Migration probabilities*. Lund studies in geography, *B*, **14**.

Langton, J. (1972). Networks and Roman roads. Comments. *Area*, **4**, 137–8.

Laux, F. (1971). *Die Bronzezeit in der Lüneburger Heide*. Hildesheim.

Leblanc, S. (1971). An addition to Naroll's suggested floor area and settlement population relationship. *American Antiquity*, **36**, 210–11.

Lee, R. B. (1969). !Kung Bushman subsistence: an input–output analysis. In Vayda, A. P. (ed.), *Environment and cultural behaviour*, pp. 47–79. American Museum Sourcebook, New York.

Lehmann, E. L. and Stein, C. (1949). On some theory of non parametric hypothesis. *Annals of Mathematical Statistics*, **20**, 28–46.

Lewis, H. S. (1968). Typology and process in political evolution. In *Essays on the problem of tribe*, pp. 101–10. American Ethnological Society, University of Washington Press, Seattle.

Liddell, D. M. (1935). Report of the Hampshire Field Club's excavations at Meon Hill. *Papers and proceedings of the Hampshire Field Club and Archaeological Society*, **13**, 7–54.

Lindgren, B. W. (1960). *Statistical theory*. Macmillan, New York.

Longacre, W. A. (1968). Some aspects of prehistoric society in east-central Arizona. In Binford, S. R. and Binford, L. R. (eds.), *New perspectives in archaeology*, pp. 89–102. Aldine Publishing Co., Chicago.

Lösch, A. (1954). *The economics of location*. Yale University Press.

Mahr, G. (1967). *Die jüngere Latenekultur des Trieren Landes*. Berliner Beiträge zur Vor- und Frügeschichte, no. **12**. Berlin.

Manby, T. G. (1965). The distribution of rough-out Cumbrian and related stone axes of Lake District origin in Northern England. *Transactions of the Cumberland and Westmorland Antiquarian and Archaeological Society*, **65**, 1–37.

Mann, H. B. and Whitney, D. R. (1947). On a test of whether one of two random variables is statistically larger than the other. *Annals of Mathematical Statistics*, **18**, 50–61.

Marshall, J. V. (1964). Model and reality in central place studies. *Professional Geographer*, **16**, 5–8.

Martin, R. L. (1974). On spatial dependence, bias and the use of first spatial differences in regression analysis. *Area*, **6**, 185–94.

Massey, F. J. Jr (1951). The Kolmogorov–Smirnov test for goodness of fit. *Journal of the American Statistical Association*, **46**, 68–78.

Mead, R. (1974). A test for spatial pattern at several scales using data from a grid of contiguous quadrats. *Biometrics*, **30**, 295–307.

Medvedkov, Y. V. (1967). The concept of entropy in settlement pattern analysis. *Papers of the Regional Science Association*, **18**, 165–8.

Meier-Arendt, W. (1966). *Die Bandkeramische Kultur im Untermaingebiet*. Habelt, Bonn.

Meillassoux, C. (1962). Social and economic factors affecting markets in Guro land. In Bohannan, P. and Dalton, G. (eds.), *Markets in Africa*, pp. 279–98. Northwestern University Press.

Menger, K. (1892). On the origin of money. *Economic journal*, **2**, 239–477.

Middleton, J. (1962). Trade and markets among the Lugba of Uganda. In Bohannan, P. and Dalton, G. (eds.), *Markets in Africa*, pp. 561–78. Northwestern University Press.

Milke, W. (1935). *Sudostmelanesien, eine ethnostatistiche Analyse*. Wuerzburg.

Modderman, P. J. R. (1970). *Linearbandkeramik aus Elsloo und Stein*. 'S-Gravenhage.

Mood, A. M. (1954). On the asymptotic efficiency of certain non-parametric two sample tests. *Annals of Mathematical Statistics*, **25**, 514–22.

Moran, P. A. P. (1950). Notes on continuous stochastic phenomena. *Biometrika*, **37**, 17–23.

Morrill, R. L. (1962). *Simulation of central place patterns over time*. Lund studies in geography, *B*, **24**.

(1963). The development of spatial distributions of towns in Sweden: an historical-predictive approach. *A.A.A.G.*, **53**, 1–14.

(1965). *Migration and the spread and growth of urban settlements.* Lund studies in geography, *B*, no. **26**.

(1970). *The spatial organisation of society.* Wadsworth, Belmont, California.

Morrill, R. L. and Pitts, F. R. (1967). Marriage, migration and the mean information field: a study in uniqueness and generality. *A.A.A.G.*, **57**, 401–22.

Mountford, M. D. (1961). On E. C. Pielou's index of non-randomness. *Journal of Ecology*, **49**, 271–6.

Naroll, R. (1961). Two solutions to Galton's problem. In Moore, F. W. (ed.), *Readings in cross-cultural anthropology.* Hraf Press, New Haven.

(1962). Floor area and settlement population. *American Antiquity*, **27**, 587–8.

Neale, W. C. (1957). The market in theory and history. In Polanyi, K., Arensberg, C. M. and Pearson, H. W. (eds.), *Trade and market in the early empires*, pp. 357–72. Free Press, Glencoe, Ill.

Neft, D. S. (1966). *Statistical analysis for areal distributions.* Regional Science Research Institute. Monograph Series, **2**.

Newall, R. (1970). The mesolithic affinities and typological relations of the Dutch Bandkeramik flint industry. Ph.D. thesis, University of London.

Newcomb, R. M. (1970). The spatial distribution pattern of hill forts in west Penwith. *Cornish Archaeology*, **9**, 47–52.

Noy, T., Legge, A. J. and Higgs, E. S. (1973). Recent excavations at Nahal Oren, Israel. *P.P.S.* **39**, 75–99.

Olsson, G. (1965). Distance and human interaction. A review and bibliography. *Regional Science Research Institute, Bibliography Series*, **2**.

(1967). Central place systems, spatial interaction, and stochastic processes. *Papers and proceedings of the Regional Science Association*, **18**, 13–45.

Ord, J. K. (1972). *Density estimation and tests for randomness, using distance methods.* Draft for lecture to Advanced Institute on statistical ecology in the United States. The Pennsylvania State University. (Mimeo.)

Orton, C. R. (1975). Applications of statistics in pottery analysis. Meeting of medieval pottery research group. (Mimeo.)

Peacock, D. P. S. (1967). Romano-British pottery production in the Malvern district of Worcestershire. *Transactions of the Worcestershire Archaeological Society*, **1**, 15–28.

(1969a). Neolithic pottery production in Cornwall. *Antiquity*, **43**, 145–9.

(1969b). A contribution to the study of Glastonbury ware from south-western Britain. *Antiquaries Journal*, **49**, 41–61.

(1971). Roman amphorae in pre-Roman Britain. In Jesson, M. and Hill, D. (eds.). *The Iron Age and its hillforts*, pp. 161–88. Southampton University.

Pearson, K. and Blakeman, J. (1906). *Mathematical contributions to the theory of evolution.* **15**. *A mathematical theory of random migration.* Drapers' Company research memoires. Biometric series, no. **3**.

Peebles, C. S. (1973). The sites and their setting. In *Moundville: the organisation of a prehistoric community and culture.* University of Windsor Press, Ontario.

Pielou, E. C. (1959). The use of point-to-plant distances in the study of the pattern of plant populations. *Journal of Ecology*, **47**, 607–13.

(1961). Segregation and symmetry in two species populations as studied by nearest neighbour methods. *Journal of Ecology*, **49**, 255–69.

(1962). The use of plant-to-neighbour distances for the detection of competition. *Journal of Ecology*, **50**, 357–68.

(1969). *An introduction to mathematical ecology.* London.

Pierson-Jones, J. (1973). Undergraduate Part II thesis presented to the University of Cambridge. Department of Archaeology, Cambridge University.

Pinder, D. A. and Witherick, M. E. (1975). A modification of nearest-neighbour analysis for use in linear situations. *Geography*, **60**, 16–23.

Pirenne, H. (1936). *Economic and social history of medieval Europe*. Routledge.

Pounds, N. J. G. (1969). The urbanisation of the classical world. *A.A.A.G.*, **59**, 135–57.

Pred, A. (1967). *Innovation diffusion as a spatial process*. University of Chicago Press.

Prothero, R. M. (1957). Land use at Soba, Zaria province, northern Nigeria. *Economic Geography*, **33**, 72–86.

Radford, C. A. R. (1954). The tribes of southern Britain. *P.P.S.*, **20**, 1–26.

Reader, D. H. (1964). A survey of categories of economic activities among the peoples of Africa. *Africa*, **34**, 28–45.

Redman, C. L. and Watson, P. J. (1970). Systematic, intensive surface collection. *American Antiquity*, **35**, 279–91.

Reece, R. (1973). Roman coinage in the western Empire. *Britannia*, **4**, 227–51.

Reilly, W. J. (1931). *The law of retail gravitation*. New York.

Renfrew, C. (1969). Trade and culture process in European prehistory. *Current anthropology*, **10**, 151–69.

(1972a). Patterns of population growth in the prehistoric Aegean. In Ucko, P. J., Tringham, R. and Dimbleby, G. W. (eds.), *Man, settlement and urbanism*, pp. 383–99. Duckworth, London.

(1972b). *The emergence of civilisation*. Methuen, London.

(ed.) (1973a). *The explanation of cultural change: models in prehistory*. Duckworth, London.

(1973b). *Before civilisation. The radiocarbon revolution and prehistoric Europe*. Cape, London.

Renfrew, C., Dixon, J. E. and Cann, J. R. (1966). Obsidian and early cultural contact in the Near-East. *P.P.S.*, **32**, 30–72.

(1968). Further analyses of Near Eastern obsidian. *P.P.S.*, **34**, 319–31.

Richmond, I. A. (1963). *Roman Britain* (2nd edn). Penguin, Harmondsworth.

Rigby, V. (1973). Potters' stamps on Terra Nigra and Terra Rubra found in Britain. *C.B.A. Research Report*, **10**, 7–24.

Rivet, A. L. F. (1964). *Town and country in Roman Britain* (2nd edn). Hutchinson, London.

Rowlands, M. J. (1970). *A study of the bronze working industries of the middle Bronze Age in southern Britain*. Ph.D. thesis, University of London.

(1971). Modes of exchange and the incentives for trade with reference to later European prehistory. *Research Seminar: Models in Prehistory*. Sheffield.

(1973). Modes of exchange and the incentives for trade, with reference to later European prehistory. In Renfrew (1973a), pp. 589–600.

Sahlins, M. D. (1965). On the sociology of primitive exchange. *A.S.A. Monograph*, **1**, 139–236.

(1972). *Stone Age economics*. Tavistock Publications, London.

Salway, P., Hallam, S. J. and Bromwich, J. l'A. (1970). *The Fenlands in Roman times*. Royal Geographical Society Research Series, no. 5.

Sherratt, A. G. (1972). Socio-economic and demographic models for the neolithic and bronze ages of Europe. In Clarke, D. L. (ed.), *Models in archaeology*, pp. 477–542. Methuen, London.

(1973). The interpretation of change in European prehistory. In Renfrew, (1973a), pp. 419–28.

Shotton, F. W. (1959). New petrological groups based on axes from the
West Midlands. *P.P.S.*, **25**, 135–43.

Shotton, F. W., Chitty, L. F. and Seaby, W. A. (1951). A new centre of
stone axe dispersal on the Welsh border. *P.P.S.*, **17**, 159–67.

Sielman, B. (1971). Der Einflusse der Umwelt aus die Neolithische
Besiedlung Südwestdeutschlands unter Besonderer Berücksichtigung der
Verhältnisse am Nördlischen Oberrhein. *Acta praehistorica et Archaeologica*,
2, 65–197.

(1972). Die frühneolithische Besiedlung Mitteleuropas. In Lüning, J. (ed.),
Die Anfänge des Neolithikums vom Orient bis Nordeuropa, **5a**, 1–65. Köln.

Simon, H. A. (1955). On a class of skew distribution functions. *Biometrika*,
42, 425–40.

Skellam, J. G. (1952). Studies in statistical ecology. I. Spatial pattern.
Biometrika, **39**, 346–62.

(1958). On the derivation and applicability of Neyman's type A
distribution. *Biometrika*, **45**, 32–6.

Smith, D. J. (1969). In Rivet, A. L. F. (ed.), *The Roman villa in Britain*,
pp. 71–125. Hutchinson, London.

Smith, R. H. T. (1969). Market periodicity and locational patterns in west
Africa. *Tenth International African Seminar*.

Soja, E. W. (1971). *The political organisation of space*. Association of American
Geographers, Commission on College Geography, Resource paper,
no. **8**.

Soudsky, B. (1962). The neolithic site of Bylany. *Antiquity*, 1962, 190.

(1968). Criteria to distinguish cultural phases – methods employed at
Bylany. Circulated seminar paper, Institute of Archaeology, University
of London.

Spratling, M. G. (1972). Southern British decorated bronzes of the pre-
Roman Iron Age. Ph.D. thesis, University of London.

Sprockhoff, E. (1930). Zur Handelsgeschichte der germanischen Bronzezeit.
Vorgeschichtliche Forschungen, **7**.

Stanford, S. C. (1972). The function and population of hillforts in the
central Marches. In Lynch, F. and Burgess, C. (eds.), *Prehistoric man in
Wales and the West*, pp. 307–319. Adams and D.

Stanislawski, M. B. (1973). Review of W. Longacre, Archaeology as
Anthropology, *American Antiquity*, **38**, 117–22.

Stead, I. M. (1967). A La Tène III burial at Welwyn Garden City.
Archaeologia, **101**, 1–62.

Steel, R. W., Fortes, M. and Ady, P. (1947). Ashanti survey 1945–6: an
experiment in social research. *Geographical Journal*, **110**, 149–79.

Stewart, J. Q. and Warntz, W. (1958). Macrogeography and social science.
Geographical Review, **48**, 167–184.

Stiteler, W. M. and Patil, G. P. (1971). Variance-to-mean ratio and
Morisita's index as measures of spatial patterns in ecological populations.
In Patil, G. P. (ed.), *Statistical Ecology*, **1**. Pennsylvania State University.

Stjernquist, B. (1966). Models of commercial diffusion in prehistoric times.
Scripta Minora, **2**, 1–43.

Stone, J. F. S. and Wallis, F. S. (1951). Third report of the sub-Committee
of the Southwestern group of Museums and Art Galleries on the
petrological identification of stone axes. *P.P.S.*, **17**, 99–158.

Struever, S. and Houart, G. L. (1972). An analysis of the Hopewell
Interaction Sphere. In *Social exchange and interaction*. Anthropological
papers of the Museum of Anthropology, University of Michigan, **46**,
47–79.

Swan, V. G. (1973). Aspects of the New Forest Late Roman pottery industry. *C.B.A.* Research Report, **10**, 117–34.

Swed, F. and Eisenhart, C. (1943). Tables for testing randomness of grouping in a sequence of alternatives. *Annals of mathematical statistics*, **14**, 66–87.

Taaffe, E. J. (1962). The urban hierarchy: an air passenger definition. *Economic Geography*, **38**, 1–14.

Taylor, C. (1971). The study of settlement patterns in pre-Saxon Britain. Circulated seminar paper, Institute of Archaeology, University of London.

(1972). The study of settlement patterns in pre-Saxon Britain. In Ucko, P. J., Tringham, R. and Dimbleby, G. W. (eds.), *Man, settlement and urbanism*, pp. 109–13. Duckworth, London.

Taylor, P. J. (1971). Distance transformations and distance decay functions. *Geographical Analysis*, **3**, 221–38.

Thomas, D. H. (1972). A computer simulation model of Great Basin Shoshonean subsistence and settlement patterns. In Clarke, D. L. (ed.), *Models in Archaeology*, pp. 671–704. Methuen, London.

Tobler, W. and Wineburg, S. (1971). A Cappodocian speculation. *Nature*, **231**, 39–41.

Vance, J. E. (1970). *The merchant's world: the geography of wholesaling.* Prentice Hall, Englewood Cliffs, N.J.

Vansina, J. (1962). Trade and markets among the Kuba. In Bohannan, P. and Dalton, G. (eds.), *Markets in Africa*, pp. 190–210. Northwestern University Press.

Vining, R. (1953). Delimitation of economic areas: statistical conceptions in the study of the spatial structure of an economic system. *Journal of the American Statistical Association*, **18**, 44–64.

Vita-Finzi, C. and Higgs, E. S. (1970). Prehistoric economy in the Mount Carmel area of Palestine: site catchment analysis, *P.P.S.*, **36**, 1–37.

von Thünen, J. H. (1875). *Der Isolierte Staat in Beziehung auf Landwirtschaft und Nationalokonomie* (3rd edn). Hamburg.

Wacher, J. S. (1964). A study of Romano-British town defences of the early and middle second century. *Archaeological Journal*, **119**, 103–13.

(1966). Earthwork defences of the second century. In Wacher, J. S. (ed.), *The Civitas capitals of Roman Britain*, pp. 60–9. Leicester University Press.

Waibel, L. (1958). *Capitulos de geografía trapical é do Brasil.* Rio de Janeiro.

Warntz, W. (1965). *Macrogeography and income funds.* Regional Science Research Institute, monograph series, no. **3**.

Warntz, W. and Neft, D. (1960). Contributions to a statistical methodology for areal distributions. *Journal of Regional Science*, **2**, 47–66.

Washburn, J. (1974). Nearest neighbour analysis of Pueblo I–III settlement patterns along the Rio Puerco of the East, New Mexico. *American Antiquity*, **39**, 315–35.

Webley, D. (1972). Soils and site location in prehistoric Palestine. In Higgs, E. S. (ed.), *Papers in economic prehistory*, pp. 169–80. Cambridge University Press, London.

Webster, G. A. (1966). Fort and town in early Roman Britain. In Wacher, J. S. (ed.), *The civitas capitals of Roman Britain.* Leicester University Press.

Wedlake, W. (1958). *Excavations at Camerton, Somerset.* Camerton Excavation Club.

Whallon, R. (1973). Spatial analysis of occupation floors: the application of dimensional analysis of variance. In Renfrew (1973*b*), pp. 115–30.

(1974). Spatial analysis of occupation floors, II, The application of nearest neighbour analysis. *American Antiquity*, **39**, 16–34.

Wheeler, R. E. M. (1943). *Maiden Castle, Dorset.* Report of the Research Committee of the Society of Antiquaries of London, no. 12.

Whitworth, W. A. (1934). *Choice and chance.* New York.

Wiessner, P. (1974). A functional estimator of population from floor area. *American Antiquity,* **39,** 343–9.

Wilcoxon, F. (1945). Individual comparisons by ranking methods. *Biometrics Bulletin,* **1,** 80–3.

Willey, G. R. and Phillips, P. (1958). *Methods and theory in American archaeology.* University of Chicago Press.

Williams, A. (1950). Excavations at Allard's Quarry, Marnhull, Dorset. *Proceedings of the Dorset Natural History and Archaeological Society,* **72,** 58–60.

Williams, B. J. (1968). Establishing cultural heterogeneities in settlement patterns: an ethnographic example. In Binford, S. R. and Binford, L. R. (eds.), *New perspectives in archaeology,* pp. 161–70. Aldine Publishing Co., Chicago.

Williamson, E. and Bretherton, M. H. (1963). *Tables of the negative binomial probability distribution.* Wiley, New York.

Wilson, A. G. (1970). *Entropy in urban and regional planning.* Pion, London.
(1971). A family of spatial interaction models and associated developments. *Environment and planning,* **3,** 1–32.

Wood, J. J. (1971). Fitting discrete probability distributions to prehistoric settlement patterns, In Gumerman, G. J. (ed.), *The distribution of prehistoric population aggregates.* Prescott College Anthropological Reports, no. 1.

Young, C. J. (1973). The pottery industry of the Oxford region. *C.B.A. Research Report,* **10,** 105–15.

Yuill, R. S. (1965). *A simulation study of barrier effects in spatial diffusion problems.* Michigan, Inter-University Community of Mathematical Geographers, Discussion Papers, no. 5.

Zipf, G. K. (1949). *Human behaviour and the principle of least effort.* Hafner, New York.

INDEX